DIVERSITY IN WORK TEAMS

DIVERSITY IN
WORK TEAMS

Research Paradigms
for a Changing Workplace

Edited by Susan E. Jackson
& Marian N. Ruderman

AMERICAN PSYCHOLOGICAL ASSOCIATION
WASHINGTON, DC

Published by
American Psychological Association
750 First Street, NE
Washington, DC 20002

Copies may be ordered from
APA Order Department
P.O. Box 2710
Hyattsville, MD 20784

In the UK and Europe, copies may be ordered from
American Psychological Association
3 Henrietta Street
Covent Garden, London
WC2E 8LU England

Typeset in Minion by University Graphics, Inc., York, PA

Printer: Braun-Brumfield, Inc., Ann Arbor, MI
Cover Designer: Berg Design, Albany, NY
Technical/Production Editor: Edward B. Meidenbauer

Library of Congress Cataloging-in-Publication Data
Diversity in work teams : research paradigms for a changing workplace / [edited
   by] Susan E. Jackson and Marian N. Ruderman.
      p.   cm.
   Includes bibliographical references and index.
   ISBN 1-55798-333-X
   1. Diversity in the workplace. 2. Work groups. 3. Organizational change. I. Jackson,
Susan E. II. Ruderman, Marian N.
HF5549.5 M5D57   1996
658.3′041—dc20
                                                                        95-38642
                                                                              CIP

British Library Cataloguing-in-Publication Data
A CIP record is available from the British Library

Printed in the United States of America
First edition

APA Science Volumes

Temperament: Individual Differences at the Interface of Biology and Behavior
Through the Looking Glass: Issues of Psychological Well-Being in Captive
Nonhuman Primates

APA expects to publish volumes on the following conference topics:

Attribution Processes, Person Perception and Social Interaction: The Legacy of Ned Jones

Changing Ecological Approaches to Development: Organism–Environment Mutualities

Children Exposed to Family Violence

Conceptual Structure and Processes: Emergence, Discovery, and Change

Genetic, Ethological, and Evolutionary Perspectives on Human Development

Global Prospects for Education: Development, Culture, and Schooling

Maintaining and Promoting Integrity in Behavioral Science Research

Marital and Family Therapy Outcome and Process Research

Measuring Changes in Patients Following Psychological and Pharmacological Interventions

Psychology Beyond the Threshold: Conference on General and Applied Experimental Psychology and a Festschrift for William N. Dember

Psychology of Industrial Relations

Psychophysiological Study of Attention

Stereotypes: Brain–Behavior Relationships

As part of its continuing and expanding commitment to enhance the dissemination of scientific psychological knowledge, the Science Directorate of the APA established a Scientific Conferences Program. A series of volumes resulting from these conferences is produced jointly by the Science Directorate and the Office of Communications. A call for proposals is issued twice annually by the Scientific Directorate, which, collaboratively with the APA Board of Scientific Affairs, evaluates the proposals and selects several conferences for funding. This important effort has resulted in an exceptional series of meetings and scholarly volumes, each of which has contributed to the dissemination of research and dialogue in these topical areas.

The APA Science Directorate's conferences funding program has supported 40 conferences since its inception in 1988. To date, 27 volumes resulting from conferences have been published.

WILLIAM C. HOWELL, PHD
Executive Director

VIRGINIA E. HOLT
Assistant Executive Director

Contents

Contributors

Alice O. Andrews, Cornell University
David J. Armstrong, RHR International, Boston
Holly Arrow, University of Illinois
Jennifer L. Berdahl, University of Illinois
Marilynn B. Brewer, Ohio State University
Paul Cole, Lotus Development Corporation, Cambridge, Massachusetts
Taylor Cox, Jr., University of Michigan
Terri D. Egan, University of Southern California,
Robin J. Ely, Harvard University
Susan E. Jackson, New York University
Roderick M. Kramer, Stanford University
Joseph E. McGrath, University of Illinois
Ann M. Morrison, New Leaders Institute, Del Mar, California
Margaret A. Neale, Northwestern University
Stella M. Nkomo, University of North Carolina at Charlotte
Gregory B. Northcraft, University of Illinois
Jeffrey T. Polzer, University of Texas
Marian N. Ruderman, Center for Creative Leadership, Greensboro, North Carolina
Tal Simons, Hebrew University of Jerusalem
Pamela S. Tolbert, Cornell University
Harry C. Triandis, University of Illinois
Anne S. Tsui, University of California, Irvine, and Hong Kong University of Science and Technology
Katherine R. Xin, University of Southern California

Preface

Interest in the topic of work team diversity has grown steadily in recent years, reflecting two significant changes in the work environment. One change occurring during the final decades of the 20th century is the face of the American workforce: The percentage of women in the work force has risen substantially; increasingly, people of color are a source of growth in the labor force; and globalization of business organizations means that more and more employees work with colleagues from different national cultures.

A second significant change occurring at this time is reflected in the shapes and forms of modern organizations. Organizations of the past were tall hierarchies that divided up the work to be done among individual employees. Today, the old structures are being reformed. As organizations seek to become more flexible in the face of rapid environmental change and more responsive to the needs of customers, they are experimenting with new, team-based structures.

The juxtaposition of these two trends challenges organizations to develop new approaches to managing employees, and at the same time, it challenges social scientists to develop better theories for understanding behavior within organizations. Traditional perspectives that assume a homogeneous workforce and a traditional organizational form are inadequate for understanding the attitudes and behaviors of people from many diverse backgrounds who are working closely together on tasks that require effective teamwork.

This volume presents several examples of research and theory relevant to understanding people working within organizations characterized by workforce diversity and teamwork. Included are the perspectives of psychologists, sociologists, and management scholars, who are carrying out studies of organizational demography, social identity, psychological distance, intergroup competition, and negotiation. Within these areas of scholarship, research and theory tend to proceed in isolation, with little attempt being made to pull together the various streams of research. By bringing together different paradigms and perspectives, we hope to encourage the integration of these research traditions. As a first step, we believe such an integration will produce a more complete picture of the state of our knowledge about teams working in the context of diversity. In the longer term, we seek to stimulate new conversations between researchers working within different traditions, with the expectation that new and creative research will soon follow.

Through the preparation of this volume, we have begun the process of cross-disciplinary integration and conversation. The authors of this volume started the process as they prepared their contributions: Before preparing the final versions of their chapters, the authors shared their work with each other in written form. In addition, they participated in a two-day conference, which provided a forum to present ideas, receive feedback, and begin learning from others. Thus, as we prepared this volume, a few bridges were built among isolated islands of intellectual activity. Opportunities for additional bridges remain, nevertheless, and we hope that readers of this volume are stimulated to join in this activity.

Preparation of this volume was greatly facilitated by the efforts of a large team of people at the Center for Creative Leadership, the American Psychological Association, and New York University, each of whom we sincerely wish to thank. At the top of our "thank you" list is Walt Tornow, who helped us transform ideas into realities. With his encouragement and support, the Center for Creative Leadership joined with New York University and the American Psychological Association to cosponsor the preparation of this volume. Walt, along with other staff members at the Center for Creative Leadership, helped us plan, organize, and facilitate a two-day conference during which the authors of this volume and other interested scholars met to exchange ideas and data. In addition to Walt's support, we are especially grateful for the assistance provided by Martha Hughes-James and Patti Hall. Their many hours of individual effort were the foundation of the total team effort. We also appreciate the support and advice of Debbie Nelson, Karen Bolyston, Karen McNeil-Miller, Luke Novelli, John Sayres, and Valerie Sessa. In addition, we thank Philip Morris Companies, Inc., and Pfizer, Inc., who made donations to the Center for

Creative Leadership in support of the conference and preparation of this volume.

We also thank New York University, who provided administrative support. In particular we thank Elina Dobin for her secretarial assistance in preparing the final manuscript for this volume.

Finally, we thank the APA staff for their support throughout this project. In particular, we thank William Howell and Virginia Holt, who worked with us during the planning of this volume on behalf of the APA Science Directorate, and Beth Beisel and Ed Meidenbauer, who guided our work through the production process at APA Books.

SUSAN E. JACKSON
MARIAN N. RUDERMAN

1

Introduction: Perspectives for Understanding Diverse Work Teams

Susan E. Jackson and Marian N. Ruderman

P sychologists have been studying group processes and productivity for over half a century. Throughout the years, the amount of attention focused on groups has varied, with a period of dormancy characterizing recent decades (Jones, 1985). Happily, the decade of the 1990s has witnessed a renewal of interest in understanding groups, especially groups formed within the context of work settings (Levine & Moreland, 1990). This renewed interest seems to be due in part to changes in how work is being organized (Jackson & Alvarez, 1993). In particular, employees who previously worked individually at their tasks are being reorganized into teams (Guzzo & Salas, 1995; Sundstrom, De Meuse, & Futrell, 1990).

Many types of teams can be found in today's workplace. Some work teams are temporary. For example, an organization struggling to control the rising costs associated with employees' health benefits might delegate responsibility for recommending alternative benefits plans to a task force made up of employees selected to represent all segments of the workforce likely to be affected by the change. Other teams are longer-lived. For example, a pharmaceutical firm may give project teams responsibility for developing a specified product (e.g., a synthetic blood substitute). Some teams may even be permanent. For example, a computer software company may organize employees into teams that have full responsibility for serving specified customers, from determining the customer's needs to developing, implementing, and evaluating products and services to meet those needs.

Regardless of whether a team is formed as a temporary task force, as a project team, or as a permanent and self-managing work unit, it is likely to bring together employees of many different types, creating diversity. By chance and by design, team members often differ from each other on a variety of dimensions, including demographics and an array of psychological and social attributes. Thus, as organizations restructure to take advantage of the potential benefits of teams, they find they must understand and effectively manage diversity in order to be successful.

This book explores how the amount and type of diversity in teams shape both internal team dynamics and team outcomes. Our assumption is that the composition of teams—that is, the amount and type of diversity within teams—is an important structural characteristic that must be understood in order to use teams effectively in work organizations. Past approaches to managing may be obsolete because managing a diverse team is a different experience from managing a monocultural team (Mayo, Meindl, & Pastor, in press). In particular, managerial techniques and styles appropriate for homogeneous teams do not work well for teams composed of people with substantially different values, perspectives, and expectations concerning how leaders should behave (James, Chen, & Cropanzano, in press).

Our objectives for this volume are to (a) contribute to a fuller understanding of the benefits and liabilities of diversity by describing some of the available theory and research evidence and (b) identify directions for future research. To achieve these objectives, this volume brings together the work of a diverse group of scholars. Rooted in the disciplines of psychology, sociology, and management, their research illustrates the variety of conceptual and methodological approaches being used to study this topic. By including diverse intellectual traditions within one volume, we hope to reveal the complex nature of work team diversity and its consequences, including cognitive, affective, and behavioral phenomena at the levels of individuals, dyads, groups, and organizations (cf. Jackson, May, & Whitney, 1995). In addition, we hope to encourage new research that crosses the artificial boundaries that separate these scientific disciplines.

THE COMPLEXITY OF DIVERSITY WITHIN WORK TEAMS

Although social scientists (especially sociologists and psychologists) have a long history of interest in group composition, the term *diversity* is not a well-established scientific construct. There is no consensus yet on what diversity means, nor is there consensus about which types of phenomena define the domain of *diversity research.*

When selecting authors to contribute to this volume, we defined the construct domain of diversity broadly to include demographic diversity (e.g., based on gender, ethnicity, age), psychological diversity (e.g., based on values, beliefs, knowledge), and organizational diversity (e.g., based on tenure, occupation, hierarchical level). By defining the domain broadly, we do not intend to suggest that all types of diversity are equivalent; however, we do intend to suggest that researchers who study these many types of diversity should be aware of each other's work and should be actively thinking about its implications for their own research.

Our eclectic approach reflects our interest in stimulating research that is applicable—that is, we hope to stimulate research that can eventually be used in organizational settings to improve the functioning of work teams and the well-being of their individual members. In organizational settings, the many different types of diversity cannot be isolated from each other—teams are composed of whole individuals. Their demographic, psychological, and organizational attributes all simultaneously contribute to the composition of their work team. Ultimately, researchers interested in understanding basic group processes and practitioners interested in organizational interventions must take this reality into account. Future research will have utility to the extent it has the potential to help a manager be effective when operating within the context of teams composed of individuals who are dissimilar in a number of different ways from the manager and from each other.

THE NATURE AND IMPORTANCE OF DIVERSITY IN WORK TEAMS

To some extent, the diversity found within work teams reflects conditions within the labor market in general. In particular, the increasing numbers of women and people of color in the workforce translate into organizations and work teams characterized by gender and ethnic diversity (Johnston & Packer, 1987; Morrison & Von Glinow, 1990). That is, as the proportions of women and people of color in the workforce increase, the composition of the workforce shifts from being relatively homogeneous to being quite diverse.

In the late 1980s, demographic projections about the changing composition of the U. S. workforce drew widespread attention to the topic of diversity. Indeed, within the past decade, an entire industry has emerged to assist organizations that had suddenly become concerned about issues related to managing diversity. As some commentators have noted, however, changes in the demographic composition of the labor market are not as dramatic as sometimes portrayed in the popular press. Furthermore, such macro-level changes occur gradually over a period of many years. Alone, such gradual changes do not explain why organizations suddenly became so concerned about diversity. Other forces also seem to be operating to make diversity a salient concern.

One such force is the advancement of women and people of color up the organizational hierarchy. Previously women and people of color were segregated into the lower levels of organizations ("Race in the Workplace," 1991; Selbert, 1987). Under conditions of segregation, an increasing reliance on teams might not have highlighted issues of diversity, but under conditions of relative integration, teams are naturally diverse—even when those teams include only managerial-level employees. For managerial teams, gender and ethnic diversity may be especially salient simply because it is new.

Increased age diversity is another inevitable, and perhaps unantici-pated, consequence of several converging trends: Improved health, longer life expectancies, changes in legal regulations governing mandatory re-tirement, declining pension benefits, and employers' increased reliance on contract and part-time workers (many of whom are semiretired) all con-tribute to increasing the proportion of older workers in the workforce. Furthermore, older employees and younger employees are more likely to work together. Modern organizations are more flat, so they have fewer hi-erarchical boundaries, resulting in less tenure- and age-based segregation. In addition, as we enter the age of "knowledge work," the roles held by younger and older employees often are reversed: Young and more recently educated employees have greater career mobility and are increasingly likely to find themselves supervising their elders (Farnham, 1989; Hirsch, 1990).

While broad, general changes at the societal level account for some of the diversity now found within organizations, work team diversity also oc-curs by design. As they seek new ways to satisfy a diverse customer base, many organizations realize the value of insuring that the diversity of their customers is represented when services and products are designed, evalu-ated, and delivered. For example, today it makes no sense to ignore the perspectives of female consumers when designing and marketing auto-mobiles. Consequently, in the auto industry, gender diversity is being de-liberately introduced into work units that were sharply segregated two decades ago. Similar market forces operate on many organizations in both the private and public sector. In their attempts to be responsive to a di-verse market of consumers, organizations often create work teams that are intentionally designed to be demographically diverse (e.g., see Sellers, 1990).

Finally, the increasing globalization of markets and economies brings cultural diversity into the growing number of organizations that conduct business beyond domestic borders (Kanter, 1991). Here again, purposeful change is occurring, with cultural integration replacing cultural segrega-tion. U.S. employees once worked almost exclusively with other U.S. citi-zens. As U.S. businesses shift from being narrowly focused on domestic markets to becoming global enterprises with operations in numerous countries (Kanter, 1991), employees around the world frequently find themselves working on projects that are staffed by a multinational team (James et al., in press).

As this volume will reveal, the scientific evidence suggests that diversity is a team characteristic that makes a difference. No single theoretical perspective adequately accounts for the full range of evidence. Nevertheless, it is clear that diversity shapes phenomena at the level of the team as a whole, including group processes and outcomes, and it also affects the experiences of the individuals within a team. The remainder of this volume offers detailed descriptions of some of this scientific evidence.

OVERVIEW OF CHAPTERS IN THIS VOLUME

The chapters that follow are of two types. In Part One, chapters 2 through 8 each describe a single theoretical or empirical approach to understanding work team diversity. The authors of these chapters illustrate how researchers working within a particular perspective approach the task of improving our understanding of work team diversity. In Part Two, the authors of chapters 9 through 12 offer their personal reflections on the chapters in Part One. Part Two is intended to sensitize readers to the strengths and weaknesses of the extant literature. In particular, they offer insights into how the choices researchers make when conducting research affect the potential applicability of their findings.

Part One: Theory and Research

The chapters within Part One differ substantially from each other. One salient dimension that differentiates these chapters is their disciplinary focus: Some are rooted firmly in social psychology; some, in sociology; and some, in organizational science, which draws on these disciplines for the purpose of understanding organizations. Associated with this multidisciplinary approach is variety in the theoretical foundations of the chapters. Thus, to understand work team diversity, the authors use concepts from social identity theory, organizational demography, negotiations theory, and theories of intergroup competition.

Second, the chapters represent different approaches to creating knowledge: One chapter presents a very broad and integrative conceptual framework intended to help scientists formulate researchable questions; others present conceptual frameworks for understanding narrowly specified phenomena. Some chapters describe empirical research—including laboratory experiments and analyses of longitudinal trends in field settings—designed to test hypotheses derived from well-developed theory; other chapters offer rich descriptive detail about how diversity affects teams.

Third, the chapters address different dimensions of diversity: Some chapters address the domain of diversity broadly defined, but most focus on a single dimension of diversity. The particular dimensions of diversity receiving detailed treatment are age, gender, ethnicity, geographic location, and functional or occupational affiliation. More specifically, the following brief overviews of the chapters in Part One should prepare readers for the full range of issues addressed by these authors.

In chapter 2, McGrath, Berdahl, and Arrow frame the conceptual domain of interest by examining the concepts of diversity and teams. Through careful analysis, they first reveal and then begin to unpack the complexity of these two concepts. After presenting readers with a clear map of the conceptual domain, the authors then describe four alternative theoretical approaches for understanding the effects of diversity within work teams: the trait approach, the expectations approach, the power differential approach, and an integrative multicultural approach. Finally, using the multicultural approach, McGrath, Berdahl, and Arrow explore the dynamics of diversity within teams, paying particular attention to the interplay between issues of diversity and changes that occur over time in team membership and group development. Thus, chapter 2 serves as a broad introduction to the scientific literature that can be used to understand team diversity.

Within the discipline of social psychology, research designed to test social identity theory has shed a great deal of light on the intergroup dynamics that arise when group members become differentiated and categorized into ingroups and outgroups. Brewer provides an overview of social identity theory in chapter 3. In addition to summarizing what has been learned through research on social identity theory, Brewer's description of a few key studies illustrates the research paradigm associated with this line of inquiry, which is based in experimental social psychology. Extrapolating from the results from this line of research, Brewer argues that the dysfunctional consequences of the categorization processes that arise in diverse teams can be reduced by emphasizing common team goals and by attending carefully to the compositional design of teams.

Chapter 4 focuses on the interpersonal dynamics that can arise among people working as members of cross-functional or multidisciplinary teams. Northcraft, Polzer, Neale, and Kramer introduce the language of negotiation into the dialogue on diversity. They explain the team dynamics that arise out of the perspectives team members adopt when engaged in disputes. Integrating social identity theory concepts with principles of effective negotiation, they generate recommendations for how to improve the functioning of diverse teams. To realize the potential of diverse teams, they argue, organizations should consider three types of interventions: educating team members about principles of effective negotiation, attending to the "social architecture" of teams, and designing an appropriate infrastructure for assessing and rewarding team performance.

Hierarchy is ubiquitous in work settings. In chapter 5, Tsui, Xin, and Egan draw our attention to how issues of diversity shape relationships between team members at different levels within the organizational hierarchy. Drawing on findings from research on organizational demography and the vertical dyad linkage model of leadership, these authors develop propositions to describe how demographic differences between supervisors and subordinates shape their relationship. Their argument is that, for the demographic characteristics of age, tenure, and education, social and organizational norms define some types of dissimilarity between supervisors and subordinates as legitimate, whereas other types of dissimilarity are less legitimate. If the demography of a dyad matches the social and organizational norms, dissimilarity should facilitate the relationship. By contrast, when the pattern of demographic dissimilarity is normatively inconsistent, the dissimilarity is likely to be disruptive. Finally, these authors consider how the composition of the work team in which the dyad is embedded creates a context that moderates the consequences of demographic dissimilarity within the dyad.

The literature on organizational demography introduced in chapter 5 also informs the discussion presented in chapter 6 by Tolbert, Andrews, and Simons. In this chapter, however, the focus shifts from dyadic relationships to the intergroup dynamics that occur within larger organizational units. The question of interest is how changes in the relative sizes of subgroups affect the relationships between the subgroups. Social contact theories predict that relationships should improve as a minority subgroup increases in size, but competition theories predict the opposite. Predictions from these two perspectives are tested by analyzing the changing proportions of women faculty members in sociology departments from the late 1970s through the late 1980s. After studying this chapter, readers will learn whether the data supported the social contact perspective or competition theories; they also will learn a great deal about the research methodology used by organizational demography researchers.

When the topic is diversity, issues of power cannot be ignored. As Ely observes in chapter 7, discussions of how diversity affects team and organizational functioning often reflect implicit assumptions about the roles available to members of the dominant majority and members of oppressed minorities. For example, members of oppressed minorities are presumed to understand the experience of oppression, and they are generally held guiltless of domination; conversely, members of the majority are presumed incapable of understanding the experience of being oppressed, and they are presumed guilty of taking advantage of their position of dominance. When the objective is understanding diversity, Ely argues, these assumptions implicitly suggest that members of oppressed groups have privileged information. Ely questions these assumptions and the roles they cast for majority and minority group members. By describing her teaching experiences and a case analysis of an ethnically diverse, nonprofit, feminist organization, she shows how insight into the issue of diversity can be gained with a shift of focus from discussing oppression to exploring the experience of dominance.

Chapter 8, the final chapter in Part One, takes readers on a journey into the reality of global work teams. As organizational consultants, Armstrong and Cole were asked to analyze the issues that arise within geographically distributed work teams. Their insightful description of events, which is based on information gathered through interviews and direct observation, uses social distance theory to interpret the consequences of geographic distance. It is interesting to see that, just as social structures give rise to ingroup–outgroup dynamics, so too can geographic structures. For distributed teams, the challenge is to create a feeling of psychological closeness among team members who experience a variety of communication difficulties. Perhaps this challenge is not so different from those faced by other types of diverse teams.

Part Two: Future Directions for Theory and Research

The chapters in Part Two reflect on the chapters in Part One. Four well-established experts who conduct research on the topic of diversity and who serve as consultants to organizations concerned about issues of diversity were asked to identify the themes running through the chapters, critique the state of the literature represented by the chapters, and offer suggestions for future research. All of this they were asked to do within just a few pages. Faced with this constraint, each of these experts chose to focus on one or two key points.

Ann Morrison, the author of chapter 9, has conducted large-scale field studies of diversity within organizations and currently serves as a consultant to organizations that are actively confronting this issue. In her daily work, she sees managers struggling to improve their relationships with subordinates, and she sees organizations struggling to reduce the negative consequences of prejudice. As a consultant, Morrison is sensitive to the importance of context when studying diversity. It is obvious to her that psychology laboratories and work organizations are two different places. In reflecting on Part One, Morrison expresses concern about the gap between research and practice. After identifying barriers to closing this gap, she offers specific suggestions for how to increase the utility of future research on diversity for people who wish to use the research to improve daily life within organizations.

Reflecting on Part One in chapter 10, Harry Triandis brings to bear his perspective as a cross-cultural researcher attuned to the very important, but often ignored, roles of cultural and historical contexts. He reminds us that diversity is a socially constructed phenomenon that can be fully understood only if we attend to the specific contexts in which it is experienced. As Triandis points out, the chapters in Part One focus on issues of diversity as experienced today within the United States. This specific context shapes what researchers look for and what they find, yet this fact is generally not acknowledged. Future theory and research on diversity will be improved to the extent that researchers understand and explicitly consider how the broader social context impinges on the people whose experiences they seek to understand.

Within the academic field of management, Taylor Cox is a pioneer whose theorizing and research on diversity within organizations has opened new windows for researchers on organizational behavior. According to Cox, the most difficult challenge to be tackled by future theory and research is that of dealing effectively with the multidimensionality of the construct. In chapter 11, after illustrating where this challenge surfaces throughout Part One, he offers suggestions for conducting new research that addresses the challenge. In addition, Cox echoes the concerns of Triandis and Morrison regarding the need to pay more attention to contexts—including organizational, societal, and historical contexts.

Stella Nkomo is another pioneer of diversity research within the field of management. In the final chapter of this volume, Nkomo asks us to revisit the fundamental question that anyone interested in diversity must address, namely: As a scientific construct, what is the meaning of *diversity*? Is diversity a construct that can be usefully construed to include a broad range of differences, such as those associated with race, gender, age, and organizational standing? Or is a more narrow focus appropriate? After highlighting the viewpoints expressed in Part One, Nkomo asserts that the goal of scientists should be to develop an approach that specifies the many dimensions of diversity and links these to their unique and common consequences. To conclude, Nkomo—like other authors in Part Two—calls future researchers into the field where they will grapple with the question of whether laboratory-tested theories are useful for developing recommendations that can be used to improve how individuals and organizations manage within the context of work team diversity.

To fully appreciate the chapters introduced here, it is necessary to read them in their entirety. We trust your interest is now piqued, and we invite you to proceed. After you have read this sampling, we hope you are stimulated to develop your own, more complete understanding of the role of diversity within work teams through additional reading, theorizing, and empirical research.

REFERENCES

Farnham, A. (1989, December 4). The trust gap. *Fortune*, 56–78.

Guzzo, R. A., & Salas, E. (Eds.). (1995). *Team decision making effectiveness in organizations*. San Francisco: Jossey-Bass.

Hirsch, J. S. (1990, February 26). Older workers chafe under young managers. *The Wall Street Journal*, pp. B1, B6.

Jackson, S. E., & Alvarez, E. B. (1993). Working through diversity as a strategic imperative. In S. E. Jackson (Ed.), *Diversity in the workplace: Human resources initiatives* (pp. 13–29). New York: Guilford Press.

Jackson, S. E., May, K. A., & Whitney, K. (1995). Understanding the dynamics of diversity in decision making teams. In R. A Guzzo & E. Salas (Eds.), *Team decision making effectiveness in organizations* (pp. 204–261). San Francisco: Jossey-Bass.

James, K., Chen, D-L., & Cropanzano, R. (in press). Culture and leadership among Taiwanese and U.S. workers: Do values influence leadership ideals? In M. N. Ruderman, M. W. Hughes-James, & S. E. Jackson (Eds.), *Selected research on work-team diversity*. Greensboro, NC: Center for Creative Leadership; and Washington, DC: American Psychological Association.

Johnston, W. B., & Packer, A. E. (1987). *Workforce 2000: Work and workers for the 21st century*. Washington, DC: U.S. Department of Labor.

Jones, E. E. (1985). Major developments in social psychology during the past five decades. In G. Lindzey & E. Aronson (Eds.), *Handbook of social psychology*, (3rd ed., Vol. 1, pp. 47–107). New York: Random House.

Kanter, R. M. (1991, May-June). Transcending business boundaries: 12,000 world managers view change. *Harvard Business Review*, pp. 151–164.

Levine, J. M., & Moreland, R. L. (1990). Progress in small group research. *Annual Review of Psychology, 41,* 585–634.

Mayo, M. C., Meindl, J. R., & Pastor, J. C. (in press). The cost of leading diversity: Effects of group diversity on leader's perceptions. In M. N. Ruderman, M. W. Hughes-James, & S. E. Jackson (Eds.), *Selected research on work team diversity.* Greensboro, NC: Center for Creative Leadership; and Washington, DC: American Psychological Association.

Morrison, A. M., & Von Glinow, M. A. (1990). Women and minorities in management. *American Psychologist, 45,* 200–208.

Race in the workplace: Is affirmative action working? (1991, July 8). *Business Week,* pp. 50–63.

Selbert, R. (1987, November 16). Women at work. *Future Scan, 554,* 1–3.

Sellers, P. (1990, June 4). What customers really want. *Fortune,* pp. 58–68.

Sundstrom, E., De Meuse, K. P., & Futrell, D. (1990). Work teams: Applications and effectiveness. *American Psychologist, 45,* 120–133.

PART ONE

Theory and Research

2

Traits, Expectations, Culture, and Clout: The Dynamics of Diversity in Work Groups

Joseph E. McGrath, Jennifer L. Berdahl, and Holly Arrow

This volume (and the conference on which it is based) tackles the problem of diversity in work groups. *Diversity* and *work group* are complex concepts. To examine the impact of diversity within work groups in a systematic way, we must first unpack the complexities and assumptions of these two concepts, and then relate them to one another in a richly articulated fashion. That is the project of this chapter.

Our concern in this chapter is not with diversity among members of an organization or among members of some general organizational category (such as the production division), but rather with diversity among interacting members of work groups. To proceed with our task, we first present a theoretical framework for the systematic analysis of behavior in work groups, building on group-theoretic ideas that have proven useful in analyzing and clarifying other issues within research on groups. In the second section, we analyze diversity as a multidimensional aspect of groups and discuss four models for studying its effects in groups. In the third sec-

Research on which this chapter is based was supported in part by NSF grants BNS 91-06501, IRI 91-07040, and IRI 93-10099 (Joseph E. McGrath, Principal Investigator) and by a National Science Foundation Graduate Research Fellowship grant to Holly Arrow.

tion, we discuss how different dimensions of diversity will affect groups over time, with and without membership changes.

THE NATURE OF WORK GROUPS

We define a work group as a dynamic system, made up of an integration of *people, purposes,* and *tools,* which become the group's *members, projects,* and *technology,* respectively (Argote & McGrath, 1993; Arrow & McGrath, 1995; McGrath, 1991; McGrath & Gruenfeld, 1993; see Figure 1). Every work group must continuously be concerned with at least three functions: (a) a *production function,* by which it makes a contribution to its embedding system (e.g., a larger organization) in exchange for that system's support of the group and its members; (b) a *member support function,* by which it makes contributions to its constituent members in exchange for their contributions to the group's activities; and (c) a *group well-being function,* by which the group maintains itself as an integral and effective system. Groups carry out all three of these functions by means of four modes of activity: project inception or goal selection activities; technical problem-

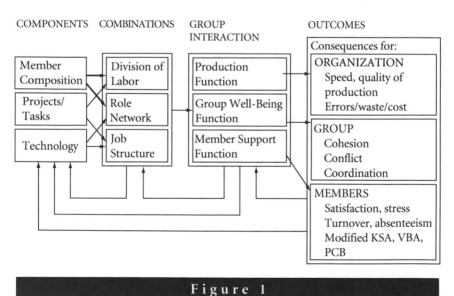

Figure 1

A framework for studying work groups.

18

solving activities; political or conflict resolution activities; and execution or goal attainment activities. These four modes apply to all three group functions.

Components of Work Groups

Members

A group's *composition* is the pattern of its members' characteristics. Members of a given collectivity may be diverse or homogeneous with respect to any of a large number of attributes. The composition of a group may be stable or may change over time as members come and go.

Projects

The group's purposes become transformed into a set of simultaneous or overlapping and interdependent *projects*, each of which can be specified in terms of a set of tasks. Group projects differ in a number of ways, one of which is especially notable: Projects differ in the extent to which they involve a demonstrably correct answer or best solution, versus seeking consensus on a preferred policy or plan. This corresponds to Laughlin's (1980) "intellective" versus "judgmental" continuum of tasks. Most projects subsume a variety of tasks and require a variety of activities—as reflected in the four modes of activity already noted (goal selection, technical problem solving, conflict resolution, and execution).

Technology

The group's tools include both the "hardware" it uses to carry out its activities and sustain itself, and the "software" of procedures and norms by which group members do their work and relate to one another. Borrowing from anthropology, we call a group's tools, rules, and procedures its *technology*.

Combinations of the Components

When studying groups, one needs to consider not only each component separately (that is, the members, the projects, and the technology), but also how those three sets of constituent elements combine, two at a time. We refer to the project–member matching as the *division of labor*, to the member–technology matching as the *role network*, and to the project–technology matching as the *job structure*. Division of labor refers to which members will carry out which parts of a set of tasks (e.g., for a baseball team, who will pitch and who will play left field). The role network refers to less formal differences in how group members relate to one another (e.g., who is the team's motivational leader and who is the locker-room clown). A job structure refers to the tasks to be done to carry out a given project, and the tools and procedures for accomplishing those tasks, without reference to any individual members (e.g., in baseball, the nine fielding positions and the nine batting-order positions constitute the job structure).

The group's composition sets limits for both its division of labor and its role network. If the array of member attributes do not fulfill the requirements of the group's division of labor, the specification of who will do what needs to change, or the members need to be changed (through training, socialization, or substitution) until there is an adequate fit. If the array of member attributes does not satisfy the requirements of its role system, either the role requirements (technology) or the group's membership must change, or some members must be socialized or trained to acquire the missing attributes. These matches (and the match between the group's technology and projects) are enacted simultaneously and continuously, a process that Poole and colleagues refer to as the group's *adaptive structuration* (Poole & Roth, 1989a, 1989b).

Any given adaptive structuration is subject to disruption if any of the components change. A change may improve or worsen the fit at one or more of those intersections. Disruption of the existing system can be an opportunity for the group to develop a new system altogether. The effects depend on the current situation, the particular changes, and the system's adaptive (or maladaptive) responses.

Types of Work Groups

Organizations create at least three kinds of work groups, distinguished by the different paths by which they originate (Arrow & McGrath, 1995; Mc-

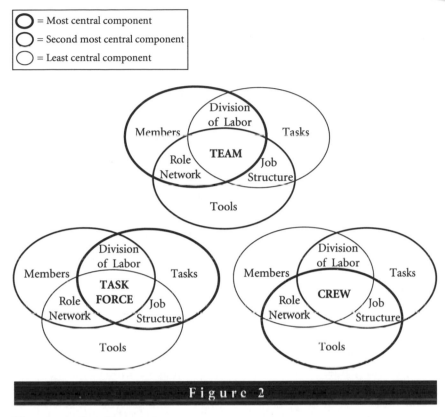

Figure 2

Three types of work groups.

Grath & Gruenfeld, 1993). These are illustrated in Figure 2. Some work groups are formed when an organization selects people, each of whom has a particular array of knowledge, skills, and abilities, and then trains, equips, and organizes them into a *team* that will be given responsibility for carrying out a particular class of projects on a continuing basis. Components of the group are incorporated in the logical sequence: members, then technology, then project.

Other work groups are formed because an organization wishes to carry out a specific project. People are assigned to a *task force*—which then selects or develops tools, rules, resources, and procedures for completing the project. The task force completes its project, then disbands. Components of the group are incorporated in the logical sequence: project, then members, then technology.

Still other work groups are formed when an organization establishes a focused technology designed to carry out a specific class of projects and then recruits personnel to provide a *crew* for that project–technology system. Components of the group are incorporated in the logical sequence: technology, then project, then members.

These three types of work groups (teams, task forces, and crews) differ in terms of which constituent element is primary (the members, the project, or the technology, respectively) and which elements, thereby, become less central and, hence, more subject to adaptation.

Our group-theoretic perspective has a number of implications for how variations in diversity may affect work groups over time. For example, the three types of groups differ in at least three important ways that relate to membership diversity: (a) the extent to which group members develop their own structure or fit into an existing structure; (b) the relative importance of member–member relations as opposed to member–project (division of labor), member–technology (role network), and project–technology (job structure) relations; and (c) the expected duration of the group with more or less the same membership, projects, and technology. These and other issues are discussed in terms of group development and change over time in the third section of this chapter, after we have discussed a number of issues related to the concept of diversity.

DIVERSITY IN WORK GROUPS

Diversity (and its opposite, homogeneity) refers to the differences (or similarities) among members of some particular collectivity—in our case, a work group. The term has most often been used to refer to demographic differences. At times, these demographic differences have been treated as though they are interchangeable—as though, for example, the effects of racial diversity in a group should be the same as the effects of differences among members on sex, religion, age, college major, or organizational tenure. When diversity is treated as a generic concept—as it is, for example, in social identity theory (see Brewer, chapter 3, this volume)—issues such as the nature of the historical relations between particular social groups are typically ignored.

A group's membership composition can be relatively homogeneous or diverse on more than just demographic characteristics. In our view, diversity on five clusters of attributes are of special importance for work groups. Group members may be relatively homogeneous or diverse on:

1. Demographic attributes (DEM) that are socially meaningful in the society in which the organization is embedded (e.g., age, race, ethnicity, gender, sexual orientation, physical status, religion, and education).
2. Task-related knowledge, skills, and abilities (KSA).
3. Values, beliefs, and attitudes (VBA).
4. Personality and cognitive and behavioral styles (PCB).
5. Status in the work group's embedding organization (ORG; e.g., organizational rank, occupational specialty, departmental affiliation, and tenure).

Attributes in these clusters differ in how easily they can be observed, either by another group member or by a third party, such as a researcher. Many demographic characteristics are immediately observable. One can make relatively accurate estimates of others' age, gender, race, ethnicity, handicapped status, and so on from merely seeing people, hearing them speak, and knowing their names. In most organizational contexts, attributes such as rank and department are also relatively easy to determine. Yet in some types of interaction (such as communication conducted via electronic mail), people can remain relatively anonymous with respect to organizational and personal demographic cues.

Attributes in the other three clusters are more difficult to assess. Individual standing on attributes in the KSA, VBA, and PCB clusters may be assessed on the basis of considerable interaction or via careful measurements such as tests and questionnaires. Individual capabilities, values, and styles are often inferred (correctly or incorrectly) from demographic cues (Newcomb, 1961). In general, however, it is relatively difficult to determine a stranger's underlying attributes, whether the stranger is a new group member or a research participant.

Attributes in these clusters also differ in how easy they are to change. For example, it is difficult or impossible to change one's sex or race, but one's values or skills are much more mutable. Implications of differences in mutability among the attribute clusters are addressed in the third section of the chapter, where we discuss the effects of diversity over time.

Diversity researchers use different frameworks for explaining how demographic diversity affects group outcomes. Below, we identify three common approaches that relate demographic diversity in groups to differences in member behavior, group interaction, and task performance. They can be regarded as three theoretical models that imply different (and sometimes opposing) predictions about diversity effects (see Figure 3). We describe these three frameworks below and then propose a more complex model that incorporates all three in a multicultural framework (see Figure 4).

Diversity Model A: A Trait Approach

This model presumes that diversity on demographic factors affects group interaction and performance only in so far as such diversity is directly linked to systematic differences in underlying attributes (KSA, VBA, and PCB; see Figure 3a). Researchers such as Northcraft, Polzer, Neale, and Kramer (chapter 4, this volume), who assert or assume that diversity on demographic characteristics implies diversity on underlying attributes related to group interaction, have taken this approach. Indeed, Murray (1989) explicitly used differences in age, tenure, and occupational and educational backgrounds as indicators of diversity on values, but did not measure values directly. Below we examine how diversity in one or more of the three clusters of underlying attributes may affect group member behavior, group interaction, and group task performance, and how various aspects of groups may modify those effects.

Group Functions and Modes of Activity

Different types of diversity may affect the ways in which groups engage in the four modes of activity (goal selection, technical problem solving, conflict resolution, and task execution) as they carry out their three functions

3a. Trait Approach:

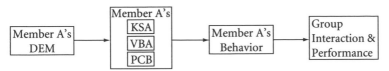

3b. Expectations Approach:

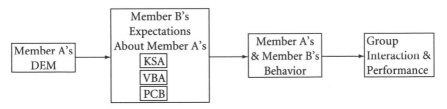

3c. Differential Power Approach:

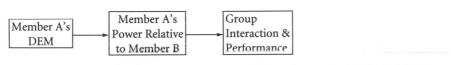

Figure 3

Three models of diversity.

(production, member support, and group well-being). For example, diversity on the capability cluster (KSA) may benefit goal selection, technical problem-solving activities, and the execution or implementation of the group's task. As members bring a broader array of knowledge, skills, and abilities to a group, the capability to generate a variety of goals and to tackle technical problems should increase, and a wide selection of skills should be available to the group for carrying out its task.

Diversity on the values cluster (VBA) may impede goal selection if members have difficulty reaching consensus, but homogeneity of values may reduce the quality of the goals selected (Janis, 1972). Similarly, if members differ in values, beliefs, and attitudes, the incidence of conflicts may increase, and these conflicts may be more difficult to resolve. Diversity of values is likely to affect the level of attraction and respect among members, ease of communication, and degree of overt conflict in the group.

Multicultural Approach:

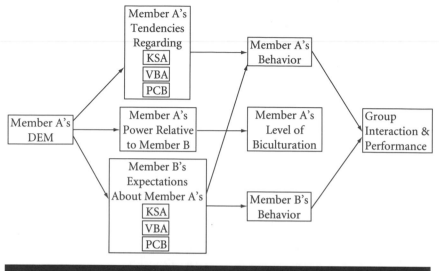

Figure 4

An integrative model for studying diversity.

Diversity on the relevant attributes in the personality cluster (PCB) may benefit a group's goal selection activities, provided the group members can communicate effectively enough to take advantage of their diverse perspectives. Homogeneity in some behavioral styles may decrease political conflicts. Yet, if members are homogeneous in certain personality traits—for example, if all group members are high in dominance—conflicts can increase.

These examples should not be construed as generic predictions for all attributes in any particular cluster. Instead, the effects will depend on the particular attribute, the type of group and task, and other features of the group's context.

Projects and Tasks

It is likely that many of the effects of different types of diversity depend in part on the types of tasks the group's project entails. The distinction between intellective and judgmental tasks (Laughlin, 1980; McGrath,

1984) is related to the technical problem solving and conflict resolution modes of activity (McGrath, 1991), respectively, for the production function. Diversity on the capabilities cluster should be associated with effective performance on intellective tasks. Diversity on the values cluster may be negatively associated with a group's efficiency (though not necessarily with its effectiveness) on judgmental tasks. Diverse ideas and perspectives provided by diversity on the capabilities and personality clusters may be advantageous for groups whose job it is to generate new products or to devise, improve, or use new procedures.

Technology

Our framework suggests that effects of diversity are likely to be in part a function of the group's technology. For example, if group members differ in their familiarity with and skills relating to the communication technology the group is using, this should affect group interaction and performance. If a group can communicate only via a computer, then those members most adept at typing and using computers may participate most in the group interaction; if a group meets face-to-face, members with strong verbal skills may participate most.

Types of Work Groups

Diversity is an aspect of membership. Thus, diversity should affect teams more than task forces and should affect crews least. For example, we would expect diversity among members on relevant attributes in the KSA, VBA, and PCB clusters to be related to how the group divides its tasks among members and what role network the group develops. Diversity on these three sets of underlying attributes should have little effect on job structure in crews.

Diversity Model B: An Expectations Approach

This model emphasizes that demographic factors affect group interaction and performance primarily because demographic differences evoke differential expectations by other group members (whether or not these expectations are justified). That is, group members make inferences, based on one another's demographic attributes, about one another's underlying attributes (KSA, VBA, and PCB). These inferences shape the expectations group members have about one another's behavior, leading to differential treatment of, and differential behavioral responses by, other group members (see Figure 3). Expectations based on demographic cues are usually thought to be more pronounced and stereotypic as the demographic attributes in question become more salient.

For example, social-role theory (Eagly, 1987) suggests that when gender is salient in a group context, group members will have sex-stereotypic expectations for one another's behavior. Expectations-states theory (e.g., Berger & Conner, 1974; Berger, Conner, & Fisek, 1974; Carli, 1991; Ridgeway, 1991) proposes that when gender is salient, it is used as a status cue to make inferences about competence (KSA), giving members who are assumed to be more competent more opportunity to participate in and influence group interaction. In another example of this approach, Lawrence (1988) proposes that it is the expectations based on age, not the actual age differences, that affect behavior toward people who are dissimilar in age. Brewer (chapter 3, this volume) and Tsui, Xin, and Egan (chapter 5, this volume) also emphasize this approach.

In sum, the expectations approach does not necessarily assert that demographic differences are linked to differences in underlying attributes, but rather that demographics are used to infer underlying attributes and subsequently shape the expectations for and behavior toward group members. If people generally behave as others expect them to based on demographic attributes, then these attributes should affect group functions and modes of activity in ways similar to those described for the trait approach when demographic attributes are salient. If, instead, group members rebel against expectations that are based on their demographic attributes, we should expect more conflict in groups where this is salient. If the expectations reflect inaccurate stereotypes, we can expect the group to perform less well because the group's division of labor and role networks will not reflect group members' actual underlying attributes.

Interestingly, this approach differs from the trait approach in its implications for the interaction of demographic attributes and communication technology. Under this model, we would expect demographic diversity among group members to have a different impact for groups communicating only via electronic technology (e.g., a computer conference group) versus groups working face-to-face (Hollingshead, McGrath, & O'Connor, 1993; McGrath & Hollingshead, 1994; Sproull & Kiesler, 1991). The relations among members are likely to be more anonymous and more impersonal in computer groups. Effects of personal and organizational demographics will, therefore, be dampened in computer groups, as group members are likely to be less aware of variation among members on those attributes (McGrath & Hollingshead, 1994).

Diversity Model C: A Differential Power Approach

Like model B, this model is silent on whether demographic differences map to differences in capabilities, values, and personality. It proposes that demographic diversity affects group interaction and performance primarily because members of different demographic categories (such as men and women) come to the group with differential power—based on differential access to resources—in both the embedding organization and the larger society within which it is operating (see Figure 3).

Various feminist theories (see Tong, 1989) and other analyses of structural and symbolic power differences between demographic groups (e.g., Tolbert, Andrews, & Simons, chapter 6, this volume; Ely, chapter 7, this volume) suggest this approach. Whether or not people differ on underlying attributes, members of dominant groups (e.g., men, European-Americans, heterosexuals, or able-bodied people) carry with them into work groups greater access to resources and more social or symbolic status and prestige. This affords members of dominant groups greater influence in shaping group interactions and outcomes than members of subordinate groups (e.g., women, African-Americans, homosexuals, or physically disabled people). Members of different demographic groups are likely to differ on some underlying attributes, given their differential sociohistorical experiences. Regardless of any "true" differences, those attributes on which they are believed to differ are likely to become "marked." The values of those attributes that are believed to be characteristic of the dominant group will be regarded more positively than those believed to be characteristic of the subordinate group (e.g., assertiveness vs. nurturance).

This model predicts that members of subordinate groups will be relatively "silenced" in group interaction and that the group will not make full use of nor reflect these members' capabilities, values, and behavioral styles. This may impede goal selection, technical problem solving, conflict resolution, and task execution. To the extent that communication technology or procedural norms dampen the salience of power-based cues, however, the detrimental effects that this differential power approach predicts should be lessened.

Diversity Model D: An Integrative Multicultural Approach

We propose a multicultural model that incorporates all three of the above models (see Figure 4). In this view, when group members are diverse on certain demographic attributes, they can be regarded as having diverse cultural identities. Those cultural identities reflect differential sociohistorical experiences and, hence, are likely to be associated with actual differences in expertise (KSA), in values (VBA), and in habits (PCB) (model A). Moreover, group members recognize those cultural identities and carry certain expectations about attributes and behaviors probably associated with them (model B). Furthermore, in many instances, the different cultural identities carry differential power and status in the organizational and cultural context in which that work group is operating. Hence, members of more dominant cultures can, and probably will, exercise more influence over the group's interaction and task performance. As a consequence, the underlying attributes of those powerful members are likely to play a greater role in shaping the group's interaction and task performance than are the underlying attributes of the less powerful members (model C). Power relations in the surrounding culture get embedded not just in people (stereotypes), but also in rules and procedures (technology) where they are harder to notice.

When culturally based differences pose problems for a work group, members of the less dominant group often bear the major burden of adjustment. Members of the less dominant group may also have greater multicultural sophistication, with a better understanding of the dominant group's culture than vice versa. Acculturation responses vary at both the societal and individual level (Triandis, 1994). A person may (a) shift toward the dominant culture (accommodation), which will downplay or minimize differences; (b) shift so far that his or her behaviors become more stereotypical of the dominant culture than is the case for most members of that culture (overshooting); or (c) emphasize the ways in which his or her own culture or subculture is different, downplaying similarities (ethnic or cultural affirmation) (Triandis, Kashima, Shimada, & Villareal, 1986). An alternative strategy is what Berry, Poortinga, Segall, and Dasen (1992) term *integration*, in which members value and draw on aspects of both cultures.

Triandis (chapter 10, this volume) has emphasized such a multicultural approach to studying the effects of diversity. He joins other cross-cultural psychologists in arguing that, under certain conditions, interaction of a cooperative nature among members of different cultural backgrounds can change harmful expectations (prejudices) (Triandis, 1980, 1994). Greater familiarity with one another as individuals, it is argued, can help dispel erroneous beliefs about members of various social categories (e.g., Tolbert, Andrews, & Simons, chapter 6, this volume).

Triandis (chapter 10 this volume) suggests that diversity researchers should study large and meaningful cultural differences within work groups, for example, by studying work groups composed of members from different countries. This approach could also be applied to the study of dominant and subordinate groups within the same country or metaculture, however. For example, Berdahl (1993) has suggested that women's experiences can be considered to form a subcultural pattern in relation to a dominant male culture. Berdahl suggests that some stable and systematic sex differences in personality and behavioral tendencies result from stable and systematic sex differences in economic and social power in society at large. These power and personality differences, in turn, translate into differences in influence and cultural dynamics in mixed-sex groups.

DYNAMICS OF DIVERSITY

This section explores the dynamics of diversity, using the multicultural model (model D) as a theoretical framework. That model includes the key factors of the other three models: heterogeneity of underlying attributes (model A), member expectations about one another (model B), and power relations (model C). These components play differentially important roles for work groups over time, depending in part on the type of group and in part on the relative stability or change in group membership composition. We also discuss processes of cultural adaptation highlighted by the multicultural model. We consider, in turn, groups whose membership remains stable over time and groups whose membership changes.

Changes in Diversity with Continuity of Membership

The effects of a given level of diversity in a work group often take time to unfold and may vary, depending on the group's stage of development. Changing effects reflect changes that occur within and between members as the group develops. Some of those changes involve a change in diversity on underlying attributes that are important to the group's activities. Others reflect changes in member expectations about one another.

Some characteristics on which members can be diverse (e.g., race and sex) are fixed; hence, diversity on such attributes will not change as long as the membership of the group remains the same. Other attributes (e.g., specific skills, beliefs, and behavioral styles) are more mutable. Group diversity on KSA, VBA, and PCB attributes changes over time through processes of integration and differentiation that are part of group development. In groups with people from different cultural or subcultural backgrounds, acculturation processes can lead to greater integration or greater differentiation.

Convergence

As newly formed groups develop norms and procedures, members' group-related values, beliefs, and attitudes are likely to converge, enhancing a sense of group identity and increasing group cohesiveness. The more interdependent member activities are and the higher the coordination needs, the more important it will be for the group to establish shared assumptions and ground rules for interaction and performance.

This convergence process operates most strongly in teams. In crews, norms, procedures, and job structures are typically established before members join, reducing uncertainty about who will be doing what, how, and why, and to some extent eliminating the need for this "team-building" activity. In task forces, the limited time horizon and prospects for future interaction limit the convergence process, but some level of value consensus must still be reached for the group to accomplish its tasks.

Teams whose members work intensively together need a common language and efficient communication procedures to perform effectively. If members have difficulty communicating because of language differences based on demographic or organizational characteristics such as national origin, level of education, or different functional specialties, the group must agree upon or develop a shared language to use in accomplishing group tasks. The intensive interaction required in finding this common ground can pull together members with quite diverse values and perspectives. The more that members differ on values and beliefs, the longer it will take to negotiate shared group norms.

One important set of beliefs highlighted by the expectations component of the model are the beliefs that members have about one another. People form impressions based on what they have heard or have observed about others, and stereotypes linked to sex, race, age, occupational specialty, and national origin play a role in these impressions. The degree of difference that members perceive will depend on their background and experience, and also on the context. For example, two Americans from New York and Georgia may see themselves as different when stationed in the United States, but see themselves as very similar if they are working together in Japan.

If group members perceive one another as similar on relevant dimensions, they are more likely to feel attracted to one another, facilitating group well-being (Newcomb, 1961). They may also presume that others will think and act as they do, and, hence, spend little time finding out about other members' assumptions. Therefore, demographically homogeneous groups should be both more cohesive and more efficient and productive in the short run, as members focus immediately on the task. Over the long run, however, members' assumption of similarity may lead to problems if they fail to notice fundamental differences until these lead to serious difficulties.

Of course, fundamental differences can also be overlooked by people from different cultures, because they simply take it for granted that "everyone knows X." Armstrong and Cole (chapter 8, this volume) give examples of overlooked differences in values and attitudes that led to problems for both culturally homogeneous and culturally diverse research and development teams.

Differentiation

Whereas diversity on group-relevant norms should decline over time as routines are established and members accumulate shared experiences, diversity on specialized skills and knowledge, and on behavioral styles related to the division of labor and role specializations, are likely to increase. Such differentiation effects should vary with group type, being most pronounced in teams with stable membership and elaborate role structures. This trend may be moderated if teams cross-train their members. It should be weaker in task forces and may not occur at all in crews, because crews often have a high and constant level of KSA and PCB diversity by design.

The tendency toward increased differentiation should also be stronger in teams and task forces that are initially more homogeneous on capabilities and behavioral styles, and weaker in groups where existing differences in job-relevant KSA and PCB are used as a basis for job and role distribution. If demographic differences are used as cues to determine the division of labor, this will limit further differentiation only if members are indeed different along stereotypic lines. Inappropriate task and role assignments can fuel both overt and unexpressed conflict (O'Connor, Gruenfeld, & McGrath, 1993). Members of teams have more at stake in these struggles than members of more ephemeral task forces, and, hence, struggles are apt to be more bitter and divisive.

In demographically homogeneous teams and task forces that are also homogeneous on skills (KSA) and behavioral styles (PCB), the division of labor and development of roles can be more difficult because they must be relatively arbitrary. In such groups, quite small differences may be used as the basis for differentiation into roles, status positions, and task assignments (Berger & Conner, 1974). For instance, once a person who is slightly more talkative has been designated as a leader, he or she may rapidly become much more dominant in the group, as behavioral patterns considered appropriate to a leader are reinforced (e.g., Whyte, 1943).

In a crew, the job structure is the most important aspect of the group system, and this structure is typically designed and then staffed with members who fill particular jobs within the group system (e.g., an airline crew). Rather than tasks being divided up by the members, people are assigned to tasks based on job descriptions.

Acculturation

When people are living in cultures different from their own, they may adopt an *integration* strategy of acculturation, in which they participate in the different culture while also maintaining their own. Berry and colleagues (1992) presented cross-cultural evidence that this is the most desirable for mental health. However, other strategies may predominate in work groups composed of culturally diverse members. Some (e.g., members of lower status social categories such as immigrants) may pursue an *assimilation* strategy, in which they adopt the new culture and repress or reject their own.

In work groups such as cross-functional teams, an analogous set of choices is available. As the engineer and marketing representative learn to translate one another's languages and concepts, they may grow increasingly similar as both adopt some aspects of the other person's "culture" (integration and convergence). They may also exaggerate their differences as a way of reaffirming their identity with their functional department.

Membership Change and Diversity

Turnover is a popular dependent variable in diversity research (Jackson et al., 1991; Wagner, Pfeffer, & O'Reilly, 1984). However, turnover—that is, membership change—can also be studied as an input variable that affects the pattern and degree of group diversity. Despite the frequency of references to "increasing diversity" (which usually means increasing demographic diversity) in the workplace, the impact of actual increases (or decreases) in the demographic diversity of existing work groups has not been a common focus of diversity research (but see Tolbert, Andrews, & Simons, chapter 6, this volume, and Allmendinger & Hackman, 1993, for notable exceptions).

The only way that diversity on fixed demographic attributes can increase in organizations is through membership change: the addition and replacement of members. All organizations that have an extended history undergo such changes in membership, and most work groups within these organizations also experience changes in membership over time.

Changes in membership composition affect the diversity of a group on all five clusters of attributes. A group that loses a member inevitably becomes more homogeneous in KSA, for example, because it loses whatever unique knowledge, skills, and abilities that member had. A group that gains a new member automatically becomes more diverse in KSA and also in tenure (ORG), with the newcomer distinguished from the "old-timers." If a member leaves and is replaced, the configuration of diversity in the group will change to the extent that the new member is unlike the old member. At the very least, the replacement member will lack much of the "institutional memory" of the person replaced (see Wegner, 1986, on transactive memory) and will be unfamiliar with that group's habitual routines (Gersick & Hackman, 1990). Indeed, differences between the new member and the member replaced may be just as important and salient to the group as any difference between the new member and the continuing members.

Newcomers to groups are necessarily different because they are new. This creates a certain amount of social distance between newcomers and old-timers. Newcomers who have transferred from elsewhere in the same organization will share much of the same corporate culture. Newcomers who are new to both the group and the embedding organization typically diverge more from other group members in beliefs and attitudes (VBA) about issues upon which the group has established norms. An inexperienced rookie, however, is likely to adapt more quickly than someone hired in who is familiar with a very different organizational culture.

To become fully functioning members of a team, newcomers must go through a period of mutual adjustment during which established members accommodate to the newcomers and the newcomers learn the ropes and take on roles in the group (Moreland & Levine, 1982, 1988, 1989). Admittance to the team is a two-stage process. The act of joining is external, obvious, and often abrupt; the second stage is internal to the group and takes time (Arrow & McGrath, 1995). High turnover among new hires (Wanous, 1982) can be interpreted as the departure of newcomers who made the first transition, but not the second.

Many organizations have increased their hiring of people who are demographically different from established group members, but find they have trouble retaining these newcomers. If new hires are different from the rest of the group on easily observable and socially meaningful demographic attributes such as sex, age, or ethnicity, the compounded social distance that members feel may make it especially difficult to integrate these new members. Jackson and colleagues (1991), for example, found that dissimilarity from other group members on age, educational background, and industry experience predicted turnover in top management teams.

However, groups that are formed from the start with a high level of diversity among members—on demographic attributes such as sex and race, and on organizational attributes such as functional specialty—should be better at accepting and socializing newcomers. Ziller (1965) proposes that the chances for successful integration of newcomers increases with greater membership heterogeneity because the newcomer is more likely to find common ground and identify with at least one other group member. Another basis for this prediction is that members of heterogeneous groups are more accustomed to dealing with differences and, thus, more accepting of the difference of being new and inexperienced.

Group Types and Membership Change

Changes in demographic homogeneity resulting from membership change should have the strongest impact on teams, because of the centrality of member–member relations in them. Change should have the least impact on crews, with task forces in the middle. Teams need the most time and energy to adjust to a loss in membership and to integrate new or replacement members. Task forces have fewer resources to devote to the socialization process and, thus, can be quite vulnerable to the impact of membership change, even though member–member relations are less developed than in teams. Crews, in contrast, are structured to absorb frequent changes of personnel with ease (Arrow & McGrath, 1995). The impact of VBA and PCB diversity (and any language differences pronounced enough to impede communication) should be greatest in those groups that have both high integration needs and that develop their own integration structures.

Member Change in Teams

The most important group structure for teams is the role network, which specifies both the social structure of the group and the set of norms and procedures that become an integral part of the group technology. Although in some teams the role of leader is assigned by outsiders, much of the role network evolves to fit the personalities, skills, and preferences of existing team members (Homans, 1950). Because teams typically work together over an extended period on a broad range of tasks, the social relations also tend to be well-developed. Integrating a member with a distinctly different set of values (VBA) may demand considerable time and energy.

A team may rely heavily on differences in personality and capabilities in developing an effective role network and division of labor. Because of the higher variability of tasks tackled by long-standing teams (as compared to crews or task forces), a team is apt to perform most effectively and provide ample member support if members have different preferences and strengths that can be matched with different phases of projects. The loss of a member who fills a tailor-made role decreases the group's PCB and KSA diversity and leaves a gap that is difficult to fill by simply recruiting a new member.

If new members are different from old members on an array of attributes, the group may need to restructure the role system and division of labor completely to accommodate the change in membership. The investment of time and energy this entails may disrupt task performance, at least temporarily, and also limit the member support available to old-timers, who are busy socializing the newcomers.

Member Change in Task Forces

In task forces, the division of labor—the matching of members to tasks—is the most important structure. Often, this structure is not determined in advance, but must be worked out by group members. Inferences about KSA, VBA, and PCB attributes based on demographic attributes may well influence the assignment of members to tasks, reflecting the expectations component of the model. Actual diversity on underlying attributes, reflecting the trait component of the model, should broaden the resource base of the group.

Because task forces are usually staffed part-time by organizational members who have different primary work groups, organizational attributes may also provide an important cue for distributing tasks. If members leave and are replaced by people from the same primary work groups, the substitute members may be treated as more or less equivalent regardless of actual differences between the departing member and the replacement. If an engineer is replaced by someone from accounting, however, differences between the two should be highly salient, as will be differences in KSA, VBA, and PCB attributes associated with (or assumed to be associated with) those functional specialties.

Member Change in Crews

Membership change is frequent in crews, but replacement members typically "know the ropes" for their job and, hence, are more truly interchangeable. A changeover in crew members, whether in a flight crew, at a switchboard, or in a restaurant's wait staff, should require minimal adjustment or socialization. In a crew work setting, which typically includes a great deal of standardization both in task activity and communication norms, diversity on the values and personality clusters should have little effect on routine task performance. In a crisis situation, however, the imported infrastructure of language and roles may prove inadequate. Unless the same people "crew" together frequently, they will not have spent the time together that is needed to be more than superficially aware of differences in their perspectives.

In crews, diversity is most apt to be considered an issue if people with lower status demographic attributes (e.g., Latina) are in high-status jobs traditionally occupied by those with higher status demographic attributes. An airline crew consisting of Latinas in the cockpit and Anglo men as flight attendants is no more demographically diverse than an airline crew with Latina flight attendants and Anglo men in the cockpit. Nonetheless, interpersonal friction may result when stereotyped assumptions about relative status, competencies, and roles are violated. (For good examples, see Whyte, 1948.) Higher status jobs cannot simply be reassigned to those with higher status demographic attributes. For an airline crew to do so would be a clear violation of member–task–technology matches that are designed into the system. In crews, the organizational attribute of functional specialty is typically a much stronger cue about job-relevant skills (KSA) than any demographic attribute. Status conflicts based on demographic differences can also, of course, occur in teams and task forces. But these two group types typically have more latitude than do crews in rearranging their own division of labor and roles to reflect demographically based status hierarchies.

Groups, Diversity, and Time

Considering demographic diversity as a dynamic property of groups raises issues of change, history, and patterning that are typically not addressed in research on diversity. Members of two groups that have the exact same demographic diversity profile may view and respond to their intragroup variety quite differently if that profile is a long-standing configuration for one group but a newly diverse configuration for the other.

A marked increase in demographic diversity confounds two kinds of change—a particular change in the pattern of member attributes and membership change as an event in and of itself. Untangling the joint effects of the two requires specific attention to membership change as an independent variable. Effects ascribed to "more diversity" may instead represent a more general response to change that can also be provoked by a marked *decrease* in member diversity that involved the same amount of turnover. It may also be the case that the key issue is not the amount of diversity at all, but rather a change in how members with different demographic attributes are distributed among roles—as in our flight crew example.

Groups may be as sensitive to alterations in the patterning of diversity as they are to relative "amounts" of diversity among members. Any turnover in membership will involve some change in the patterning of diversity in the group. Tsui, Xin, and Egan (chapter 5, this volume) tackle some of the complexities involved in the patterning of diversity in the static case, focusing on vertical dyads. Brewer (chapter 3, this volume) adds a dynamic element by reconfiguring groups to alter the patterning of roles among members. Tolbert, Andrews, and Simons (chapter 6, this volume) take a more macro perspective, investigating both a broader period of time and a larger aggregate of people than the small interacting groups we have focused on in this chapter.

DIVERSITY IN ORGANIZATIONS IS POLITICAL

"Diversity in the workplace" has become a catch phrase, widely and loosely used to refer to "increasing" demographic diversity by the popular press, by authors of popular literature about work organizations, and by researchers of work organizations. Diversity is often referred to both as (a) an implied desideratum, to justify affirmative action and related policies in regard to race, ethnicity, gender, disability, and age; and (b) an implied barrier to effective task performance and overall organizational effectiveness.

The issue of diversity in organizations is intensely controversial and political, and, inevitably, this permeates the conduct of research on diversity issues. Because diversity is a complex matter, one cannot ask all of the important questions at once. In any research endeavor, what answers one comes to depends on what questions one asks and how those questions are asked—that is, how the researcher construes the problem domain at the outset. Such construals are closely intertwined with the researcher's prior beliefs, values, and so forth, and those initial construals of the problem shape and limit what the researcher can find and how results are likely to be interpreted. Such initial construals of the problem are carried, in part, in terms of the models described above—that is, they depend upon which sets of assumptions are being made about diversity effects. They are also carried in terms of which diversity clusters, and which dimensions within those clusters, are the focus of research.

Thus, when researchers or practitioners assert that demographic diversity is good for groups, they often refer to a group's need for a wide range of knowledge, skills, abilities, and cognitive perspectives. This line of reasoning is based on a trait model: Demographically diverse groups are more likely to have diverse capabilities (KSA).

In contrast, when researchers or practitioners assert that demographic diversity is bad for groups, they often refer to a group's need for consensus on values in order to achieve agreement on goals, norms, and procedures. This reasoning is also built on a trait model, but focuses on different clusters of attributes: Demographically homogeneous groups are more likely to be homogeneous in beliefs, attitudes, and values and in behavioral styles.

At the same time, other cases for and against demographic diversity are built on arguments based on expectations and power analyses. Some military spokesmen, for example, have argued that demographic diversity is bad for military groups because existing (demographically homogeneous) group members (e.g., European-American heterosexual males) would not accept or be able to work effectively with members of different demographic categories (e.g., African-Americans, women, or homosexuals). Members of demographically subordinate groups would presumably encounter difficulties working with members of demographically dominant groups who are prejudiced against them.

In our view, researchers cannot avoid the political issues embedded in their work and so should confront those issues directly. Furthermore, they are likely to make much more effective progress on the problem if they work from a model that is more inclusive of the alternative sets of assumptions and that tries to reckon with a broad range of attributes and a broad range of aspects of the problem. Doing so, however, increases the complexity of the problem and the difficulty of conducting research. That complexity is even further increased when research attempts to take into account the dynamics of diversity and its myriad effects over time.

REFERENCES

Allmendinger, J., & Hackman, J. R. (1993). *The more the better? On the inclusion of women in professional organizations* (Working paper #94-005). Boston: Harvard University Business School, Division of Research.

Argote, L., & McGrath, J. E. (1993). Group process in organizations: Continuity and change. In C. Cooper & I. T. Robertson (Eds.), *International review of industrial and organizational psychology* (pp. 333–389). London: John Wiley.

Arrow, H., & McGrath, J. E. (1995). Membership dynamics in groups at work: A theoretical framework. In B. M. Staw & L. L. Cummings (Eds.), *Research in organizational behavior* (Vol. 17, pp. 373–411). Greenwich, CT: JAI Press.

Berdahl, J. L. (1993). *Toward a theory of gender: Feminist subculture within male culture.* Unpublished manuscript, University of Illinois, Urbana-Champaign, IL.

Berger, J., & Conner, T. L. (1974). Performance expectations and behavior in small groups: A revised formulation. In J. Berger, T. Conner, & M. H. Fisek (Eds.), *Expectations states theory: A theoretical research program* (pp. 85–110). Cambridge, MA: Winthrop.

Berger, J., Conner, T., & Fisek, M. H. (Eds.). (1974). *Expectations states theory: A theoretical research program.* Cambridge, MA: Winthrop.

Berry, J. W., Poortinga, Y. H., Segall, M. H., & Dasen, P. R. (1992). *Cross-cultural psychology: Research and applications.* New York: Cambridge University Press.

Carli, L. L. (1991). Gender status and influence. In E. J. Lawler, B. Markowsky, C. Ridgeway, & H. A. Walker (Eds.), *Advances in group processes,* (Vol. 8, pp. 89–113). Greenwich, CT: JAI Press.

Eagly, A. H. (1987). *Sex differences in social behavior: A social-role analysis.* Hillsdale, NJ: Erlbaum.

Gersick, C. J. G., & Hackman, J. R. (1990). Habitual routines in task-performing groups. *Organizational Behavior and Human Decision Processes, 47,* 65–97.

Hollingshead, A. B., McGrath, J. E., & O'Connor, K. M. (1993). Group task performance and communication technology: A longitudinal study of computer-mediated versus face-to-face work groups. *Small Group Research, 24,* 307–333.

Homans, G. C. (1950). *The human group.* New York: Harcourt, Brace & World.

Jackson, S. E., Brett, J. F., Sessa, V. I., Cooper, D. M., Julin, J. A., & Peyronnin, K. (1991). Some differences make a difference: Individual dissimilarity and group heterogeneity as correlates of recruitment, promotions, and turnover. *Journal of Applied Psychology, 76,* 675–689.

Janis, I. L. (1972). *Groupthink: Psychological studies of policy fiascoes* (2nd ed.). Boston: Houghton-Mifflin.

Laughlin, P. R. (1980). Social combination processes of cooperative problem-solving groups on verbal intellective tasks. In M. Fishbein (Ed.), *Progress in social psychology* (Vol. 1, pp. 127–155). Hillsdale, NJ: Erlbaum.

Lawrence, B. S. (1988). New wrinkles in the theory of age: Demography, norms, and performance ratings. *Academy of Management Journal, 31,* 309–337.

McGrath, J. E. (1984). *Groups: Interaction and performance.* Englewood Cliffs, NJ: Prentice Hall.

McGrath, J. E. (1991). Time, interaction, and performance (TIP): A theory of groups. *Small Group Research, 22,* 147–174.

McGrath, J. E., & Gruenfeld, D. H. (1993). Toward a dynamic and systemic theory of groups: An integration of six temporally enriched perspectives. In M. M. Chemers & R. Ayman (Eds.), *The future of leadership research: Promise and perspective* (pp. 217–243). Orlando, FL: Academic Press.

McGrath, J. E., & Hollingshead, A. B. (1994). *Groups interacting with technology.* Newbury Park, CA: Sage.

Moreland, R. L., & Levine, J. M. (1982). Socialization in small groups: Temporal changes in individual-group relations. In L. Berkowitz (Ed.), *Advances in experimental social psychology* (Vol. 15, pp. 137–192). New York: Academic Press.

Moreland, R. L., & Levine, J. M. (1988). Group dynamics over time: Socialization and development in small groups. In J. McGrath (Ed.), *The social psychology of time: New perspectives.* Newbury Park, CA: Sage.

Moreland, R. L., & Levine, J. M. (1989). Newcomers and old-timers in small groups. In P. B. Paulus (Ed.), *Psychology of group influence* (pp. 141–186). Hillsdale, NJ: Lawrence Erlbaum.

Murray, A. I. (1989). Top management group heterogeneity and firm performance. *Strategic Management Journal, 10,* 125–141.

Newcomb, T. M. (1961). *The acquaintance process.* New York: Holt, Reinhart & Winston.

O'Connor, K. M., Gruenfeld, D. H., & McGrath, J. E. (1993). The experience and effects of conflict in continuing work groups. *Small Group Research, 24,* 362–382.

Poole, M. S., & Roth, J. (1989a). Decision development in small groups IV: A typology of decision paths. *Human Communication Research, 15,* 323–356.

Poole, M. S., & Roth, J. (1989b). Decision development in small groups V: Test of a contingency model. *Human Communication Research, 15,* 549–589.

Ridgeway, C. (1991). The social construction of status value: Gender and other nominal characteristics. *Social Forces, 70,* 367–386.

Sproull, L., & Kiesler, S. (1991). *Connections: New ways of working in the networked organization.* Cambridge, MA: MIT Press.

Tong, R. (1989). *Feminist thought: A comprehensive introduction.* Boulder, CO: Westview Press.

Triandis, H. C. (1980). Introduction to handbook of cross-cultural psychology. In H. C. Triandis & W. W. Lambert (Eds.), *Handbook of cross-cultural psychology* (Vol. 1, pp. 1–14). Boston: Allyn & Bacon.

Triandis, H. C. (1994). *Culture and social behavior.* New York: McGraw-Hill.

Triandis, H. C., Kashima, Y., Shimada, E., & Villareal, M. (1986). Acculturation indices as a means of confirming cultural differences. *International Journal of Psychology, 21,* 43–70.

Wagner, W. G., Pfeffer, J., & O'Reilly, C. A., III. (1984). Organizational demography and turnover in top-management groups. *Administrative Science Quarterly, 29,* 74–92.

Wanous, J. P. (1982). *Organizational entry: Recruitment, selection, orientation and socialization of newcomers.* Reading, MA: Addison-Wesley.

Wegner, D. M. (1986). Transactive memory: A contemporary analysis of the group mind. In B. Mullen & G. R. Goethals (Eds.), *Theories of group behavior* (pp. 185–208). New York: Springer-Verlag.

Whyte, W. F. (1943). *Street corner society.* Chicago: University of Chicago Press.

Whyte, W. F. (1948). *Human relations in the restaurant industry.* New York: McGraw-Hill.

Ziller, R. C. (1965). Toward a theory of open and closed groups. *Psychological Bulletin, 64,* 164–182.

3

Managing Diversity: The Role of Social Identities

Marilynn B. Brewer

L arge work organizations, and work groups within those organizations, can be defined as social groups in at least two senses. First, a
work group is a *bounded social category* in that we can specify who is a
member or participant and who is not. Second, a work group is characterized by *social interdependence* in that both collective and individual outcomes are influenced by what other individuals in the group do. Because
of these properties, work groups and organizations are potential *social
identities* for those who see themselves as members. The purpose of this
chapter is to review the consequences of different social identities within
an organization for the functioning of diverse work teams.

Social identity theory (Hogg & Abrams, 1988; Tajfel, 1978; Turner,
Hogg, Oakes, Reicher, & Wetherell, 1987) provides a social psychological
perspective on the origins and consequences of group identification. According to this perspective, identification with a social group involves two
key ingredients: first, that membership in the social group is an important, emotionally significant aspect of the individual's self-concept, and
second, that collective interests are of concern to the individual, above
and beyond their implications for personal self-interest (Brewer, 1991).

47

In effect, then, social identities are extensions of the self; social identity entails "a shift towards the perception of self as an interchangeable exemplar of some social category and away from the perception of self as a unique person" (Turner et al., 1987, p. 50).

Social identity theory posits that such group identification has both cognitive and motivational underpinnings. Group identification arises, first of all, from basic cognitive processes of social *categorization*. Although almost all sources of variation among human beings can be conceived of as continuous dimensions, there is a strong tendency to simplify our cognitive representations of the social world by dividing persons into discrete social categories. Once such categories have been defined and labeled, processes of category *accentuation* are set into motion. Differences between categories are exaggerated while individual differences within categories are minimized (Tajfel & Wilkes, 1963).

The cognitive processes of categorization and category accentuation apply to perceptions of objects in the physical world just as they do to the perception of social groups. However, social categorization has a special feature that distinguishes it from object categorization in a profound way: The individual perceiver is a member of some social categories and not of others. Thus, all social categorizations implicitly involve a further distinction between *ingroups* (categories to which the perceiver belongs) and *outgroups* (categories to which the perceiver does not belong). Social categories, in effect, create we–they, us–them distinctions. When such categorizations also have emotional significance for an individual's self-concept, the motivational components of ingroup–outgroup distinctions are engaged. These include ingroup loyalties and favoritism, implicit intergroup rivalries, and negative stereotypes and distrust of outgroup members (Brewer, 1979; Schopler & Insko, 1992; Tajfel, 1970).

SOCIAL IDENTITY AND DIVERSITY

Social identity theory provides one perspective on conceptualizing the effects of diversity within organizational settings. Implicit in the concept of *diversity* is social category identities. Individual differences in technical ability, social skills, physical attributes, and so forth, have always been part of the structure of organizations and of work group composition, but such differences did not become represented as issues of diversity until categorical distinctions among groups of individuals were recognized. Thus, the study of diversity in organizations and work groups is equivalent to the study of category differentiation within those settings. Categorical distinctions can involve both demographic differences among work group members (e.g., gender, ethnicity, age) and organizational distinctions (e.g., production, engineering, marketing).

The influence of demographic and organizational category diversity on work group performance can take a number of different forms (see McGrath, Berdahl, & Arrow, chapter 2, this volume). Figure 1 provides a schematic representation of diversity effects that places the role of social identity factors in context with other influences on group process and outcomes. In this chapter, I am focusing solely on the effects of social categorization processes per se (the first arrow in Figure 1), apart from the influences of real or expected category differences in roles, status, values, or behavior.

LEVELS OF SOCIAL IDENTITY
WITHIN ORGANIZATIONS

In an earlier program of research (Brewer & Kramer, 1986; Kramer & Brewer, 1984, 1986), I proposed that any social category could be represented in terms of three different levels of social identity. At one level, a social category is a collection of interdependent *individuals* (e.g., the individual faculty members in a particular university); at another level, it may be conceptualized as a single, *superordinate* social entity (e.g., the university as a whole); in yet a third possibility, the superordinate unit is subdivided into constituent *subgroups* (e.g., academic departments within a university). This differentiation into subgroup identities is the one of most relevance to research on diversity. Although individuals within the various subunits may be interdependent at the superordinate level, interdependence within the subgroups is more psychologically salient than that

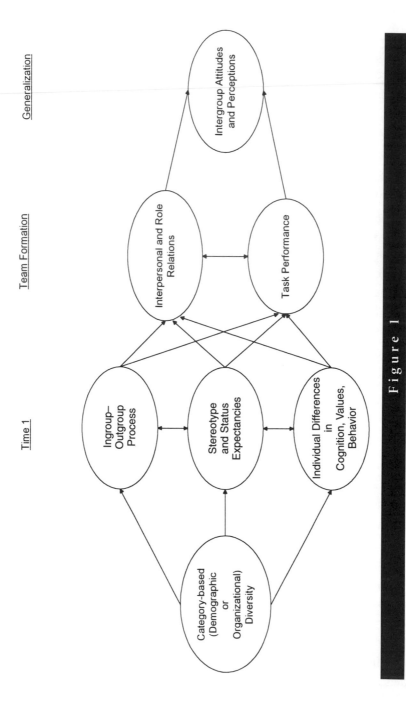

Figure 1

Influences of diversity on team process and outcomes.

between subgroups. Such subgroup differentiation creates ingroup–outgroup distinctions within any organizational unit. These distinctions engage processes of intergroup discrimination and distrust, and interfere with social identification with the organization as a whole.

Crosscutting and Nested Differentiation

The differentiation of any superordinate collective, such as an organization, into distinct categories can take several different forms. The two forms that are most relevant for issues of work group diversity are portrayed in Figure 2. The form represented in Figure 2a is one where the relevant social categorizations are *external* to the organization and overlap only partially with membership in the organization itself. This is the situation represented by diversity defined in terms of demographic categories such as gender, ethnicity, or age. The form represented in Figure 2b is one where the salient categories are interdependent subgroups nested within a superordinate unit. This is most characteristic of organizations divided into functional units such as departments or divisions that are not only outcome interdependent at the superordinate level, but also functionally interdependent at the subordinate level.

The overlapping or crosscutting category identities represented in Figure 2a are not inherently problematic for organizational interests. They become relevant only when external constituencies come to be equated with *within organization* subcategories, either because members of these categories are perceived as having separate subgroup interests (e.g., women executives as opposed to male executives), or because category distinctions become correlated with functional distinctions within the organization (e.g., male executives and female clerical staff, White supervisors and Black assembly line workers). It is this last form of organizational diversity (where external constituencies and internal functional divisions converge) that has the most problematic implications for the structure and performance of effective work groups within organizational contexts. When work teams are formed within large organizations, such teams are frequently (by intent) composed of employees from distinct, previously segregated divisions, functional units, or demographic categories. As a consequence,

2a. External/Crosscutting

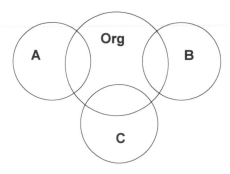

2b. Hierarchical/Nested

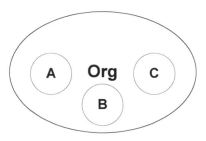

Figure 2

Alternative models of subgroup differentiation.

the formation of teams in work organizations frequently resembles the nested subgroup differentiation represented in Figure 2b.

The rationale for team composition in most organizational settings is the general idea that individuals from diverse backgrounds will bring different perspectives to the group task and enhance creativity and performance. The common goals and cooperative interdependence characteristic of work teams should provide a context for breaking down barriers to communication and exploiting the benefits of diverse skills and perspectives. However, various aspects of intergroup relations—ingroup loyalties, implicit intergroup rivalries, and negative stereotypes and distrust of outgroups—often conspire to impede coordination among members of diverse work teams and reduce effective performance (see Armstrong & Cole, chapter 8, this volume; Northcraft, Polzer, Neale, & Kramer, chapter 4, this volume).

Subgroup Differentiation and Social Dilemmas

A series of experiments by Kramer and Brewer (1984) demonstrates how subgroup differentiation can interfere with effective cooperative behavior within social groups. In these experiments, subjects were assigned to teams facing a social dilemma situation. Social dilemmas were particularly suited to our research interests because they are situations of collective interdependence in which individual self-interest is in conflict with collective welfare. Thus, the choices that an individual makes in such situations reflect the relative importance placed on outcomes for the group as a whole.

One example of a social dilemma situation is the choice faced by individuals under conditions of gradual depletion of a common resource, such as petroleum, rain forests, or water supplies in drought-stricken regions. The more endangered the resource becomes, the more each individual with access to the resource has a self-interested motivation to harvest and hoard as much as possible while the supply exists. However, if each individual behaves in this way, the collective consequence is rapid depletion of the resource without opportunity for replenishment, to the ultimate detriment of everyone's individual interests. Collective welfare is preserved only if each individual restrains self-interest on behalf of the common good. However, if any one individual exercises self-restraint while others in the collective do not, the individual's sacrifice makes no difference to the collective outcome. The value of individual cooperation is meaningful only when aggregated at the collective level.

Most analyses of social dilemmas assume only two levels of decision making—the individual person and the collective as a whole. However, in many real-world social dilemma situations, the group that shares the common resource is one that does not correspond to salient social identities of the constituent individuals. Instead, differentiated subgroups within the collective are the most salient units of social identification. Under these conditions, individuals may well care about interests beyond their own personal outcomes, but implicit competition between subgroups may interfere with the individual's ability or willingness to make choices that benefit all members of the collective, irrespective of subgroup membership.

Kramer and Brewer (1984) designed a computer-based laboratory analogue of a resource depletion dilemma in order to assess the psychological effects of social identity on individual choice behavior. The laboratory paradigm placed six-person heterogeneous groups in a situation in which each individual made decisions about use of a common resource pool via a system of linked computer terminals. Each terminal was located in a private cubicle, so group members had no opportunity to see each other or to communicate. Participants were told that they would share (along with the other five participants) access to a resource pool initially containing 300 points, with each point being worth a specified amount of money. On each of a series of trials, each group member had the opportunity to take up to 10 points from the common pool. Points were put into a private "account," where they accumulated cash value. After all six participants had decided how much to take on that trial (decisions being made privately and without knowing what others in the group had decided), the computer would subtract the total number withdrawn from the existing pool size, multiply the remaining amount by a "replenishment factor" of approximately 1.1, and issue a report on the new pool size prior to the next trial. Participants expected that the succession of choice trials would continue as long as any points remained in the pool, up to 2 hours.

The resource task was structured so that optimal utilization of the common pool (moderate withdrawals by all group members on each trial) would sustain the pool at 300 points and maximize collective outcomes in the long run. However, if group members individually took more than the optimal number of points on average, the pool would begin to shrink and could never be replenished to its original size. As the pool size decreased, the optimal utilization point also decreased, setting in motion a pattern of gradual depletion. As the experiment progressed, participants received feedback that the pool was being depleted to a critically low point.

We were particularly interested in how individuals moderated their own withdrawals in response to this depletion situation. Because their potential choices ranged from 0 to 10, the extremity of their decisions on each trial reveals the extent to which they were motivated by pure self-interest, pure collective interest, or some compromise between the two.

Kramer and Brewer (1984) conducted three different experiments in which the six individuals who shared the collective resource in each experimental session were members of two three-person subgroups. Individual resource utilization decisions were made under conditions either in which a superordinate social collective identity had been made salient (i.e., all participants in the session shared a common social categorization) or in which the respective subgroup identities had been made salient (i.e., the collective was subdivided into two distinct social categories that shared the same common resource pool). Across all three experiments, as the resource pool approached depletion, subjects in the subgroup identity conditions consistently harvested significantly more of the common resource (to the detriment of all) than did subjects who had only a superordinate social identity. In the latter conditions, individuals were able to suppress individual self-interest for the sake of preserving a collective good, but this capacity for self-restraint was eliminated when subgroup differentiation was introduced. Mere categorization into distinct sets had this detrimental effect on collective interests.

The results of the Kramer and Brewer resource dilemma experiments are particularly impressive because there was no objective conflict of interest between the subgroups created in the experimental setting. Although the resource dilemma pits individual self-gain against the welfare of the collective as a whole, the mutual interdependence among individuals was equivalent within and between subgroups. Nonetheless, the mere fact of differentiation altered the capacity for individuals to act in the interests of the collective as a whole. Once an ingroup–outgroup categorization had been made salient, interdependence at the superordinate level had little impact on individual behavior.

Although work groups in an organizational setting do not operate under the conditions of anonymity represented in the social dilemma experiments, such work groups are often characterized by potential conflicts among individual self-interest, subgroup interests, and interests of the group as a whole. If subgroup identities are salient, implicit social competition may interfere with effective work group cooperation, as in the Kramer and Brewer experiments. The purpose of the remainder of this chapter is to review recent research from experimental social psychology that may shed some light on how to structure and manage work teams to diminish potential detrimental effects of diversity in the short and long run.

LESSONS FROM THE LABORATORY

In the last decade, a number of experimental paradigms have been developed to study the effects of intergroup contact within cooperative work groups in the laboratory (Bettencourt, Brewer, Croak, & Miller, 1992; Gaertner, Mann, Dovidio, Murrell, & Pomare, 1990; Gaertner, Mann, Murrell, & Dovidio, 1989; Marcus-Newhall, Miller, Holtz, & Brewer, 1993; Miller, Brewer, & Edwards, 1985). Although details of experimental procedures vary, the basic design of these experiments begins with the creation of two distinct, but arbitrary, social categories to which participants in a session are assigned, ostensibly on the basis of some psychological test. The two categories (with three to four members each) are then separated and given some period of time to engage in discussion or work together as segregated social groups (the "ingroup formation" stage of the research paradigm).

By the close of the first phase of the experiment, assessments of mutual perceptions by members of the two categories usually reveal the typical pattern of ingroup favoritism and outgroup derogation elicited by category differentiation. At this point, the researchers remove participants from their ingroups and create four- or six-person work teams composed of representatives from each of the two categories. The newly formed teams are given a task that requires cooperative interaction to reach a common goal. Various aspects of the structure or composition of, or instructions to, these work teams are systematically varied to determine what structural and psychological conditions are most effective in reducing intergroup bias and discrimination within the teams and in general.

From these experiments, two models have emerged that seem to be particularly promising for application to work groups. One capitalizes on the effects of superordinate social identities, and the other focuses on the relationship between social category identity and role relationships in a task group.

Common Ingroup Identity

One possible consequence of team formation is the creation of a new social identity for team members. When this form of recategorization is successful, ingroup loyalties and concern for collective welfare are transferred from the original subgroups to the team as a whole. This is the basis of the "common ingroup identity model" espoused by Gaertner and his colleagues (Gaertner, Dovidio, Anastasio, Bachman, & Rust, 1993) as a means to reduce intergroup bias in contact situations. The model has been tested in a series of experimental studies to assess the conditions under which two previously segregated work groups can be successfully merged in a superordinate unit.

Gaertner's experimental manipulations have focused on situational variables that enhance or reduce the perceptual salience of subgroup identities during the combined work team experience. Symbolic features such as group names and colors, or seating patterns that influence proximity and who interacts with whom, have been varied to control relative salience. Consistently, conditions that enhance the salience of the common team identity and reduce the salience of subcategory identities are found to diminish or eliminate ingroup bias in evaluation of fellow team members. To the extent that participants perceive the combined team as a single entity, rather than an aggregate of two separate groups, evaluations of former outgroup members become more positive. Such a merger of group identities would be represented in organizational settings where two departments are successfully merged into a new functional unit, or previously segregated male and female work groups are integrated in a single working unit.

In Gaertner's model, superordinate social identities are created through the merger of subgroups into a single, common category that replaces the original category differentiation. An alternative route to superordinate group identity involves making salient an inclusive categorization in which both groups have common membership. Two competing departments, for instance, may be reminded of their common interest in the success of the organization as a whole, or heterogeneous work teams may be created with accountability to the larger organization. This model does not require eliminating subgroup distinctions, but relies instead on enhancing the relative salience of common group membership over differentiated categories.

In a modification of the Kramer and Brewer (1984) social dilemma experiments, Brewer and Schneider (1990) demonstrated that enhancing subgroup members' awareness of their interdependence within a superordinate collective effectively reversed the negative effects of subgroup differentiation in the resource dilemma situation. When the group members were made aware of their shared membership in a superordinate organization, cooperative choices were significantly increased. In fact, under these conditions, groups divided into subunits were actually *more* cooperative than undifferentiated groups. Under the right conditions, subgroup loyalties can be engaged to enhance individuals' sense of responsibility and efficacy in ways that promote collective interests.

Crossing Categories and Functions

Although both experimental and field studies have demonstrated the power of superordinate social identities to alter intergroup dynamics in cooperative settings, there are a number of reasons that common ingroup formation is an unstable solution to the problems of managing diverse work teams. The common ingroup model relies heavily on the relative salience of alternative category representations, which means it is highly situation specific. As contexts change, as new individuals enter the work group, and so forth, the salience of superordinate category membership may diminish. At the same time, subgroup identities remain available as a primary basis for group loyalties and attachment. This is particularly likely when the superordinate category is a large collective, the psychological "presence" of which is difficult to maintain.

Unfortunately for the common ingroup model, cognitive factors combine with motivational forces to reduce individual identification with large, superordinate groups relative to smaller, distinct subgroups. Brewer's (1991) "optimal distinctiveness theory" postulates that social identity is driven by two opposing social motives at the individual level: the need for inclusion and the need for differentiation. Human beings strive to belong to groups that transcend their own personal identity, but at the same time, they need to feel special and distinct from others. To satisfy both of these motives simultaneously, individuals seek inclusion in *distinctive* social groups where the boundaries between those who are members of the social category and those who are excluded can be clearly drawn.

Large, diverse social organizations are not likely to have the properties necessary to engage strong social identification and ingroup loyalties. Within such organizational contexts, distinct subgroups are more likely to satisfy members' needs for group identification. If work groups are formed within such organizations, individual group members are likely to be closely identified with their subgroup affiliations. Thus, psychological mechanisms conspire to reestablish subgroup differentiation and awareness of ingroup–outgroup distinctions within diverse work groups, and the idea of eliminating fundamental ingroup identities within the work group context may be idealistically naive. In effect, superordinate category identity and awareness of interdependence may be necessary conditions for effective functioning of diverse work teams, but they may not be sufficient to produce enduring changes in work relationships.

In a recent program of research, Norman Miller and I have been experimenting with ways of structuring the role relationships within work groups to change intergroup attitudes and perceptions. Our objective is to determine how task requirements within a cooperatively interdependent social group can be exploited to break down intergroup barriers without threatening group identities.

Cooperative work teams are often composed and structured in such a way that roles or functions within the team are correlated with subgroup category identities. Members of Subgroup A all play one role, while members of Subgroup B play a different role. For instance, one or two individuals are drawn from a particular departmental unit or demographic category in order to contribute skills or perspectives that are specialized to that category. As long as role differentiation and category differentiation within the work team converge, they are essentially redundant. There is no need to individuate the characteristics or contributions of category members because they are functionally equivalent or interchangeable. As a consequence, the experience of interdependent cooperative interaction within the work team may ultimately reinforce category distinctions and associated category stereotypes.

In contrast with the usual convergence of category and role are task structures in which roles are systematically (or randomly) crossed with category membership. For instance, subtasks can be created that combine the technical skills of engineers and computer scientists, or male and female marketing experts may be represented on the same team. Under these conditions, the job of getting the task done requires team members to differentiate between members of the respective social categories according to their role or contribution to the team goal. Even if subgroup category identities are highly salient, this categorization is not sufficient to identify the team member's functional position in the work group. Instead, each individual's contribution is necessarily separately evaluated in relation to the collective goal.

The comparative effects of convergent and crosscutting role assignments were tested in a laboratory experiment by Marcus-Newhall, Miller, Holtz, and Brewer (1993). The purpose of the experiment was to assess the effectiveness of crosscutting categories and roles in cooperative work teams for reducing ingroup bias in how the performance and contribution of fellow team members are perceived and evaluated.

Using the basic experimental paradigm described at the beginning of this section, members of two artificially created social categories ("overestimators" and "underestimators") were assigned to a four-person work team to complete a problem-solving task. The team consisted of two overestimators and two underestimators whose category identities were visibly salient throughout the session because of colored labels and ID tags.

The team task was structured in such a way that it required input from two specialized roles or expertise to be achieved. The problem given to the teams was to identify the seven most important traits or characteristics that should be used to select potential astronauts for NASA. The job requirements of an astronaut include both technical competencies and social–emotional skills. At the initial stages of the team task, individual team members were given one of two scripts to read. Two received a script describing the social–emotional demands placed on an astronaut during a typical space flight, whereas the other two received a script describing the cognitive and technical demands of being part of a space flight crew. Thus, two of the team members acquired expertise in one aspect (social–emotional) of the astronaut job, whereas the others had expertise in the complementary aspects (cognitive and technical) of the job.

Assignment of team members to the respective roles constituted the primary experimental manipulation. For half of the teams, roles and category membership were convergent in that the two overestimators read one script (social or technical), while the two underestimators read the other prior to team discussion. For the remaining half, the scripts were systematically assigned to one overestimator and one underestimator prior to interaction.

Once the differential role assignments had been established, the four members of the team worked together to reach consensus on a single list of seven traits to be submitted as their team product. Teams expected their products to be evaluated against a standard developed by NASA, as a measure of the quality of their performance. (No such evaluation was actually made.) While the results were ostensibly being "scored," team members individually completed a series of questionnaires assessing their ratings of the group experience, evaluations of team members, perceived similarity among members of the team, and trait ratings of overestimators and underestimators in general. The perceived contribution of each team member to the group product was assessed by a reward allocation measure in which each team member distributed chips to each of the other team members from a set of chips of up to 100 for each participant.

Of particular interest was the presence of biased evaluations of fellow team members who were members of the subject's own subgroup (ingroup) compared with those who were outgroup members. Indices of ingroup bias on the evaluative and allocation measures were obtained by subtracting mean evaluations (or reward allocations) of ingroup team members from mean evaluations of outgroup members for each individual subject. In addition, we were interested in the effect of team role assignment structure on the perception of differences between ingroup and outgroup members. When ingroup–outgroup differentiation is salient, members of the same group are perceived to be more similar in personality and values than members of different groups. From ratings of interpersonal similarity following team interaction, we computed a similarity index that represented the perceived similarity of team members across category identities relative to within-category similarity. Higher values on this index reflect greater individuation of team members, irrespective of group membership.

The results of the experiment comparing convergent and crosscutting task assignments are summarized in Table 1 in terms of mean outcomes on the various dependent measures. The direction of results on each of the dependent variables supported the hypothesis that crosscutting role assignments results in less intergroup differentiation and less ingroup bias following contact in a cooperative team experience. These effects were particularly pronounced on measures of reward allocation and intergroup differentiation or similarity. (The evaluative bias measures in this experiment were generally low and relatively insensitive to experimental conditions.) In general, the crosscutting of categories and task assignment succeeded in reducing intergroup discrimination even under conditions where ingroup–outgroup categorization was salient and meaningful.

The results of this experiment indicate that the assignment of roles and functions in a work team can have a critical impact on whether subgroup identities are reinforced or overridden in the work group context. To avoid the potentially disruptive effects of ingroup bias and intergroup competition, task structures should cross functional and demographic categories. Of course, in many work contexts, role assignments cannot easily be randomly distributed. Thus, the larger organizational context from

Table 1

Effects of Team Structure and Role Assignment

| | Experimental Condition | |
	Crosscutting	Convergent
Post-task Measures:		
Trait evaluation bias[a]	0.11	0.17
Reward allocation[a]	0.06	3.27
Similarity index[b]	4.00	3.50

[a]Difference between mean ingroup rating/allocation minus mean outgroup rating.
[b]Higher index scores indicate greater differentiation in similarity ratings. Mean rating of intergroup similarity on 1–9 scale. (Reprinted from Marcus-Newhall et al., 1993.)

which work groups are composed introduces potentially important constraints on the possible role structures of such work teams.

SOME IMPORTANT CAVEATS AND DIRECTIONS FOR FUTURE RESEARCH

The results of social psychological experiments manipulating social category identity alone have potentially useful implications for how work teams can be structured and managed to reap the benefits of diversity without the costs of intergroup conflict. However, there are a number of reasons that the translation of findings from basic research to application in real-world settings still requires additional research and theory.

First of all, the focus of social psychological experiments has been almost exclusively on the consequences of cooperative contact for intergroup attitudes and perceptions. In other words, the attention of social psychologists has been directed to using cooperative work teams as a technology for improving intergroup relations, regardless of the success or failure of the team experience itself. As a consequence, there has been little or no assessment made of the effects of group composition and structure on group process or performance. It is still a matter of inference whether the conditions that result in more positive intergroup evaluations also promote more effective group functioning in either the short or long run.

There is, in fact, reason to believe that the structural arrangements that lead ultimately to better intergroup relations also elicit initial resistance to team formation and negative attitudes toward the cooperative task. When social identification with subgroup categories is high, the prospect of cooperative interdependence between the ingroup and outgroup raises a threat to group identity (Hewstone & Brown, 1986). As a consequence, individual group members approach team work with, at best, mixed motives. On the one hand, there are personal and collective incentives for the team to perform well, but there is also a strong reluctance to rely on outgroup contributions to achieve group goals, or to share the benefits of successful achievements with outgroup members. The crosscutting of role assignments (which reduces the contribution to the team product that can be clearly attributable to the ingroup) may well exacerbate the sources of resistance to cooperative team efforts. Thus, it is extremely important to learn more about the impact of team structure and role relationships on process and performance across time. It is very likely that short-term deficits in team functioning may be a necessary price to pay for longer term effectiveness (see also McGrath et al., chapter 2, this volume).

A second critical factor to take into consideration, as mentioned above, is the larger organizational context in which the formation and structuring of work teams take place (see Armstrong & Cole, chapter 8, this volume). If demographic categories and work roles are correlated in the organization as a whole, this places important constraints on the feasibility of forming work teams in which categories and functions are effectively crossed. Furthermore, the structural characteristics of the organization will influence how roles are perceived within the work team. Social psychological experiments with crosscutting categories indicate that if categories are normally correlated, individuals whose category membership crosscuts the usual structure are rejected as outgroup members by both ingroups (Eurich-Fulcer & Schofield, 1995). This means, for instance, that in an organizational context in which work roles such as engineering are correlated with sex, the woman engineer on a work team is likely to be regarded neither as a woman nor as an engineer. Such psychological rejection of crosscutting roles would certainly undermine the beneficial effects of diversity obtained in laboratory studies. Thus, the concept of crosscutting roles and categories must be extended beyond the structuring of work teams to the structure of the organization as a whole.

A third potentially important limitation of social psychology experiments for application to organizational settings is the absence of attention to status relationships among social groups. The creation of arbitrary social identities in the laboratory setting precludes any history of status differentials among the categories under study. Although the processes of ingroup bias and favoritism may lead members of each group to perceive that their group is better than the outgroup, these biases are symmetric in the absence of any objective status hierarchy. Furthermore, the structure of work teams is carefully designed to bring the groups together under equal-status conditions, even if differentiated roles are involved.

In large-scale organizations in the real world, there is an objectively recognized status hierarchy that complicates the nature of intergroup relations and mutual perceptions among subgroups. Furthermore, the nature of the status hierarchy is often such that category identity, functional roles, and position within the organization are largely convergent. Such preexisting status relationships can be expected to moderate the effects of work team structure and function and, at a minimum, cannot be ignored within the work context.

As an initial attempt to address the role of status relationships in a laboratory experiment, Marcus-Newhall (1992) undertook a replication of the earlier experiment on crosscutting role assignment in the context of a preexisting status hierarchy. The groups recruited to participate in her experiment were members of UCLA sororities, specifically two sororities that were widely recognized as the highest status groups on campus and two that were among those in the middle ranks of the status system. Preliminary results from this experiment indicate that participation in cooperative teams with crosscutting role assignment did succeed in reducing status-related biases in intergroup perceptions, compared with cooperative experiences that involved convergent role assignments that reinforced ingroup biases on the part of high-status group members in particular. Thus, the crossing of category and role contributions to team efforts may prove to be especially important when status relationships between participating subgroups are asymmetric.

Studying the interaction between role assignment and intergroup status relationships brings our experimental work in contact with sociological research on status expectancies and work group performance, as represented by Cohen (1984) and Ridgeway (1988). Convergent findings derived from these different lines of research highlight the importance of bringing multidisciplinary perspectives to the task of applying the findings of basic research to issues of managing diversity in the workplace.

REFERENCES

Bettencourt, B. A., Brewer, M. B., Croak, M., & Miller, N. (1992). Cooperation and the reduction of intergroup bias: The role of reward structure and social orientation. *Journal of Experimental Social Psychology, 28,* 301–319.

Brewer, M. B. (1979). In-group bias in the minimal intergroup situation: A cognitive–motivational analysis. *Psychological Bulletin, 86,* 307–324.

Brewer, M. B. (1991). The social self: On being the same and different at the same time. *Personality and Social Psychology Bulletin, 17,* 475–482.

Brewer, M. B., & Kramer, R. M. (1986). Choice behavior in social dilemmas: Effects of social identity, group size, and decision framing. *Journal of Personality and Social Psychology, 50,* 543–549.

Brewer, M. B., & Schneider, S. (1990). Social identity and social dilemmas: A double-edged sword. In D. Abrams & M. Hogg (Eds.), *Social identity theory: Constructive and critical advances* (pp. 169–184). London: Harvester-Wheatsheaf.

Cohen, E. G. (1984). The desegregated school: Problems in status power and interethnic climate. In N. Miller & M. Brewer (Eds.), *Groups in contact: The psychology of desegregation* (pp. 77–96). New York: Academic Press.

Eurich-Fulcer, R., & Schofield, J. W. (1995). Correlated versus uncorrelated social categorizations: The effect on intergroup bias. *Personality and Social Psychology Bulletin, 21,* 149–159.

Gaertner, S., Dovidio, J., Anastasio, P., Bachman, B., & Rust, M. (1993). The Common Ingroup Identity Model: Recategorization and the reduction of intergroup bias. In W. Stroebe & M. Hewstone (Eds.), *European Review of Social Psychology* (Vol. 4, pp. 1–26). Chichester, England: Wiley.

Gaertner, S., Mann, J., Dovidio, J., Murrell, A., & Pomare, M. (1990). How does cooperation reduce intergroup bias? *Journal of Personality and Social Psychology, 59,* 692–704.

Gaertner, S., Mann, J., Murrell, A., & Dovidio, J. (1989). Reducing intergroup bias: The benefits of recategorization. *Journal of Personality and Social Psychology, 57,* 239–249.

Hewstone, M., & Brown, R. (1986). Contact is not enough: An intergroup perspective on the "contact hypothesis." In M. Hewstone & R. Brown (Eds.), *Contact and conflict in intergroup encounters* (pp. 1–44). Oxford, England: Blackwell.

Hogg, M., & Abrams, D. (1988). *Social identifications: A social psychology of intergroup relations and group processes.* London: Routledge.

Kramer, R. M., & Brewer, M. B. (1984). Effects of group identity on resource use in a simulated commons dilemma. *Journal of Personality and Social Psychology, 46,* 1044–1057.

Kramer, R. M., & Brewer, M. B. (1986). Social group identity and the emergence of cooperation in resource conservation dilemmas. In H. Wilke, D. Messick, & C. Rutte (Eds.), *Psychology of decisions and conflict* (Vol. 3, pp. 205–230). Frankfurt, Germany: Verlag Peter Lang.

Marcus-Newhall, A. (1992). *Crosscutting and convergence of category membership with role assignment: Under which intergroup situational features will each lead to reduced bias?* Unpublished doctoral dissertation, University of Southern California, Los Angeles.

Marcus-Newhall, A., Miller, N., Holtz, R., & Brewer, M. B. (1993). Cross-cutting category membership with role assignment: A means of reducing intergroup bias. *British Journal of Social Psychology, 32,* 125–146.

Miller, N., Brewer, M. B., & Edwards, K. (1985). Cooperative interaction in desegregated settings: A laboratory analogue. *Journal of Social Issues, 41,* 63–79.

Ridgeway, C. (1988). Gender differences in task groups: A status and legitimacy account. In M. Webster & M. Foschi (Eds.), *Status generalization: New theory and research* (pp. 188–206). Stanford, CA: Stanford University Press.

Schopler, J., & Insko, C. (1992). The discontinuity effect in interpersonal and intergroup relations: Generality and mediation. In W. Stroebe & M. Hewstone (Eds.), *European Review of Social Psychology* (Vol. 3, pp. 121–151). Chichester, England: Wiley.

Tajfel, H. (1970). Experiments in intergroup discrimination. *Scientific American, 223,* 96–102.

Tajfel, H. (1978). The psychological structure of intergroup relations. In H. Tajfel (Ed.), *Differentiation between social groups: Studies in the social psychology of intergroup relations.* London: Academic Press.

Tajfel, H., & Wilkes, A. L. (1963). Classification and quantitative judgment. *British Journal of Psychology, 54,* 101–113.

Turner, J. C., Hogg, M., Oakes, P., Reicher, S., & Wetherell, M. (1987). *Rediscovering the social group: A self-categorization theory.* Oxford, England: Basil Blackwell.

4

Diversity, Social Identity, and Performance: Emergent Social Dynamics in Cross-Functional Teams

Gregory B. Northcraft, Jeffrey T. Polzer,
Margaret A. Neale, and Roderick M. Kramer

P roblems cut across boundaries in organizations, and piecemeal solutions that do not also cross those boundaries prove to be time-
consuming and ineffective (Lipnack & Stamps, 1993). The ability of any
individual specialist to appreciate all the relevant aspects of a boundary-
spanning problem is limited (Fuller, 1993), and the complexity of modern-
day organizational problems may be beyond the reach of a single mind
(Over, 1982; Trist, 1977). Thus, organizations have come to appreciate the
value of *sound interfunctional coupling*, that is, close interaction between
diverse functional areas within a firm (Shanklin & Ryans, 1984). They have
embraced organizational forms and practices that themselves embrace a
diversity of opinions, values, and perspectives.

This chapter addresses the use of cross-functional or multidisciplinary
teams (e.g., Larson & Gobeli, 1988) as vehicles for incorporating diversity
into organizational problem solving. A central goal of this chapter is to
introduce the language of negotiation (e.g., Fisher & Ury, 1981; Neale &
Bazerman, 1991) into the dialogue concerning diversity in organizations.
The language of negotiation provides a calculus for concretely conceptualizing the fit among the cognitive and physical resources that diverse col-

leagues bring to a team. The language of negotiation is particularly useful because the assembling of a successful diverse team is metaphorically and literally equivalent to negotiating a successful agreement. The language of negotiation also clarifies the manner in which team members' social identity concerns affect team dynamics. Finally, conceptualizing the management of diverse teams in the terms of negotiation and social identity suggests some ways to improve team functioning.

DIVERSITY

Organizational diversity typically is justified in terms of the advantage of characteristic variety within a workforce (e.g., Cox & Blake, 1991; Northcraft & Neale, 1993). However, the rhetoric of diversity often confuses two different levels of variety. On the one hand is variety among participants' category memberships, which include demographic (e.g., gender, race, ethnicity) and organizational (e.g., hierarchical rank, departmental affiliation) characteristics (e.g., Mandell & Kohler-Gray, 1990; McGrath, Berdahl, & Arrow, chapter 2, this volume). Legal and moral imperatives have often focused organizations on creating *representative* category membership diversity within their workforces (e.g., workforce demographic variety that mirrors the demographic mix of the local labor market). However, from the viewpoint of accomplishing an organization's work goals, this type of diversity in the workforce's category memberships is less valuable than variety in *functional* characteristics (such as cognitive and physical resources), for which individuals' category memberships are often taken (perhaps incorrectly) as cues (e.g., Eagly, 1987; Tsui, Xin, & Egan, chapter 5, this volume).

McGrath et al. (chapter 2, this volume) have noted several different types of diversity that fit under this functional-characteristics umbrella, including differences among individuals in knowledge, skills, and abilities (KSAs); values, beliefs, and attitudes (VBAs); and personality, cognitive style, and behavioral style (PCBs). Individuals' access to different networks (e.g., Ibarra, 1992) and different physical resources (e.g., clerical support, funding, technologies) also represents a potentially functional type of workforce variety. Variety in the cognitive and physical resources that individuals bring to the organization is functional if it improves the likelihood of *synergy:* the ability of coworkers to do better or accomplish more working together than any of them could alone. The benefits of synergy come in two domains: *effectiveness* and *efficiency.*

Effectiveness refers to an organization's ability to accomplish its core goals, purposes, or mission (Northcraft & Neale, 1994). In terms of effectiveness, cognitive variety is the wellspring of creativity (e.g., Amabile, 1983; Triandis, Hall, & Ewen, 1965). Creative solutions to difficult problems are more likely to emerge if a variety of problem restructurings can be brought to bear (Maier, 1930). It is a multiplicity of perceptions that produces creativity (Hoffman, 1959), and the emerging appreciations that come from cognitive cross-fertilization provide insights into complex problems. Souder (1987) likened organizational innovation to a mosaic to which "each party contributes enlightened pieces of insight" (p. 77). Discussion of diverse opinions and perspectives allows diverse individuals to pool information and combine ideas, and also can help clarify, organize, and even prioritize ideas (Rohrbaugh, 1979).

It should not be surprising that integration of diverse perspectives is considered a necessity in organizational innovation (Moenaert & Souder, 1990). Scientists benefit most from contact with *dissimilar* colleagues (Pelz, 1956), and the highest levels of creativity are found in organizations that encourage differences in opinions and diversity in backgrounds among their people (Goddard, 1985). Notice that it is not variety among individuals' category memberships (e.g., a mix of genders or a variety of professional affiliations) that produces synergy; it is the variety in values, perspectives, and so on that we associate (perhaps incorrectly) with a healthy mix of gender and professional affiliations that affords the promise of innovative idea cross-fertilization.

Workforce diversity also can contribute to an organization's successful monitoring of and interaction with the environment. Greater diversity among individuals' network contacts (e.g., Lipnack & Stamps, 1993; Tushman, 1977) makes it more likely that any useful new information will be discovered and brought to the organization. Greater network diversity also makes it more likely that prospective clients will discover the organization (e.g., see Ely, chapter 7, this volume). This raises the issue of dealing with a turbulent or fast-moving environment (e.g., Donnellon, 1993; Trist, 1977). Greater network-contact diversity in an organization means more opportunities to monitor environmental turbulence; greater workforce diversity in skills and knowledge means more skills available to address that turbulence when identified—what Cox and Blake (1991) refer to as the *system-flexibility* advantage of workforce diversity.

An organization's workforce variety also plays an important functional role on the efficiency side. *Efficiency* refers to an organization's ability to maximize its productivity per unit of labor and capital resources (Northcraft & Neale, 1994). Both portfolio theory (Sharpe, 1970) and macro-perspectives on diversification (e.g., Davis & Thomas, 1993) emphasize the importance of variety to the long-term success of an organization. A diversity of knowledge and skills within an organization's workforce means that more aspects of the organization's tasks can be attended to by specialists (individuals who are specifically skilled at or interested in particular aspects of the task). With better fit in role assignment or division of labor (e.g., McGrath et al., chapter 2, this volume), the organization's accomplishment of its goals should be quicker and more correct (e.g., Jones & Vroom, 1964; Moenaert & Souder, 1990; Souder, 1987). Generally, knowledge and skill diversity among an organization's participants provides more opportunities for the organization's products to be both correct and comprehensive (Amabile, 1983; Miller & Hamblin, 1963). Such efficiencies become increasingly more difficult to attain by individuals working alone as the complexities of science, technology, and engineering push well past any individual's grasp (Over, 1982; Price, 1963).

Interestingly, this last benefit poses something of a paradox. Knowledge and skill diversity among an organization's participants promotes efficiency if individual specialists take charge of particular aspects of a project because specialists presumably can do a job better and faster than nonexperts. Task specialization does promote efficiency, but often by insulating specialists from the interaction of different values, attitudes, styles, and personalities that can be beneficial to effectiveness. Therefore, some apparently counterproductive redundancy in skills and task assignments needs to occur to allow cross-fertilization of ideas (Trist, 1977) and thereby prevent increases in an organization's efficiency from coming at the expense of effectiveness.

What should be obvious as well is that not all of the benefits of functional diversity are reaped in the present. Finding appropriate fits and cross-fertilization among a workforce's diverse knowledge and skills, values and attitudes, and personalities and styles may take time and effort. In fact, the greater the diversity in a group's cognitive resources, the less efficient that group may be at getting down to work at the tasks at hand (Northcraft & Neale, 1993). To realize the long-term benefits of enhanced efficiency and effectiveness, diverse groups and organizations must be able to bear some short-term costs—costs directly attributable to working with and through the diversity that represents the potential for competitive advantage.

Finally, McGrath et al. (chapter 2, this volume) note that the potential benefits of diversity need not always be conceptualized as a matter of finding fits between static tasks and the resources and demands of an organization's workforce. Tasks also can be *enacted* (Weick, 1977) or reconstrued specifically to take full advantage of the diversity at hand.

TEAMS

Whereas efficiency and effectiveness represent the bottom-line justifications for pursuing workforce diversity, *teams* provide the mechanism for realizing those benefits (Donnellon, 1993; Larson & Gobeli, 1988). Cross-functional teams are small collections of representatives from diverse functional specializations (i.e., diverse category memberships) that provide an apparently manageable way to bring diverse cognitive resources to bear on a project (Lawrence & Lorsch, 1967). Pinto and Pinto (1990) have suggested that some tasks can be accomplished only by teams and that teams that exhibit higher levels of cross-functional cooperation have significantly higher project success (Pinto, 1989). Overall, cross-functional teams have demonstrated extraordinary successes (e.g., Dumaine, 1990) and have been successfully adopted in a variety of fields, including ecology and environmental assessment (Fuller, 1993), medicine (Pinto & Pinto, 1990), banking and financial services (Bantel & Jackson, 1989; Deutsch, 1990), and education (Clemson, 1990; Gilliam & Coleman, 1981). Perhaps the prototype for cross-functional cooperation occurs in manufacturing, where the interface between marketing and research-and-development is critical and can be addressed by cross-functionally cooperative teams (e.g., Donnellon, 1993; Moenaert & Souder, 1990; Myers & Wileman, 1989; Persico, 1989; Young, 1979).

Unfortunately, the performance-enhancing potential of cross-functional teams is not always realized (Deutsch, 1990; Hoerr, 1989). Although teams certainly have problems working together that do not arise from diversity among team members (e.g., Persico, 1989; Wetlaufer, 1994), it is often, paradoxically, the diversity within teams that makes it difficult for them to realize efficiency and effectiveness gains over individuals. The positive conflict (e.g., Tjosvold, 1991) among team members' cognitive resources (i.e., knowledge and skills, values and attitudes, and personalities and styles) is what makes cross-functional teams valuable. These conflicts (and others that similarly stem from differences among team members' social category memberships) are also what make it difficult for diverse team members to work together effectively (Epton, Payne, & Pearson, 1985). The heterogeneity of a team often negatively influences its dynamics (e.g., Ibarra, 1992; Pfeffer, 1983) in ways that can eventually lead to turnover or dissolution of the group (e.g., O'Reilly, Caldwell, & Barnett, 1989).

THE LANGUAGE OF NEGOTIATION

The language of negotiation provides team members with a way to think and talk about the potentially disruptive conflicts they encounter in trying to bring together their diverse cognitive and physical resources. Negotiation is a process that multiple parties use to decide what each will give and take in an exchange (Bazerman & Carroll, 1987). In the case of diverse teams, *giving* includes those cognitive and physical resources that team members bring and contribute to the team; *taking* includes what each team member receives in exchange, such as, for example, the satisfaction of having fully discharged one's obligations to the team. At the heart of the giving and taking of negotiation are three different types of issues (Thompson, 1990): distributive, congruent, and integrative issues.

Distributive issues are points in dispute that are apparently of equal value to both parties and for which the parties' settlement preferences are diametrically opposed. For example, Issue A in Table 1 is a distributive issue; Issue A is worth up to 750 points to both parties, and Team Member #1 prefers Option A-1, whereas Team Member #2 prefers Option A-5.

Congruent issues are those for which the disputing parties' preferences are not really in conflict. Issue D in Table 1 is a congruent issue; both Team Member #1 and Team Member #2 prefer settlement Option D-1.

Finally, *integrative* issues are those for which the disputing parties'

Table 1

Diverse Values

| Option | Team Member #1 | | | |
	Issue A	Issue B	Issue C	Issue D
1	750	1000	100	500
2	600	800	80	400
3	450	600	60	300
4	300	400	40	200
5	150	200	20	100

| Option | Team Member #2 | | | |
	Issue A	Issue B	Issue C	Issue D
1	150	20	200	500
2	300	40	400	400
3	450	60	600	300
4	600	80	800	200
5	750	100	1000	100

Note. The numbers listed by option per issue represent the value to that team member of accepting that option for that issue. Higher numbers signify more valuable issues and options.

preferences are diametrically opposed, but which the parties value differently. In Table 1, Issue B and Issue C are integrative issues. For Issue B, Team Member #1 prefers Option B-1 and Team Member #2 prefers Option B-5, but Issue B is a more important issue to Team Member #1. For Issue C, Team Member #1 prefers Option C-1 and Team Member #2 prefers Option C-5, but Issue C is a more important issue to Team Member #2. Integrative issues offer disputants a way to trade off concessions on less important issues in exchange for concessions on more important issues. The result is beneficial for both parties. In Table 1, an agreement to Option B-1 and Option C-5 is better for both Team Member #1 (1020 points) and Team Member #2 (1020 points) than a "meet halfway" compromise (Option 3 on both issues, yielding 660 points to each disputant).

The relevance of negotiation to the management of diverse teams is that assembling a successful team is like negotiating a good agreement. Good agreements are negotiated when disputing parties discern what resources and demands each brings to the table, and discover positive ways to integrate those resources and demands. Integration does not mean that everyone gets everything (e.g., task assignments, outputs) that he or she wants; it does mean that disputants get more than they give, by giving concessions on less important issues in exchange for getting concessions on more important ones. The concept of negotiated integration—finding a positive fit among apparently conflicting positions, values, and beliefs— is what can make diversity "value-added" for teams and organizations.

The concept of negotiated integration clarifies how it may be possible, if not desirable, for team members to retain their diverse individualities while simultaneously collaborating successfully. A successful cross-functional team is like a well-negotiated agreement because both entail discovering good fits among diverse and apparently conflicting positions. In diverse teams, this discovery process may itself entail some actual negotiating or some enacting of tasks to create opportunities for positive integration among team members.

In real-life terms, integration of diverse values, beliefs, and attitudes may mean shaping a team's output (e.g., juggling aspects of a new product proposal) to satisfy team members' apparently conflicting agendas (e.g., low cost, high quality, fast production). Integration of diverse knowledge and skills may mean assigning each team member to a portion of the task for which she or he is particularly qualified and motivated. Team members may fail to realize that their interests are integrative or even congruent when discussions focus on *what* outcomes individuals prefer rather than *why* they prefer those outcomes (Fisher & Ury, 1981). Moving a team's dialogue away from team members' desired outcomes to the interests and concerns underlying those desires allows team members to discover or create new outcomes that mutually satisfy their apparently conflicting interests (congruence) or that satisfy each team member's most critical concerns even when they are in conflict (integration).

Some of the difficulties that diverse team members encounter in working together may stem from the lack of *any* congruence that can provide a platform for exploring possible integrative fits among their resources and demands. For example, groups from different functional backgrounds are likely to have different ways of talking about even the same things (e.g., Donnellon, 1993; Tannen, 1990), as well as differences in what they are interested in talking about. Given the importance of effective communication to the discovery of integrative resolutions to conflict, and, hence, successful coaction (e.g., Tjosvold & Deemer, 1980), these linguistic barriers create substantial problems for heterogeneous teams whose members are trying hard to work together (Triandis, Kurowski, & Gelfand, 1994). In general, this suggests that the added value of diversity—in negotiation terms, the positive integration of team members' diverse resources and demands—must be predicated on some core of congruence (in knowledge and skills, values and attitudes, or personalities and styles) among team members.

Cooperation theory (Deutsch, 1949; Tjosvold, 1984) suggests that groups work best together (*cooperate*) if they share congruent objectives. Congruent objectives create positive orientation toward others (Tjosvold, 1984) and promote a useful flow of information concerning the team's task (Zander & Wolfe, 1964). Such communication can help team members discover possibilities for positive integration of their cognitive and physical resources. In contrast, team members' commitments to their own individual (nonteam) goals will substantially interfere with coordination of the team's coaction activities (Pettigrew, 1973).

If diverse team members believe that their goals and objectives are distributive, derogation and hostility (e.g., Sherif, Harvey, White, Hood, & Sherif, 1961), as well as distrust and poor communication (e.g., Pearson, Ball, & Deuch, 1985; Souder, 1980), are likely to result. Perhaps as a reflection of this, the amount of turnover that a team experiences often is a function of that team's heterogeneity, and the probability that any individual will leave is a function of the difference between that individual and the rest of the team (Jackson et al., 1991). In contrast, homogeneous teams experience fewer false starts on their tasks and typically take a shorter time to reach completion (Moos & Speisman, 1962).

To understand the factors that may derail diverse teams in the completion of their tasks, it is important to understand how nominal diversity (personal and organizational social category membership such as race and departmental affiliation) may interfere with a team's ability to discover integrative fits among its functional diversity (i.e., the team's diverse cognitive and physical resources). A key issue here is team members' identification with and consequent commitment to the social categories in which their nominal diversity places them. In the next section of this chapter, we explore social identity theory and the impact of team members' subgroup identification and commitment on team functioning.

SOCIAL IDENTITY THEORY

According to social identity theory (e.g., Ashforth & Mael, 1989; Tajfel & Turner, 1986), individuals tend to see themselves and others as belonging to social categories. Individuals categorize themselves and others on the basis of how closely their individual characteristics match the prototypes of various groups (Turner, 1985). The tendency to categorize the social world is driven by a need for cognitive parsimony (Brown, 1986; Bruner, Goodnow, & Austin, 1956), but it is the need for self-esteem (Tajfel & Turner, 1986), belongingness, and uniqueness (Brewer, 1991) that lead people to prefer certain categorizations over others. Thus, although categorization is largely a cognitive process (Ashforth & Mael, 1989; Turner,

1987), the process of identifying with a group includes affective and evaluative components as well (Tajfel, 1978). Identifying with groups leads an individual's self-concept to contain both personal and social identities (Leary, Wheeler, & Jenkins, 1986; Markus & Kunda, 1986; Markus & Wurf, 1987).

A variety of factors can influence the categorization process, including the salience of the outgroup (Turner, 1981), the status or size of ingroups and outgroups (Mullen, Brown, & Smith, 1992), and the distinctiveness of the characteristics that distinguish one subgroup from another (Oakes & Turner, 1986). Observable and immutable nominal diversity, such as diversity on personal demographic characteristics (e.g., gender, race), plays a critical role in social categorization (Messick & Mackie, 1989; Tsui, Xin, & Egan, chapter 5, this volume), as does diversity in formal organizational demographic characteristics (e.g., marketing vs. research-and-development subgroup membership; e.g., Baron & Pfeffer, 1989; Yoon, Baker, & Ko, 1994). Competition also can lead to social categorization (Brown & Ross, 1982); for example, in the context of an organization, differentiated compensation schemes that emphasize individual performance might catalyze the salience of subgroup identification boundaries.

Regardless of which boundaries team members use to categorize themselves and others, some categories will include the categorizing team member (ingroups), whereas other categories (outgroups) will not. These social categorization and identification processes may have few behavioral manifestations and implications as long as there is little interdependence or need for subgroups to interact. Crossfunctional teams, however, are designed specifically to provide an arena in which latent conflicts among values and attitudes, and personalities and styles are likely to surface. As team members interact, they can confirm the objective differences in values, attitudes, personalities, and styles that members of other subgroups bring to the team. Socialization, experiences, knowledge, and the focus of attention are likely to differ more across personal and organizational demographic subgroups than within them and so would be expected to create a certain amount of parochialism within subgroups (Dougherty, 1992;

Pfeffer, 1981). The potential clash of subgroup parochialism is precisely how diversity adds value—that is, if the team manages to integrate these differences (Lawrence & Lorsch, 1967).

Unfortunately, intergroup anxiety—the discomfort or apprehension that individuals experience when interacting with members of a different social category (Kramer, 1989; Stephan & Stephan, 1985)—is a natural consequence of social identification processes. People tend to like and are more comfortable around those with whom they are most similar (Berscheid, 1985; Sears, Freedman, & Peplau, 1985). Not surprisingly, then, nominal diversity (i.e., diversity of personal and organizational demographics) significantly influences coalition formation within teams (e.g., Tolbert, Andrews, & Simons, chapter 6, this volume).

Schneider's *attraction–selection–attrition* model of organizational membership (1983) provides a striking example of how team members' social categorizing can affect team functioning. The idea behind Schneider's model is that we are attracted to similar others and, therefore, are likely to select similar others to join our groups and organizations. Those similar others are most likely to be comfortable in the group and, therefore, will remain over time; dissimilar others will experience the discomfort and alienation of being different and eventually leave the group. Work group homogenization also occurs as a natural process of interaction over time because of assimilation; as the amount of interaction among team members increases, each member of the team mutually influences the thinking and perspective of others (Northcraft & Neale, 1993). Over time, the diversity in cognitive resources (i.e., values and attitudes, knowledge and skills, and personalities and styles) that offers integrative potential is dissipated by interaction. These perspectives foreshadow a homogenization of a team's functional characteristic diversity over time (George, 1990; McGrath et al., chapter 2, this volume). Interestingly, it is this process of homogenization of cognitive resources within a workforce that gives an organization its unique character (Schneider, 1987). However, if diversity is functional, homogenization of a workforce's functional diversity presents a threat to organizational competitiveness.

There is a subtle but important conceptual distinction underlying research on social identity that is relevant for analyzing the effects of diversity in cross-functional teams. In their seminal studies on intergroup conflict, the primary argument of Sherif and his colleagues (e.g., Sherif et al., 1961) is that intergroup conflict is *resource based:* that is, it reflects distributive conflicts in the cognitive and physical demands and resources that members bring to a team. Therefore, changing the nature of the resource acquisition process (e.g., by creating a superordinate goal) should decrease conflict among subgroups in an organization. Sherif et al. have proposed an essentially economic theory of intergroup relations, contending that conflicts among subgroups arise from natural goal incompatibility and consequent competition for scarce resources. Tajfel and his colleagues (e.g., Tajfel, 1978; Tajfel & Turner, 1986), on the other hand, have demonstrated that people exhibit ingroup favoritism even if there is no objective goal incompatibility or competition for scarce resources (i.e., there is no economic basis for conflict). Tajfel and Turner have argued that resource-based factors are sufficient, but not necessary, to produce intergroup conflict. Merely categorizing people is enough to elicit discrimination between subgroups (e.g., see Brewer, chapter 3, this volume).

The importance of this insight to the dynamics of cross-functional teams is that behavior is affected by both the objective structure of a team's resources and by social–psychological mechanisms of subgroup identification. Although these two sets of factors are surely related in practice, they are conceptually distinct. Subgroups may find real conflicts among the cognitive and physical resources and demands that they bring to the team, but biases stemming from social categorization and identification processes will exacerbate those conflicts. In the extreme, social categorization and identification processes may even create the illusion of distributive conflicts where there are none.

The issue for cross-functional teams is that social categorization and identification processes provide a means for subgroup members to misconstrue potentially positive (integrative or even congruent) cross-functional interaction as distributive cross-functional competition. Individuals acting as members of social-category subgroups tend to behave more competitively (Brewer, 1991; Brewer & Silver, 1978) and focus more on relative gain (i.e., on winning) compared with individuals acting alone (McCallum et al., 1985). Team members typically overestimate their similarity to members of their ingroup and their differences from outgroup members (Tajfel & Wilkes, 1963; Taylor, Fiske, Etcoff, & Ruderman , 1978). Furthermore, subsequent information processing about ingroup and outgroup members is often biased to confirm these impressions, resulting in a potentially vicious cycle of self-fulfilling prophecy (e.g., Sutton & Woodman, 1989).

The tragedy of misconstrued conflict stemming from subgroup categorization and identification is captured in Tjosvold's comment that "it is not so much commitment to one's [sub]group goals that disrupts coordination, but the tendency for [sub]groups to assume, unless clearly convinced otherwise, that their goals are negatively linked" (1984, p. 752). Tjosvold's comments suggest that the problems arising in teams from subgroup categorization and identification may be based on two perceptual biases. The first is the *fixed pie bias* (e.g., Bazerman & Neale, 1983). Cooperation theory assumes that goals are either congruent or distributive. Collaboration theory (e.g., Trist, 1977) and negotiation theory (e.g., Neale & Bazerman, 1991), however, posit a third option, namely, the possibility of integration. Unfortunately, the very parochialism of perspective that allows the possibility of functional diversity in cross-functional teams may also lead those individuals to assume that the issues they value most are also valued most by others on the team (e.g., Bazerman & Neale, 1983; Thompson & Hastie, 1990). This will lead team members to misconstrue issues in conflict (such as Issue B or Issue C in Table 1) as being distributive rather than integrative.

The second bias is the *incompatibility error* (e.g., Thompson & Hastie, 1990). Even when there is no reason for disagreement on an issue (e.g., Issue D in Table 1), stereotypes, distrust, and poor communication among subgroups in conflict (e.g., Deutsch, 1949) may lead team members to misconstrue these points of conflict as distributive as well. This can result in meaningless arguing and posturing where there is no real conflict.

The problem here is that team members tend to categorize themselves and others on the basis of social category diversity, such as personal and organizational demographics. These processes of social categorization and identification often reflect real differences in values, attitudes, personality and styles—differences that represent a valuable resource for the organization. Social categorization and identification processes become divisive, however, if they lead team members to believe that the functional conflicts among different subgroups in the team are distributive. These processes are divisive if a subgroup believes it can achieve its goals only at the expense of other subgroups represented in the team, when, in fact, these goals may be integrative or even congruent. This can lead to competition rather than collaboration among subgroups in the team.

Research on social identification processes confirms that subgroup members tend to make exactly this assumption about other subgroups. Once subgroups suspect that their goals are distributive, dysfunctional conflict becomes somewhat inevitable (e.g., Ginn & Rubenstein, 1986). Groups perceiving themselves to be in goal conflict will exhibit distrust, and communication and helping behaviors will deteriorate appropriately (Brewer, chapter 3, this volume; Deutsch, 1949; Souder, 1987). The perception of distributive incongruence polarizes subgroups and produces a separatism that undermines the potential benefits of diversity.

REALIZING THE BENEFITS

The picture painted here is that cross-functional teams offer enormous potential in principle that is difficult to realize in practice. But the problem is that social identification processes may lead team members to expect conflicts with other team members where there are no conflicts and to perceive all real conflicts as distributive, which, in turn, promotes defensiveness and competition along social identity lines. What mechanisms are likely to increase an organization's likelihood of successfully integrating cross-functional diversity? Social identity theory provides three potential avenues to overcome barriers to successful collaboration in the context of diversity: team education, architecture, and infrastructure.

Team Education

Rideout and Richardson (1989) suggested that appreciation of differences among participants is key to the success of a diverse working group. To that should be added that the most important appreciations can be the messages of the fixed pie bias and the incompatibility error: Not all conflicts are win or lose distributive conflicts, and sometimes differences do not translate into conflicts at all. A cross-functional team that appreciates the positive constructive potential of differences in values and attitudes, personalities and styles, and knowledge and skills is probably more likely to welcome the expression of those differences, thereby making the benefits more attainable. Simply put, if the benefits of diversity are inaccessible because of faulty perceptions, organizations must change those perceptions.

Education about other team members (and the nondistributive nature of their goals and the resources and demands they bring to a team) can also be accomplished successfully through job rotation programs (e.g., Northcraft, Griffith, & Shalley, 1992; Weinrauch & Anderson, 1982). Successful job rotation programs can be used strategically to give workers experiences in other functions and, thereby, dramatically decrease the "culture shock" of dealing with the issues, language, and perspectives of another subgroup when cross-functional teams are formed. In effect, job rotation programs help develop a multifunctional workforce in which cross-functional communication and cooperation are easy.

Team Architecture

Perlmutter's (1965) notion of *social architecture* may also play a role in improving the probability that a cross-functional team will realize the benefits of its membership diversity. Social architecture can be used to create an appropriate climate for cross-disciplinary cooperation, in which commonalities and complementarities among values and goals can be identified. Certainly, an organization does not want to select team members whose perspectives and values tend toward compatibility, for fear of undermining any possible diversity advantages. On the other hand, there may be some *meta*-characteristics that would help the process along, such as choosing individuals who value team collaboration and indirect or vicarious achievement over those who prefer direct achievement and individual contribution (George, 1977).

Social architecture may also refer to the physical arrangements and how they affect the collaborative spirit of diverse team members. A long-standing tradition of psychology research has shown that friendship choices are often a function of proximity (e.g., Armstrong & Cole, chapter 8, this volume; Festinger, Schachter, & Back, 1950; Nahemow & Lawton, 1975). Put simply, environmentally stimulated casual interaction is likely to promote familiarity and mutual adjustment that will help diverse individuals see the commonalities and complementarities beyond their surface conflicts. Physical proximity can increase casual contact that, if neutral or favorable, can ameliorate negative stereotyping and increase liking (Amir, 1969; Zajonc, 1968). Levi-Strauss found that cross-functional team meetings work best if the furniture is arranged as a horseshoe in which all participants can see each other clearly (Laabs, 1992). These no tions have implications not only for the management of cross-functional teams (e.g., nonwork social gatherings and closer temporary quarters enhance the probability of casual interaction), but also for the general physical design of factories and offices, where such configurations may help to break down prejudice and encourage intellectual cross-fertilization.

Finally, social architecture can also refer to the structure of reporting relationships in an organization (i.e., who reports to whom). Cross-functional teams, which can require individuals to report to multiple bosses in different departments, may fail simply because of their novelty in otherwise functionally segregated organizations. Cross-functional reporting relationships (such as those created in matrix organizations) render cross-functional communication more common (Reeves, 1985), thereby making the establishment of cross-functional teams less novel and less threatening.

Team Infrastructure

In many cases, the difficulties experienced in cross-functional groups can be blamed on the performance appraisal and reward systems that fail to support cooperative efforts (e.g., Edwards & Sproull, 1983; O'Dell, 1989). Performance appraisal and compensation schemes, if poorly designed, create short-term distributiveness even where groups' long-term interests coincide. Donnellon (1993) noted that any performance appraisal and compensation system that is based on *individual* achievement should beg questions about whether individuals have an incentive to withhold team contributions in order to receive individual credit later. In general, if the objective of a cross-functional team is cooperation and collaboration, the performance appraisal and compensation for team members must be team oriented (Walton & Dutton, 1969). If distributive values represent a major roadblock to cooperation among cross-functional groups, a compensation scheme that creates distributive outcomes (e.g., by rewarding only individual accomplishment in the team rather than team accomplishment) can only decrease the probability of successful cross-functional cooperation.

It is important for cross-functional teams to have sufficient time to be able to coalesce as a team. The greater the diversity of team members, the longer it will probably take for the team to discover congruencies that can provide a foundation for interaction and to work out the integrative fits among conflicting positions. The five-stages model of group development (Tuckman & Jensen, 1977) suggests that groups must go through the five stages of forming, storming, norming, performing, and adjourning. In the first three stages, diverse teams are likely to take longer to work through their real and apparent conflicts than are relatively homogeneous teams. Mannix and Loewenstein (1994) have suggested that a short-term time horizon can make the additional demands of cross-functional diversity too costly to explore. Under these circumstances, team members may simply avoid or submerge their conflicts with each other or simply compromise away (rather than integrate) the positive potential of those conflicts. The result is less of a "salad" (Kilborn, 1990)—the desired mix in which the identity of individual components remains intact, but intermingled to form positive contributions to the whole.

CONCLUSIONS

There is no doubt that cross-functional teams can represent a substantial ally in the fight for corporate efficiency and effectiveness. At Rubbermaid, the use of cross-functional teams increased sales 50% above projections (Dumaine, 1990). However, if organizations are going to realize the benefits, they must understand—and manage—the psychological baggage that potentially fruitful collaborators bring to cross-functional teams.

Social identity theory provides a helpful framework for thinking about that psychological baggage. Individuals need to understand who they are and who others are (Ashforth & Mael, 1989), and they often satisfy this need through their social categorization and identification with groups. Group categorization and identification, whether based on organizational (e.g., marketing, research-and-development) or personal (e.g., race, age, gender) characteristics, present practical barriers to the successful interaction of potentially constructive collaborators. For example, diverse past socialization experiences can result in differences among team members' values, skills, and personal styles. These differences represent the competitive advantage of diverse groups: the wellsprings of creativity and improved efficiency that can be realized only if the practical impediments they represent can be overcome.

The problem here is twofold. Social identity processes may lead team members to misperceive themselves as functionally different from others on the team who are in other social categories. Social identity processes also may lead team members to misperceive real conflicts with team members as distributive rather than integrative. Teams that are diverse in terms of personal and organizational demographics can work well together if they realize (a) that nominal diversity need not imply functional diversity and (b) that functional diversity need not be distributive. Properly managed, diverse cross-functional teams will come to understand their interactions as less distributive.

Organizations can also make interactions less distributive through proper organization of the infrastructure. Through the infrastructure, the social identity processes that create problems can be harnessed to help address them. Social categorization and identification processes often revolve around team members' concerns that resources will be distributed along nominal diversity lines. Therefore, realignment of team members' performance appraisal and reward contingencies—for instance, by explicitly rewarding group facilitation by individual and group achievement—makes clear the nondistributive nature of interactions with diverse others. This should help team members recast their social categories along more productive boundaries. Recategorization from subgroups to one aggregate causes a reduction in intergroup bias (Gaertner, Mann, Murrell, & Dovidio, 1989) and should assist the exploration and discovery of further positive integrations of differences among team members.

Albert and Whetten (1985) distinguished between holographic and ideographic organizations. In holographic organizations, individuals across subunits share a common identity; in ideographic organizations, individuals' social identities are subunit specific. Significantly, organizations must begin to integrate the needs of the organization and its members, the needs of different groups within the organization, and even the needs of the organization and its larger societal environment (Ackoff, 1974). In the context of an organization that attends to these integrations, the distinction between holographic and ideographic organizations becomes a false dichotomy. The fact that individuals feel the pull of multiple group memberships (Allen, Wilder, & Atkinson, 1983) does not suggest that a choice needs to be made. In the age of diversity, it is possible to be African American, from marketing, and a team player, all at the same time. A good organization makes multiple identity allegiance possible; a great organization makes multiple identity allegiance valuable.

REFERENCES

Ackoff, R. L. (1974). *Redesigning the future.* New York: Wiley.

Albert, S., & Whetten, D. A. (1985). Organizational identity. In L. L. Cummings & B. M. Staw (Eds.), *Research in organizational behavior* (Vol. 7, pp. 263–295). Greenwich, CT: JAI Press.

Allen, V. L., Wilder, D. A., & Atkinson, M. L. (1983). Multiple group membership and social identity. In T. R. Sarbin & K. E. Scheibe (Eds.), *Studies in social identity* (pp. 92–115). New York: Praeger.

Amabile, T. M. (1983). The social psychology of creativity. *Journal of Personality and Social Psychology, 45,* 357–376.

Amir, Y. (1969). Contact hypothesis in ethnic relations. *Psychological Bulletin, 71*, 319–342.

Ashforth, B. E., & Mael, F. (1989). Social identity theory and the organization. *Academy of Management Review, 14*, 20–39.

Bantel, K. A., & Jackson, S. E. (1989). Top management innovations in banking: Does the composition of the top team make a difference? *Strategic Management Journal, 10*, 107–124.

Baron, J., & Pfeffer, J. (1989). *The social psychology of inequality*. Unpublished manuscript, Stanford University.

Bazerman, M. H., & Carroll, J. S. (1987). Negotiator cognition. In L. L. Cummings & B. Staw (Eds.), *Research in organizational behavior* (Vol. 9, pp. 247–288). Greenwich, CT: JAI Press.

Bazerman, M. H., & Neale, M. A. (1983). Heuristics in negotiation: Limitations to dispute resolution effectiveness. In M. Bazerman & R. Lewicki (Eds.), *Negotiating in organizations* (pp. 51–67). Beverly Hills, CA: Sage.

Berscheid, E. (1985). Interpersonal attraction. In G. Lindsey & E. Aronson (Eds.), *Handbook of social psychology* (Vol. 2, pp. 413–484). New York: Random House.

Brewer, M. B. (1991). The social self: On being the same and different at the same time. *Personality and Social Psychology Bulletin, 17*, 475–482.

Brewer, M. B., & Silver, M. (1978). Ingroup bias as a function of task characteristics. *European Journal of Social Psychology, 8*, 393–400.

Brown, R. J. (1986). *Social psychology*. New York: Free Press.

Brown, R. J., & Ross, G. F. (1982). The battle for acceptance: An investigation into the dynamics of intergroup behavior. In H. Tajfel (Ed.), *Social identity and intergroup relations* (pp. 155–178). Cambridge, England. Cambridge University Press.

Bruner, J. S., Goodnow, J. J., & Austin, G. A. (1956). *A study of thinking*. New York: Wiley.

Clemson, S. (1990). Four models of collaborative teacher education: A comparison of success factors and maturation. *Action in Teacher Education, 12*, 31–37.

Cox, T., & Blake, S. (1991). Managing cultural diversity: Implications for organizational competitiveness. *Academy of Management Executives, 5*, 45–56.

Davis, R., & Thomas, L. G. (1993). Direct estimation of synergy: A new approach to the diversity–performance debate. *Management Science, 39*, 1334–1335.

Deutsch, C. H. (1990, August 26). Teamwork or tug of war? *The New York Times*, Section 3, p. 27.

Deutsch, M. (1949). An experimental study of the effects of cooperation and competition upon group process. *Human Relations, 2,* 199–231.

Donnellon, A. (1993). Crossfunctional teams in product development: Accommodating the structure to the process. *Journal of Product Innovation Management, 10,* 377–392.

Dougherty, D. (1992). Interpretive barriers to successful product innovation in large firms. *Organization Science, 3,* 179–202.

Dumaine, B. (1990, May 7). Who needs a boss? *Fortune, 121,* 52–59.

Eagly, A. H. (1987). *Sex differences in social behavior: A social role analysis.* Hillsdale, NJ: Erlbaum.

Edwards, M. R., & Sproull, J. R. (1983, March). Making performance appraisal perform: The use of team evaluation. *Personnel,* 28–32.

Epton, S. R., Payne, R. L., & Pearson, A. W. (1985). Contextual issues in managing cross-disciplinary research. In B. W. Mar, W. T. Newell, & B. O. Saxberg (Eds.), *Managing high technology: An interdisciplinary perspective* (pp. 209–230). Amsterdam: North Holland/Elsevier Science.

Festinger, L., Schachter, S., & Back, K. (1950). *Social pressures in informal groups.* New York: Harper & Row.

Fisher, R., & Ury, W. (1981). *Getting to yes.* New York: Houghton-Mifflin.

Fuller, K. (1993, March). A team activity. *Landscape Design, 218,* 20–21.

Gaertner, S., Mann, J., Murrell, A., & Dovidio, J. (1989). Reducing intergroup bias: The benefits of recategorization. *Journal of Personality and Social Psychology, 57,* 239–249.

George, J. M. (1990). Personality, affect, and behavior in groups. *Journal of Applied Psychology, 75,* 107–116.

George, W. W. (1977). Task teams for rapid growth. *Harvard Business Review, 55,* 71–81.

Gilliam, J. E., & Coleman, M. C. (1981). Who influences IEP committee decisions? *Exceptional Children, 47,* 642–644.

Ginn, M. E., & Rubenstein, A. H. (1986). The R&D production interface: A case study of new product commercialization. *Journal of Product Innovation Management, 3,* 158–170.

Goddard, R. W. (1985). Bringing new ideas to light. *Management World, 14,* 8–11.

Hoerr, J. (1989, July 10). The payoff from teamwork. *Business Week, 3114,* 56–62.

Hoffman, L. R. (1959). Homogeneity of member personality and its effects on group problem-solving. *Journal of Abnormal and Social Psychology, 58,* 27–32.

Ibarra, H. (1992). Homophily and differential returns: Sex differences in network structure and access in an advertising firm. *Administrative Science Quarterly, 37*, 422–447.

Jackson, S. E., Brett, J. F., Sessa, V. I., Cooper, D. M., Julin, J. A., & Peyronnin, K. (1991). Some differences make a difference: Individual dissimilarity and group heterogeneity as correlates of recruitment, promotions, and turnover. *Journal of Applied Psychology, 76*, 675–689.

Jones, S. C., & Vroom, V. H. (1964). Division of labor and performance under cooperative and competitive conditions. *Journal of Abnormal and Social Psychology, 68*, 313–320.

Kilborn, P. (1990, October 4). A company recasts itself to erase years of job bias. *The New York Times*, p. C21.

Kramer, R. M. (1989). "The more the merrier?" Social psychological aspects of multi-party negotiations in organizations. In R. Lewicki, M. Bazerman, & B. Sheppard (Eds.), *Research on negotiations in organizations* (Vol. 3, pp. 307–332). Greenwich, CT: JAI Press.

Laabs, J. L. (1992, December). HR's vital role at Levi Strauss. *Personnel Journal*, 35–46.

Larson, E. W., & Gobeli, D. H. (1988). Organizing for product development projects. *Journal of Product Innovation Management, 5*, 180–190.

Lawrence, P. R., & Lorsch, J. W. (1967). *Organization and environment.* Boston: Harvard University Press.

Leary, M., Wheeler, D., & Jenkins, T. (1986). Aspects of identity and behavioral preferences: Studies of occupational and recreational choice. *Social Psychology Quarterly, 49*, 11–18.

Lipnack, J., & Stamps, J. (1993). *The teamnet factor: Bringing the power of boundary crossing into the heart of your business.* Essex Junction, VT. Oliver Wright.

Maier, N. R. F. (1930). Reasoning in humans. *Journal of Comparative Psychology, 10*, 115–141.

Mandell, B., & Kohler-Gray, S. (1990). Management development that values diversity. *Personnel, 67*(3), 41–47.

Mannix, E. A., & Loewenstein, G. F. (1994). The effects of interfirm mobility and individual versus group decision making on managerial time horizons. *Organizational Behavior and Human Decision Processes, 59*, 371–390.

Markus, H., & Kunda, Z. (1986). Stability and malleability of the self-concept. *Journal of Personality and Social Psychology, 51*, 858–866.

Markus, H., & Wurf, E. (1987). The dynamic self-concept: A social psychological perspective. *Annual Review of Psychology, 38*, 299–337.

McCallum, D., Harring, K., Gilmore, R., Drenan, S., Chase, J., Insko, C., & Thibaut,

J. (1985). Competition and cooperation between groups and between individuals. *Journal of Experimental Social Psychology, 21,* 301–320.

Messick, D., & Mackie, D. (1989). Intergroup relations. *Annual Review of Psychology, 40,* 45–81.

Miller, L. K., & Hamblin, R. L. (1963). Interdependence, differential rewarding, and productivity. *American Sociological Review, 28,* 768–778.

Moenaert, R. K., & Souder, W. E. (1990). An information transfer model for integrating marketing and R&D personnel in new product development projects. *Journal of Product Innovation Management, 7,* 91–107.

Moos, R. H., & Speisman, J. C. (1962). Group compatibility and productivity. *Journal of Abnormal and Social Psychology, 65,* 190–196.

Mullen, B., Brown, R., & Smith, C. (1992). In-group bias as a function of salience, relevance, and status: An integration. *European Journal of Social Psychology, 22,* 103–122.

Myers, P. W., & Wileman, D. (1989). Learning in new technology development teams. *Journal of Product Innovation Management, 6,* 79–88.

Nahemow, L., & Lawton, M. P. (1975). Similarity and propinquity in friendship formation. *Journal of Personality and Social Psychology, 32,* 205–213.

Neale, M. A., & Bazerman, M. H. (1991). *Cognition and rationality in negotiation.* New York: Free Press.

Northcraft, G. B., Griffith, T. L., & Shalley, C. (1992). Building top management muscle in a slow-growth environment: How different is better at Greyhound Financial Corporation. *Academy of Management Executives, 6,* 32–41.

Northcraft, G. B., & Neale, M. A. (1993). Negotiating successful research collaborations. In J. K. Murnighan (Ed.), *Social psychology in organizations* (pp. 204–224). Englewood Cliffs, NJ: Prentice Hall.

Northcraft, G. B., & Neale, M. A. (1994). *Organizational behavior: A management challenge.* Hinsdale, IL: Dryden Press.

Oakes, P. J., & Turner, J. C. (1986). Distinctiveness and the salience of social category memberships: Is there an automatic perceptual bias towards novelty? *European Journal of Social Psychology, 16,* 325–344.

O'Dell, C. (1989, November). Team play, team pay—New ways of keeping score. *Across the Board,* pp. 38–45.

O'Reilly, C. A., Caldwell, D. F., & Barnett, W. P. (1989). Work group demography, social integration, and turnover. *Adminstrative Science Quarterly, 34,* 21–37.

Over, R. (1982). Collaborative research and publication in psychology. *American Psychologist, 37,* 996–1001.

Pearson, A. W., Ball, D. F., & Deuch, W. (1985). Managing the R&D/Marketing interface: A problem of interdisciplinarity. In B. W. Mar, W. T. Newell, & B. O. Saxberg (Eds.), *Managing high technology: An interdisciplinary perspective.* Amsterdam: North Holland/Elsevier Science.

Pelz, D. C. (1956). Some social factors related to performance in a research organization. *Administrative Science Quarterly, 1,* 310–325.

Perlmutter, H. (1965). *Towards a theory and practice of social architecture.* London: Tavistock.

Persico, J. (1989, January). Team up for quality improvement. *Quality Progress, 33,* 33–37.

Pettigrew, T. (1973). *The politics of organizational decision making.* London: Tavistock.

Pfeffer, J. (1981). *Power in organizations.* Marshfield, MA: Pitman.

Pfeffer, J. (1983). Organizational demography. In L. L. Cummings & B. M. Staw (Eds.), *Research in organizational behavior* (Vol. 5, pp. 299–357). Greenwich, CT: JAI Press.

Pinto, M. B. (1989). Predictors of cross-functional cooperation in the implementation of marketing decisions. *AMA Educator's Proceedings, 55,* 154–158.

Pinto, M. B., & Pinto, J. K. (1990). Project team communication and cross-functional cooperation in new program development. *Journal of Product Innovation Management, 7,* 200–212.

Price, D. J. (1963). *Little science, big science.* New York: Columbia University Press.

Reeves, E. I. (1985). Spacecraft design and development at TRW: Matrix management applied. In B. W. Mar, W. T. Newell, & B. O Saxberg (Eds.), *Managing high technology: An interdisciplinary perspective* (pp. 57–73). Amsterdam: North Holland/Elsevier Science.

Rideout, C. A., & Richardson, S. A. (1989). A teambuilding model: Appreciating differences using the Myers-Briggs type indicator with development theory. *Journal of Counseling and Development, 67,* 529–533.

Rohrbaugh, J. (1979). Improving the quality of group judgment: Social judgment analysis and the Delphi technique. *Organizational Behavior and Human Performance, 24,* 73–92.

Schneider, B. (1983). An interactionist perspective on organizational effectiveness. In L. L. Cummings & B. M. Staw (Eds.), *Research on organizational behavior* (Vol. 5, pp. 1–31). Greenwich, CT: JAI Press.

Schneider, S. C. (1987). Information overload: Causes and consequences. *Human Systems Management, 7,* 143–153.

Sears, D. O., Freedman, J. L., & Peplau, L. A. (1985). *Social psychology.* Englewood Cliffs, NJ: Prentice Hall.

Shanklin, W. L., & Ryans, J. K. (1984). Organizing for high-tech marketing. *Harvard Business Review, 62,* 164–171.

Sharpe, W. (1970). *Portfolio theory and capital markets.* New York: McGraw-Hill.

Sherif, M., Harvey, O. J., White, B. J., Hood, W. E., & Sherif, C. W. (1961). *Intergroup conflict and cooperation: The Robber's Cave experiment.* Norman, OK: University of Oklahoma Book Exchange.

Souder, W. E. (1980, July). Promoting an effective R&D/marketing interface. *Research Management, 23,* 10–15.

Souder, W. E. (1987). *Managing new product innovation.* Lexington, MA: Lexington Books.

Stephan, W. E., & Stephan, C. (1985). Intergroup anxiety. *Journal of Social Issues, 41,* 157–175.

Sutton, D. D., & Woodman, R. W. (1989). Pygmalion goes to work: The effects of supervisor expectations in a retail setting. *Journal of Applied Psychology, 74,* 943–950.

Tajfel, H. (1978). *Differentiation between social groups: Studies in the social psychology of intergroup relations.* San Diego, CA: Academic Press.

Tajfel, H., & Turner, J. C. (1986). The social identity theory of intergroup behavior. In S. Worchel & W. G. Austin (Eds.), *Psychology of intergroup relations* (pp. 7–24). Chicago: Nelson-Hall.

Tajfel, H., & Wilkes, A. (1963). Classification and qualitative judgment. *British Journal of Social Psychology, 54,* 101–114.

Tannen, D. (1990). *You just don't understand: Men and women in conversation.* New York: Ballantine Books.

Taylor, S. E., Fiske, S. T., Etcoff, N. L., & Ruderman, A. J. (1978). Categorical and contextual bases of person memory and stereotyping. *Journal of Personality and Social Psychology, 36,* 778–793.

Thompson, L. (1990). An examination of naive and experienced negotiators. *Journal of Personality and Social Psychology, 59,* 82–90.

Thompson, L., & Hastie, R. M. (1990). Social perception in negotiation. *Organizational Behavior and Human Decision Processes, 47,* 98–123.

Tjosvold, D. (1984). Cooperation theory and organizations. *Human Relations, 37,* 743–767.

Tjosvold, D. (1991). *The conflict-positive organization.* Reading, MA: Addison-Wesley.

Tjosvold, D., & Deemer, D. K. (1980). Effects of controversy within a cooperative or competitive context on organizational decision making. *Journal of Applied Psychology, 65,* 590–595.

Triandis, H. C., Hall, E. R., & Ewen, R. B. (1965). Member heterogeneity and dyadic creativity. *Human Relations, 18,* 33–55.

Triandis, H. C., Kurowski, L. L., & Gelfand, M. J. (1994). Workplace diversity. In H. C. Triandis, M. Dunnette, & L. Hough (Eds.), *Handbook of industrial and organizational psychology* (Vol. 4, pp. 769–827). Palo Alto, CA: Consulting Psychologists Press.

Trist, E. (1977). Collaboration in work settings: A personal perspective. *Journal of Applied Behavioral Science, 13,* 268–278.

Tuckman, B. W., & Jensen, M. A. C. (1977). Stages of small group development revisited. *Group and Organization Studies, 2,* 419–427.

Turner, J. C. (1981). The experimental social psychology of intergroup behavior. In J. C. Turner & H. Giles (Eds.), *Intergroup behavior* (pp. 66–101). Chicago: University of Chicago Press.

Turner, J. C. (1985). Social categorization and the self-concept: A social cognitive theory of group behavior. In E. J. Lawler (Ed.), *Advances in group processes* (Vol. 2, pp. 77–102). Greenwich, CT: JAI Press.

Turner, J. C. (1987). *Rediscovering the social group: A self-categorization theory.* New York: Basil Blackwell.

Tushman, M. L. (1977). Special boundary roles in the innovation process. *Administrative Science Quarterly, 22,* 587–605.

Walton, R. E., & Dutton, J. M. (1969). The management of interdepartmental conflict: A model and review. *Administrative Science Quarterly, 14,* 73–84.

Weick, K. E. (1977). Enactment processes in organizations. In B. M. Staw & G. R. Salancik (Eds.), *New directions in organizational behavior* (pp. 267–300). Chicago: St. Clair Press.

Weinrauch, D. J., & Anderson, R. (1982). Conflicts between engineering and marketing units. *Industrial Marketing Management, 11,* 291–301.

Wetlaufer, S. (1994). The team that wasn't. *Harvard Business Review, 72,* 22–38.

Yoon, J., Baker, M., & Ko, J. (1994). Interpersonal attachment and organizational commitment: Subgroup hypothesis revisited. *Human Relations, 47,* 329–351.

Young, H. C. (1979). Effective management of research–market teams. *Research Management, 22,* 7–12.

Zajonc, R. B. (1968). Attitudinal effects of mere exposure. *Journal of Personality and Social Psychology* (Monograph suppl.), *9,* 2–27.

Zander, A., & Wolfe, D. (1964). Administrative rewards and coordination among committee members. *Administrative Science Quarterly, 9,* 50–69.

5

Relational Demography: The Missing Link in Vertical Dyad Linkage

Anne S. Tsui, Katherine R. Xin, and Terri D. Egan

H ow to effectively manage a demographically diverse workforce is a
matter of concern for both practicing managers and management
scholars. Much of the research on demographic diversity in organizations
has been conducted at the work group level (Tsui, Egan, & Xin, 1994).
There has been relatively little analysis of such diversity in supervisor–
subordinate dyads. This is somewhat surprising, especially given the existence of a large body of literature in the last two decades on what have
been referred to as vertical dyad linkage or leader–member exchange theories about relationships between supervisors and subordinates. Graen
and Scandura argued that "the dyadic approach, by employing the small-
est unit of interpersonal organization—two participants and their interrelationships—can go beyond the one-person team and can reveal the variation in the internal teamwork components of a work group" (1987,
p. 176). An important factor in how well a team works is the relationship
that a team leader has with each individual team member. An important
job of a team leader is to learn what makes some relationships high quality and others low quality. Fahr, Podsakoff, and Organ (1990) also noted
the relevance of study at the dyad level. They argued that much of the

evolving employment contract between the individual and the organization derives from the relationship between the individual and his or her immediate supervisor. Therefore, an understanding of the relationship between an individual (such as a team member) and his or her immediate supervisor (team leader) is of great importance not only in improving the effectiveness and quality of the work team, but also in improving employee and organization relationships.

The purpose of this chapter is to fill a void in both the literature on organizational demography and the literature on vertical dyad linkage. The basic thesis of this chapter is that similarities or differences in demographic attributes such as age, sex, race, and educational or functional background are important cues not only for forming instantaneous interpersonal attraction, but also for inferring qualities related to subordinate performance by the superior and to supervisory supportiveness by the subordinate. We argue that relational demography, therefore, is important for predicting the quality of the exchange relationship in a dyad and, consequently, in a team. These predictions are based on a process of self- and other-categorization, as well as theories of roles, status, and norms associated with differences in demographic attributes. We draw evidence to support these predictions from empirical research on vertical dyads and from recent studies on relational demography. We also analyze implications of the group's compositional demography on the effect of relational demography in the superior–subordinate dyad.

VERTICAL DYAD LINKAGE RESEARCH

In the last two decades, Graen and his colleagues have developed and researched a new approach to the study of leadership by focusing on the dyadic relationship between superiors and subordinates. This approach, originally called vertical dyad linkage (VDL) theory (Dansereau, Cashman, & Graen, 1973), has been known more recently as leader–member exchange (LMX) theory (Graen, Novak, & Sommerkamp, 1982). With grounding in role theory and social exchange theory, VDL or LMX theory contends that leaders do not use the same style or set of behaviors to influence all subordinates. Instead, unique exchange relationships develop with each member in the group (Graen & Cashman, 1975). The basic hypothesis in VDL theory is that leaders categorize subordinates into two groups: the ingroup (characterized by high trust, interaction, support, and formal and informal rewards) and the outgroup (characterized by low trust, interaction, support, and formal and informal rewards). Furthermore, these group memberships tend to "develop fairly quickly and remain stable after they have formed" (Dienesch & Liden, 1986, p. 621). Given the tendency of superiors to categorize subordinates, it seems important to know who will become ingroup members and what factors influence this initial categorization. How, when, and why does this initial assignment occur?

Exchange Relationship: Quick Formation

One interesting point discovered in VDL studies is that, apparently, the quality of the relationship between a leader and a specific member is determined very early in the relationship (Dockery & Steiner, 1990). Furthermore, the quality of the relationship (good or poor), once established, tends to persist. For example, Liden, Wayne, and Stilwell (1993) looked at the relationships between 166 newly hired employees and their supervisors. Leader perceptions during the first week were generally consistent with the relationship assessed 6 months later. Similar conclusions can be drawn from a study of 192 hospital employees (Vecchio, Griffeth, & Hom, 1986) and another study with 96 individuals in a laboratory setting (Day & Crain, 1992). In a 13-year longitudinal study of 85 Japanese managers, Wakabayashi, Graen, and Uhl-Bien found that a number of these managers had been identified "early in their careers" as having a "high quality relationship with their supervisors" and had been given preferential attention (1990, p. 1102). Most of those with this higher quality relationship progressed further and faster in their careers. Another study, by Graen, Orris, and Johnson (1973), noted that "as early as the second week" supervisors categorized some newly hired employees into a lower performing group (p. 415). The supervisors saw some employees "as poorer performers from the very beginning" (p. 416).

In summary, on the basis of this accumulated evidence, two conclusions may be drawn: (a) The quality of the leader–member exchange relationship is established quite quickly and early, and (b) the initial quality of the relationship tends to persist over the long term. Given these conclusions, an important question that seems obvious but remains unanswered in the existing literature is what determines this initial categorization. Before exploring possible answers to this question, we first review the implications of ingroup and outgroup categorization of subordinates by their superiors. In other words, we must address the "so what?" question first.

Outcomes of Ingroup and Outgroup Categorization

In general, research has found that members of the ingroup enjoy a significantly better relationship with their supervisors than do members of the outgroup. According to Graen and Cashman (1975), supervisors exchange positional and personal resources for collaboration from their subordinates. Ingroup members, in exchange for their collaboration and loyalty, enjoy better access to information, influence, opportunity for challenging tasks, decision-making latitude, and supervisory support.

A number of studies have shown a positive association between high-quality leader–member exchange and high job satisfaction. For example, Graen, Novak, and Sommerkamp (1982) reported improvement in overall job satisfaction after the subject group received leader–member exchange training. This study also reported "significant ($p = 0.003$) and strong (15.1%) effects on quantity of production" by subordinates reporting a high-quality exchange relationship with their superiors (p. 125). Liden and Graen (1980) reported that subordinates having higher quality leader–member relationships (i.e., ingroup members) were more likely to be rated as good performers than subordinates having a poor-quality relationship (i.e., outgroup members). This same study, however, did not find a difference in job satisfaction between ingroup subordinates and outgroup subordinates. A study of 192 hospital employees by Vecchio,

Griffeth, and Hom (1986), on the other hand, did show a positive correlation between high-quality relationship and job satisfaction. Another study of 45 dyads in a business organization confirmed that higher quality leader–member exchange relationships were positively associated both with higher performance ratings and with higher levels of subordinate satisfaction with supervisors (Vecchio & Gobdel, 1984).

In yet another study, Duarte, Goodson, and Klich (1993) attempted to decouple objective performance from performance ratings. Their research on 261 telephone company supervisor–subordinate dyads did not conclusively show a clear positive connection between the quality of the exchange and performance. However, the authors reported that ingroup employees received higher performance appraisal ratings than would have been predicted by objective production criteria alone. In other words, subordinates who were ingroup members tended to receive high subjective ratings regardless of their actual objective performance. Outgroup employees, on the other hand, received ratings more closely tied to objective production criteria. Although the supervisors did not seem to show a negative bias against the outgroup members, a positive bias by the supervisors toward ingroup members was suggested.

However, is bias the only factor involved? Duarte et al. (1993) suggested that part of the answer may lie in what performance really means to some supervisors. Perhaps ingroup employees engage in more extrarole behavior than outgroup members. These employees may go beyond the formal job description by providing support, advice, and loyalty to the leader and to the unit. These extrarole behaviors may, in fact, be valid performance indicators from the perspective of supervisors. Two recent reports, one by Manogran and Conlon (1993) and another by Wayne and Green (1993), provided some evidence to support the idea that the quality of the exchange relationship in the dyad may be associated with several measures of organizational citizenship behavior.

VDL as a Mutual Exchange Process

The initial VDL theory seemed to imply that only leaders determine the fate of the subordinates in terms of the quality of exchange between the two members in the dyad. Later modification of the theory emphasized mutuality and reciprocity in the exchange process. In other words, both the leader and the subordinate can influence the nature of the exchange by what they bring to the relationship in terms of predispositions and actual behaviors. In a review of the research on LMX theory, Dienesch and Liden (1986) summarized how both members of the dyad may influence the relationship along three dimensions: perceived contribution, loyalty, and affect. Each member may have perceptions about the amount, direction, and quality of work that the other member puts forth toward the mutual goals of the dyad (contribution). Each member may express different levels of public support for the goals and the personal character of the other member (loyalty). Members may also have different amounts of affection for each other primarily on the basis of interpersonal attraction rather than work or professional values (Dienesch & Liden, 1986). The degrees of perceived contribution, loyalty, and affect by leader or subordinate influence the behavior of the other member in the dyad. In other words, subordinates, as much as leaders, can influence the quality of the exchange by their predisposition to cooperate and their reactions to their perception of the leader's behavior and attitude.

Dienesch and Liden further stated that during the initial stage of interaction, both leader and member bring their "unique physical characteristics, attitudes, appearance, abilities, personality, experience, age, and background to the meeting" (1986, p. 626). For example, when a particular individual characteristic is especially salient to a leader, the leader may make an immediate judgment about the member and may bypass, ignore, or discount later behavior that may contradict the initial judgment. A racially prejudiced leader may immediately categorize a member on the basis of race stereotypes. A racially prejudiced subordinate may form similar impressions of a racially different supervisor. In other words, both the leader and the member may be susceptible to the influence of visible cues associated with various demographic variables such as age, gender, race, or other physical attributes, as well as stereotypes associated with knowledge of the individual's socioeconomic, educational, or cultural background.

Preliminary Evidence on the Importance of Demographic Factors

Whereas the impact of demographic characteristics of both supervisor and subordinate at the dyad level has not been systematically researched, there is some preliminary evidence to suggest their importance. For example, Larwood and Blackmore (1978) found that supervisors tend to be biased in favor of members of their own sex. Duchon, Green, and Taber (1986) also found that gender can be used to predict ingroup and outgroup status. Fairhurst (1993) found that female leaders communicate with female subordinates somewhat differently than they do with male subordinates. Further analysis of conversations shows different discourse patterns associated with different qualities of exchange relationship with employees of both genders. McClane (1991) studied 26 groups, expecting to find that leaders were giving extra negotiating latitude to members similar to them on a variety of characteristics (locus of control, least preferred coworker, need for power, need for achievement, and gender). The expected preferential behavior did not occur, except when member and leader were similar in need for power. This finding suggests that gender similarity between supervisor and subordinate may not always influence the exchange relationship. Liden (1985) studied 35 female bank employees and collected information about their preferences for managers. Eighty percent of these female employees showed a preference for male managers. This finding may lead one to conclude that gender similarity provides no advantage. However, Liden drew quite a different conclusion. The female superiors in the bank may well have been less experienced and less influential, thus less desirable as champions or mentors. This suggests that at least for this sample of female bank tellers, rank or position may be more important than gender in determining the attractiveness of a supervisor.

Tsui and O'Reilly (1989) explicitly tested the effect of demographic differences in the vertical dyad, which they referred to as relational demography, on several perceptual measures obtained from both the supervisors and the subordinates. They found "subordinates in the mixed-gender dyad were rated to perform more poorly and were liked less well than the subordinates in the same-gender dyads. Furthermore, subordinates in the mixed-gender dyads also reported higher levels of role ambiguity and role conflict" (p. 414). They reported many additional analyses with interesting findings. For example, they found that subordinates with less education than their supervisors were liked better than subordinates with more education. Furthermore, supervisors liked subordinates with shorter job tenure than themselves more than they liked subordinates with either the same or longer job tenures. These additional findings suggest that both demographic similarities and differences may be important in influencing the dyadic relationship.

A more recent study (Tsui & Egan, 1994) provided further evidence on the complex effect of difference in race and age on the quality of relationship in the dyad. They found that White supervisors rated non-White subordinates lower than White subordinates on citizenship behavior. White subordinates were rated the highest on citizenship behavior by non-White supervisors. There were no differences in the level of subordinates' citizenship behavior rated by supervisors in same-race dyads. In terms of age, older subordinates were rated much lower by younger than by older supervisors on citizenship behavior. In fact, older subordinates were rated the highest by older supervisors on citizenship behavior among all of the groups.

In another recent study, Liden et al. (1993) looked at 166 newly hired employees and their supervisors. This study found neither demographic similarity nor subordinate performance to have any significant impact on the exchange relationship. The results of this study on demographic variables may be confounded by the method. Liden et al. combined the absolute difference values of several demographic variables and converted them into one demographic similarity index. This may be problematic. The influence of demographic similarity and dissimilarity is a very complex phenomenon. Different demographic variables may have different effects or even the same outcome variable. Combining all the relational demographic variables into one index may wash out the differential effects of different demographic factors.

In summary, the VDL literature reveals that the initial categorization (of subordinates into in- versus outgroup members by the leader) appears to be one of the most significant, yet least understood, parts of the relationship development process. This literature also reveals the potential importance of a number of demographic factors. Physical, observable, immutable personal and background characteristics of the members of the dyad may play a critical role in the initial categorization process. Furthermore, leadership is a mutual exchange process (Dienesch & Liden, 1986). The subordinate also contributes to the quality of the relationship by engaging in categorizing the leader.

In the next section, we describe the role of demographic similarity and dissimilarity (i.e., relational demography) in the vertical dyad by drawing on a variety of theoretical perspectives, including social identity theory and its associated social categorization process, the similarity-attraction theory, research on cross-race mentoring, homophily theory, and the idea of social category norms. We use these theories to provide insight into how relational demography may influence the quality of leader–member exchange, at least in the initial stage of the relationship. First, we analyze the dynamics of demographic similarities; then we discuss the dynamics associated with demographic dissimilarities. Finally, we analyze the group's compositional demography as a context in moderating the effect of relational demography on the exchange relationship in the vertical dyad.

DYNAMICS OF DEMOGRAPHIC SIMILARITY IN THE VERTICAL DYAD

As an employee enters into an employment relationship, both the supervisors and the subordinate have expectations about each other (Kotter, 1973). The subordinate may have expectations about the type of work to be performed, the contributions to be made, how she or he will be treated by the supervisor, and the types of tangible and intangible rewards that he or she will receive in return. The supervisor may have expectations about the type of work the subordinate is able to perform, contributions that the subordinate is able and willing to make, how dependable or reliable the subordinate will be in completing task assignments, and the type of tangible and intangible rewards the supervisor is willing and able to give in return. Most of the expectations regarding work assignments and rewards can be and often are discussed openly between the supervisor and the subordinate. However, although the explicit discourse may be very extensive and comprehensive, it is likely that some expectations may remain unspoken because of reluctance by either member of the dyad or unconscious bias held by either or both parties. Expectations such as the supervisor's skepticism about the real ability or potential of the employee to perform challenging assignments or about the employee's dependability, or the subordinate's doubt in the supervisor's true interest or sincerity in employee development, are often undiscussed topics.

How are these initial expectations formed? According to some theorists (e.g., Zajonc, 1980), some of these early expectations are heavily influenced by the initial affect that develops between two individuals. Affect influences future information processing and evaluation. In other words, subsequent information search, evaluation, and integration are used to confirm rather than disconfirm earlier affective impressions, resulting in a vicious cycle of self-fulfilling prophecy (Hogan, 1987; Merton, 1948; Sutton & Woodman, 1989). Other theorists would argue that these expectations are influenced by stereotypes that are cognitive information about typical traits and behaviors of people in a particular category. Affect is a consequence of such cognition (e.g., Lazarus, 1984). There has been no resolution to the debate on the primacy of affect versus cognition, and it is not our intention to attempt a resolution in this chapter. Consistent with several other theorists (e.g., Pittman & Heller, 1987; Tomkins, 1981), our view is that affect and cognition coexist, although the bases of their initial formation may be different. Social identity theory and the social categorization process may explain the quick formation of initial cognitions or expectations based on demographic similarity, and the similarity attraction theory may explain the quick formation of initial affect between the two parties, also based on demographic similarity. Affect and cognition jointly influence the nature of the exchange relationship in the dyad.

Social Identity and the Social Categorization Process

Social identity refers to the notion that individuals have some collective awareness of themselves as belonging to various groups that share some common identity (Tajfel & Turner, 1986). The theory maintains that people derive their identity in great part from the social categories to which they belong. To simplify perception and to reduce the infinite variability of stimuli into a more manageable number of distinct categories, people also engage in a process of categorization by which objects and people are classified on the basis of similarities and differences with reference to self. Through social categorization, others are perceived either as members of the same category as self or as members of a different category.

It can be seen, then, that social identity theory and the social categorization process help explain how individuals categorize others and how they categorize themselves (Turner, 1985, 1987). Insofar as the self-categorization process permits the individual to assume a positive social identity (Ashforth & Mael, 1989; Tajfel & Turner, 1986), the individual will seek to maximize intergroup distinctiveness and to see outgroup members as less attractive. The group that contains the self is likely to be perceived as special and regarded positively. This ingroup bias or accentuation effect was observed even in groups with minimal or near-minimal categorizations (Tajfel, 1982). As illustrated by Brewer's studies (see chapter 3, this volume), categorizing people even on the basis of arbitrary criteria can have powerful effects. For example, arbitrary categorization can lead group members to perceive outgroup members as less trustworthy, honest, and cooperative than members of their own groups (Brewer, 1979).

Citing work from numerous social psychologists spanning several theoretic schools, Turner (1985) concluded that "there is a strong implication that the general process underlying mutually cooperative intentions and expectations is the extent to which players come to see themselves as a collective or a joint unit, to feel a sense of 'we-ness' of being together in the same situation facing the same problems" (p. 34). In general, it appears that social identity theory and the social categorization process predict that leaders and members who are different in personality, attitudes, and demographic characteristics may find it more difficult to maintain a sense of "we-ness"; hence, it is less likely that these subordinates will be categorized as belonging to the ingroup. Leaders may tend to view subordinates in the same social category as themselves as more attractive and view those subordinates in a different social category as less attractive. Subordinates engage in a similar process. They most likely will find those supervisors who belong to the same social categories as themselves to be more attractive than those in different social categories. The other individual (i.e., the supervisor or the subordinate) is found to be attractive because association with him or her (i.e., categorizing self or the other in the same psychological group) contributes to the individual's positive social identity and high self-esteem, both of which are assumed to be fundamental human needs (Brockner, 1988; Tajfel & Turner, 1986). Affect in this case, although resulting from the cognition of stereotypic behaviors, attitudes, and social status of individuals in certain social categories, also contributes to further accentuation of these attributes.

Demographic Similarity, Interpersonal Attraction, and Homophily

Social categorization based on demographic similarity is conceptually related to the similarity-attraction paradigm (Berscheid & Walster, 1969; Bryne, 1971; Harrison, 1976). The basic tenet of the similarity-attraction theory is that affect develops on the simple awareness that the other individual is similar to oneself in some basic attitudes. Later research found attraction to occur with similarity in a variety of other variables, including leisure time activities (Werner & Parmelee, 1979) and socioeconomic background (Byrne, Clore, & Worchel, 1966). Presumably, similarity in demographics leads to an inference or assumption about similarity in values, beliefs, and attitudes. Such perceived or assumed similarity enhances attraction because of the self-enhancing motivation similar to that predicted by social identity theory. Furthermore, a presumed knowledge of the other individual's values, beliefs, and attitudes leads to a sense of predictability, comfort, and confidence regarding the other individual's likely behavior in the future. "Social homogeneity in the workplace makes communication easier, behavior more predictable and fosters relationships of trust and reciprocity" (Ibarra, 1992, p. 423). In the case of the dyad, demographic similarity, especially on those dimensions that are important social categories for social identity, will facilitate the development of a high-quality exchange relationship.

Recent work on mentoring (e.g., Murray, 1982; Thomas, 1990) and network homophily (e.g., Ibarra, 1992) has suggested that gender and race are important demographic variables for interpersonal attraction. Murray found that African American managers with same-race mentors were more satisfied with their career advancement than were African American managers with White mentors. Murray reasoned that race served as a positive source of identification in same-race developmental relationships, an explanation consistent with social identity theory. Thomas surveyed over 300 developmental relationships and reported that subordinates in cross-race relationships expressed much less psychosocial support from their mentors than subordinates in same-race relationships. In a study of network structure, Ibarra found that men were likely to form homophilous ties across multiple networks (i.e., both professional and social networks), whereas women were more likely to form homophilous ties in the social network. An interesting finding of this study is that whereas women tended to have more cross-gender ties in their instrumental (i.e., professional) network, they were less successful in benefiting from these cross-gender ties than men whose instrumental network tended to be homophilous. It is unknown, on the basis of this study, if women would benefit from homophilous instrumental ties as much as men. However, if social support is an important dimension of the exchange relationship in a vertical dyad, homogeneity in gender may be beneficial for both men and women subordinates, a prediction consistent with both social identity theory and the similarity-attraction paradigm.

Propositions Based on Demographic Similarity

On the basis of the above conceptual analyses and preliminary empirical evidence, we propose that both the supervisor and the subordinate will use demographic attributes such as gender, race, educational background, and even occupation or function to infer similarities in values, beliefs, and attitudes. In many cases, social stereotypes associated with the social categories defined by these demographic factors provide information for inferring similarities and compatibility. The supervisor may use this information to infer performance and dependability by the subordinate. The subordinate may use this information to infer consideration and supportiveness by the supervisor. The perceived compatibility and assumed similarities lead to ingroup categorization by both members. Ingroup categorization further leads to accentuation of similarity among ingroup members and differences with outgroup members. Interaction among ingroup members is likely to be characterized by high loyalty, mutual affect, and supportive behavior toward each other—the key dimensions of a high-quality exchange relationship.

The above conceptual analysis suggests several illustrative propositions on the relationship between demographic similarities and the quality of the dyadic exchange relationship:

Proposition 1. Subordinates who are of the same race or gender as their superiors will perceive a higher level of support and consideration by their superiors and will express a higher level of liking for their superiors (i.e., a higher quality exchange relationship) than will subordinates who differ from their superiors in race or in gender.

Proposition 2. Superiors who are of the same race or gender as their subordinates will perceive a higher level of loyalty and contribution by their subordinates and will express a higher level of liking for their subordinates than will superiors who differ from their subordinates in race or in gender.

Research has found a differential magnitude in the effects of gender and race, with Whites and men showing larger negative effects for increased demographic difference from others than non-Whites and women (Tsui, Egan, & O'Reilly, 1992). However, even though the magnitude of the effect may be different, the direction of the effects of these two demographic variables remains the same.

Proposition 3. Subordinates who are similar to their superiors in educational background (e.g., major or college) and training (e.g., occupation or function) will perceive a higher level of support and consideration by their superiors and will express a higher level of liking for their superiors than will subordinates who differ from their superiors in these demographic factors.

Proposition 4. Superiors who are similar to their subordinates in educational background (e.g., major or college) and training (e.g., occupation or function) will perceive a higher level of loyalty and contribution by their subordinates and will express a higher level of liking for the subordinates than will superiors who differ from their subordinates in these demographic factors.

DYNAMICS OF DEMOGRAPHIC DIFFERENCES IN THE VERTICAL DYAD

The preceding section focused on the psychological and social psychological processes that lead individuals to attach positive valence to interacting with others who are similar on specific demographic attributes. However, it is likely that differences in certain demographic attributes between leaders and followers will be both expected and valued. In other words, a different dynamic may operate on dissimilarity in the dyad on some demographic factors. We draw on theories of roles, social norms, and status associated with specific social categories to analyze the dynamic of demographic differences in the vertical dyad.

Social Categories, Roles, Status, and Norms

Sociologists such as Linton (1940, 1942) and Parsons (1942) proposed that members of social systems use age and sex to classify individuals into categories and match them with a particular role and status. This matching process among age or sex category, role, and status produces shared beliefs (norms) about the standard age or sex of members holding a particular position within the social system. More recently, Lawrence (1988) proposed that within organizations there are norms regarding the level of status attainment that can be expected of individuals in certain age categories. Individuals who attain certain status slower or faster than the norm may be viewed negatively by others. On the basis of these ideas, we suggest that in organizational contexts, social categories of age, educational level, and tenure in the organization or the department are used as bases for classifying individuals into particular roles and status levels.

Beyond age, educational level, and tenure norms for particular roles and status levels within the organization, we further propose that there are also norms surrounding these social categories in relation to others. For example, the fact that a supervisor is 40 years of age may have one meaning in and of itself. But, the meaning of being 40 years old may change if it is considered relative to the age of a 50-year-old subordinate. Similarly, although a 30-year-old supervisor may seem young within the context of age norms, the additional information that subordinates are all in their early 20s suggests a new interpretation of the supervisor's age. In this case, a 30-year-old supervisor may be as acceptable to a 20-year-old subordinate as a 50-year-old supervisor would be to a 40-year-old subordinate. The relational aspect of age norms is emphasized here.

Demographic Differences and Status Inequalities in the Vertical Dyad

The supervisor–subordinate relationship is characterized by inequalities in power, status, and benefits afforded to each of the members. To remain consistent with notions of meritocracy, organizational members expect these inequalities to have some legitimate bases. Thus, if someone is in a position of authority, subordinates expect that he or she is different from them in terms of the capacity to lead. Just as some demographic attributes are used as a means of inferring desired similarity in attitudes, values, and group interests, certain demographic attributes are also used as a means of inferring desired differences in levels of experience, skills, training, intelligence, and wisdom. Capacity to lead may be inferred indirectly from attributes such as age (wisdom), organizational tenure (experience), or educational level (training and knowledge).

Demographic similarities or differences in the vertical dyad that are incongruent with expected status and role configurations may be interpreted in one or more of the following ways: (a) The subordinate may be perceived as slow in terms of advancement and development; (b) the supervisor may be perceived as an exceptional individual who transcends common organizational role and status norms based on age, educational level, and organizational tenure; or (c) the subordinate may perceive the supervisor as having attained a position that he or she does not deserve. Each of these interpretations has implications for both the attitudes and behaviors of the subordinate and the superior and how they interact with each other.

An example is the case of the subordinate with a relatively younger supervisor. In this situation, the subordinate may perceive that the supervisor does not have the level of wisdom, training, experience, or knowledge necessary to be a leader. This perception may, in turn, influence the subordinate's belief regarding the supervisor's ability to perform as a leader (e.g., garnering needed resources and using upward influence within the organization). Younger supervisors (relative to middle-aged or older subordinates) may also be perceived as less likely to fulfill what Dalton, Thompson, and Price (1977) referred to as the mentor role in the organization. Thus, desirable supervisory behaviors aimed at guiding and developing subordinates may be less likely to occur. Finally, if the subordinate feels that the leader is not deserving of his or her position of authority—particularly relative to the subordinate's age and tenure—perceptions of inequity may occur, which, in turn, may negatively affect the subordinate's attitudes and behaviors.

The older employee being led by a younger individual with a master's degree in business administration is an excellent case to illustrate the point. The younger superior may perceive the older subordinate as lacking up-to-date business management knowledge, whereas the older subordinate may perceive the younger superior as lacking company and practical knowledge that can be acquired only by years of actual working experience. Consequently, the younger supervisor may be predisposed to negatively evaluate the older subordinate. He or she may have less confidence in the ability of the older subordinate to perform well or make an important contribution to the new business environment's demands. The older subordinate may be predisposed to be less cooperative and supportive of the younger supervisor. Thus, differences in age that are consistent with relational age norms of status and power may contribute to the quality of exchange in the superior–subordinate dyad, whereas differences in age that are inconsistent with the relational age norms may not facilitate a high-quality exchange relationship.

Similar dynamics may be expected with regard to differences in educational level and company or departmental tenure. The example above suggests that status and power may be associated with educational level. Therefore, it may be expected that a supervisor will have more education than a subordinate. An individual with long company or departmental tenure may not willingly accept a new supervisor brought in from outside. However, a new subordinate brought in from outside the company may be highly acceptable to the supervisor, especially if the subordinate is recruited by the supervisor. Superior–subordinate relationships may be strained if the superior is promoted from among a group of peers, especially those who have similar company or departmental tenure.

Propositions Based on Demographic Differences

In summary, we propose that the exchange relationship will be negatively affected by the absence of expected differences in age, organizational tenure, and educational level between a supervisor and a subordinate. The following propositions are offered to illustrate the dynamic of legitimate demographic differences in the vertical dyad. Given the potential interaction among different demographic variables, these propositions focus on the main effect of each relational demographic variable and assume constancy of all other demographic factors.

Proposition 5. Subordinates who are younger than their superiors will perceive a higher level of support and consideration by their superiors and will express a higher level of liking for their superiors (i.e., a higher quality exchange relationship) than will subordinates who are older than their superiors.

Proposition 6. Superiors who are older than their subordinates will perceive a higher level of loyalty and contribution by their subordinates and will express a higher level of liking for their subordinates than will superiors who are younger than their subordinates.

Proposition 7. Subordinates who have less education and training than their superiors will perceive a higher level of support and consideration by their superiors and express a higher level of liking for their superiors than will subordinates who have more education than their superiors.

Proposition 8. Superiors who have more education than their subordinates will perceive a higher level of loyalty and contribution by their subordinates and will express a higher level of liking for their subordinates than will superiors who have less education than their subordinates.

Proposition 9. Subordinates who have shorter company or departmental tenure than their superiors will perceive a higher level of support and consideration by their superiors and will express a higher level of liking for their superiors than will subordinates who have longer company or departmental tenure than their superiors.

Proposition 10. Superiors who have a longer company or departmental tenure than their subordinates will perceive a higher level of loyalty and contribution by their subordinates and will express a higher level of liking for their subordinates than will beliefs, superiors who have a shorter company or departmental tenure than their subordinates.

GROUP DEMOGRAPHY AS CONTEXT

Up to this point, we have focused on understanding the impact of similarities and differences in demographic variables on the character of the exchange relationship between the supervisor and the subordinate. However, this dyadic relationship takes place within a broader context. The chapter by Tolbert, Andrews, and Simons (chapter 6, this volume) provides some interesting perspectives on group proportions. For example, results from their empirical study suggest that increasing representation of women in a group leads to an increasingly negative environment for these women. They further suggest that group proportions affect not only the attitudes and actions of minority members, but also the attitudes and actions of majority members as well. Thus, it seems that a likely starting point to understand the potential influence of context embedment on the supervisor–subordinate relationship is the demographic composition of the work group in which both individuals claim a common membership. By introducing the notion of group composition as the context, we are asking the following fundamental question: Will the demographic composition of the work group moderate the impact of relational demography on the quality of leader–member exchange at the dyad level?

When Demographic Similarities Are Attractive

Drawing from a variety of theoretic and empirical sources, we have proposed that, in general, supervisors and subordinates who are similar to one another on attributes such as race, gender, and educational or functional background are likely to enjoy more positive exchange relationships than those who differ on the same attributes. This is because similar others are viewed as more attractive sources of interaction and are more likely to be evaluated positively than dissimilar others. Central to understanding the potential impact of work group composition on the effects of similarities and differences at the dyad level is the notion that the work group is a source of social identity. Contextualizing the supervisor–subordinate dyad in the work group presents the possibility that both positive and negative aspects of social identification with the work group may moderate the impact of relational demography on the exchange relationship in any of the vertical dyads in the small group.

Figure 1 presents two scenarios—same-gender dyad versus different-gender dyad—that we will use to illustrate the potential moderating effect of work group demography. In each scenario, we will focus on the same supervisor–subordinate dyad embedded in work groups characterized by different degrees of heterogeneity on gender.

In scenario 1, we first focus on the nature of the relationship between the female subordinate and female supervisor in a predominantly female work group (i.e., low group heterogeneity; dyad 1). An isolated analysis at the dyad level suggests that similarity in gender results in a positive impact on the exchange relationship (as suggested by propositions 1 and 2).

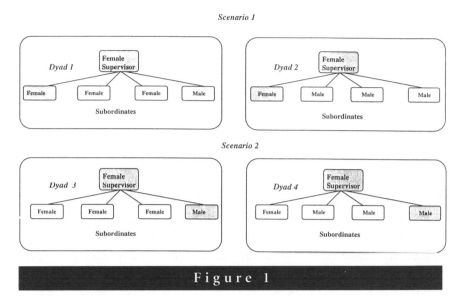

Figure 1

Dyadic demographic similarity in the context of group demography.

However, is this relationship likely to change on the basis of the fact that there are two other women in the work group? Several theoretic perspectives suggest that in this scenario the subordinate woman would be likely to identify and affiliate with other women in the work group (Bryne, 1971; Tajfel, 1982). Similarly, the female supervisor has multiple women with whom to interact and identify. We argue that in this case the salience of gender similarity between the supervisor and the subordinate may be diluted for both parties.

In contrast, for the female subordinate in dyad 2 of scenario 1, a situation of relatively high heterogeneity in group composition, we suggest that the reduced opportunity for social interaction with similar others may enhance the attractiveness of the only other female in the group for both the subordinate and the supervisor—thus accentuating the positive effect of relational similarity on gender in this vertical dyad. In essence, we argue that in a context characterized by increased opportunity for social identification with members of the same social category, the salience and value of any one particular relationship is somewhat diluted. Relatedly, if there are fewer opportunities for social identification, the value of the same relation may be stronger.

Now, turning our attention to the male subordinate with the female supervisor (dyads 3 and 4 in scenario 2), we examine the potential of group heterogeneity strengthening the negative impact of demographic difference on the dyad. In dyad 3, we have one man with a female supervisor in a predominantly female work group (i.e., low heterogeneity in group composition). From the male subordinate's perspective, opportunity for gender-based identification with work group members is absent, so the importance of his relationship with the female supervisor may be increased. He may be more likely to offer extra attention and support to the female supervisor. Furthermore, evidence on the relative treatment of male versus female tokens (Schreiber, 1979) suggests that men in predominantly female groups are generally treated quite positively. Therefore, the negative effect of being different in gender in this dyad may be weakened by the relatively low level of heterogeneity in this work group.

Dyad 4 is in the context of higher group heterogeneity in gender. In this scenario, the male subordinate has the opportunity to develop relationships with same-gender peers, a situation that provides group identity and solidarity. This subordinate is less likely to identify with the female supervisor than is the male subordinate in dyad 3. Some researchers in both gender and race relations have observed that heterogeneity increases intergroup conflict (Blalock, 1957; Pettigrew, 1980). Viewing the work group as a whole, gender heterogeneity is higher for dyad 4 than for dyad 3. Thus, we expect the negative effect of gender difference to be stronger for dyad 4 than for dyad 3.

Although we have used gender similarity and difference as an example to illustrate the moderating role of group-level demography, we suggest that the same logic applies to demographic attributes such as race and functional or educational background. In general, we propose that both the positive and the negative effect of relational demography on leader–member exchange is enhanced in heterogeneous work groups. Thus, the following proposition is offered:

Proposition 11. Work group heterogeneity will strengthen the positive effect of similarity and the negative effect of dissimilarity in demographic attributes such as gender, race, and educational or functional background on the quality of the exchange relationship in the supervisor–subordinate dyad.

When Demographic Differences Are Legitimate

Our earlier exploration of the influence of roles, status, and norms suggested that in certain situations, differences in demographic attributes such as age, educational level, and organizational or departmental tenure are both expected and valued in the supervisor–subordinate relationship. How does group demography affect the expected or legitimate differences in the vertical dyad? In this situation, the primary conceptual question is the following: What, if any, impact does group composition have on how dyadic differences affect roles, status, and norms? Figure 2 provides an illustration of four dyads that may be useful in understanding this question.

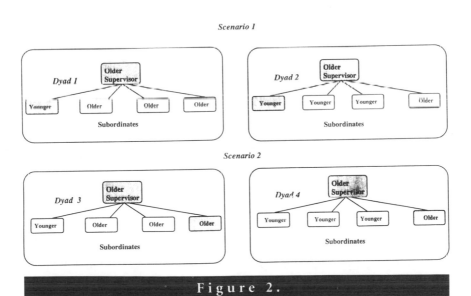

Figure 2.

Dyadic demographic differences in the context of group demography.

In scenario 1, there are two dyads characterized by an expected relational difference in age, but with different degrees of group heterogeneity in age. In both cases, the subordinate is younger than the supervisor. In the first dyad, the work group consists of predominantly older workers. Here one may expect the properties of the expected relational age norm at the dyad level to be enhanced by the relative scarcity or uniqueness of the age of the subordinate. Because most of the other workers are of an older age, this young worker may be perceived as an exceptional person who has achieved a position that usually takes many years of effort to attain. In contrast, for dyad 2 (a relatively heterogeneous work group), the presence of other young subordinates may diminish the value of being young for any one subordinate.

Scenario 2 presents us with two dyads in which the relational age norm is violated. The subordinate is similar to the supervisor in age. With respect to dyad 3, the relative frequency of other older subordinates may suggest that for this work group, having older individuals in subordinate roles is not unusual. Thus, status, role, and relational age norm expectations may be less salient in this situation. By extension, this may result in a relatively lower negative impact of age similarity in the vertical dyad. In contrast, the older subordinate in dyad 4 is surrounded by younger coworkers. Thus, the negative impact of an absence of expected age difference in this dyad may be heightened by the age-role deviance of the subordinate. However, there is also a different dynamic operating on dyad 4 in this scenario. In this case, similarity in age between the two members in dyad 4 may serve to neutralize the negative effect of the violation of the age-difference norm. The older supervisor and the older subordinate may identify with each other and form a solidarity between them in the midst of all of the other younger individuals in the group. In this case, heterogeneity in age may not heighten the negative impact of age similarity in the dyad. Preliminary findings from the study by Tsui and Egan (1994), mentioned above, are supportive of this similarity-attraction dynamic.

In summary, in cases where demographic differences are expected and legitimate, we suggest that work group heterogeneity will weaken the positive effect of the difference on the dyad, but that it will not necessarily strengthen the negative effect of no difference. We argue that a similar dynamic operates on other demographic variables such as educational level or company and departmental tenures. The following general proposition is offered:

Proposition 12. Work group heterogeneity will weaken the positive effect of differences in demographic attributes such as age, educational level, and company or departmental tenure on the quality of the exchange relationship in the supervisor–subordinate dyad.

CONCLUSION, IMPLICATIONS, AND FUTURE DIRECTIONS

In this chapter, we have argued for the importance of relational demography in the initial formation of the exchange relationship in the vertical dyad. Demographic variables, especially those that are immediately visible, are cues for inferring underlying attributes, such as values, beliefs, attitudes, abilities, and motivation. Furthermore, they represent different social categories that members may use to categorize both self and others. Whereas similarity of some demographic variables increases attraction between the two members, dissimilarity on some other variables is desired. We have offered a number of propositions to illustrate the dynamic of both demographic similarities and dissimilarities and their effects on the quality of the exchange relationship between the two members. Moreover, we have shown how the effect of relational demography on the dyad exchange relationship may be heightened or weakened in the context of different degrees of demographic heterogeneity at the work group level.

The purpose of this chapter is to highlight one aspect of the vertical dyad theory that has been ignored in previous research: How and why are subordinates categorized into ingroup and outgroup members? Existing research provides evidence on the "quick formation" nature of the exchange relationship. Furthermore, initial categorization appears to persist over time. These findings of vertical dyad research suggest two important implications: (a) The limited opportunity to exchange information and to interact before the formation of the relationship suggests the important influence of demographic and background factors that are immediately available to either member. (b) There are a large number of social–psychological and sociological theories suggesting the importance of social categories associated with various demographic variables in an individual's tendency to categorize others into ingroup and outgroup members. Thus, our emphasis on relational demography in the vertical dyad is both empirically and theoretically grounded. Our conceptual analyses further suggest the importance of group demography as a context. Group composition in terms of relative degree of heterogeneity may either strengthen or weaken the effect of relational demography at the dyad level.

Implications for the Work Team

Clearly, relational demography in the vertical dyad has important implications for the work team as a whole. The anatomy of a work team consists in part of a number of relationships between the team leader and team members. These relationships have the potential to affect the effectiveness of the work team through their influence on the attitudes and behaviors of both leaders and followers. However, beyond these individual effects, we suggest that there is an aggregate level effect of these relationships that influences the overall well-being of the team itself. In short, the ability of the team as a whole to develop into a high-performance unit is most likely constrained by the quality of the exchange relationships among the members. This notion is supported by recent work described by Vasudevan and Graen (1994).

What are some of the practical implications of the potential impact of demographic differences on the exchange relationship? Should managers expect that increased contact with those who are different will mitigate the potentially negative impact? Recent work by Tolbert, Andrews, and Simons (chapter 6, this volume) supports decades of research showing that merely placing diverse individuals into contact with each other is not enough to facilitate positive interaction—in fact, it may lead to declining relationships. Thus, we suggest a more active approach.

One active approach is through supervisory training. Scandura and Graen (1984) reported that supervisory training in active listening skills, exchange of expectations, and exchange resources resulted in significant increases in the degree of supervisor support and perceived member availability, especially in individuals who initially had low-quality relationships. The outcome was an increase in both productivity (weekly output records) and job satisfaction. Awareness of relational and group compositional effects on the expectations and the quality of relationships, as suggested in this chapter, may be included in supervisory training so that the leader–member exchange relationship can reach its full potential.

Although rarely articulated directly by organizational demographers, at the heart of much of our discourse about the impact of diversity or differences on organizational life are issues of power played out in the arena of domination and subordination. (Ironically, much of the discussion of leadership in this chapter has been framed in terms of the supervisor and the subordinate.) One method for addressing these dynamics—that is, by increasing awareness of them—is proposed by Ely (chapter 7, this volume). In contrast with past diversity training, which has focused on understanding the perspective of those who are traditionally considered diverse (i.e., women and people of color), Ely's dominant identity awareness training acknowledges the importance of understanding the dominant group identity and experiences for both the dominant and the diverse.

Future Conceptual Development

What we have proposed is preliminary at best. There are a number of conceptual issues that require further work. First, we have not addressed the potential interaction among multiple demographic factors. Would the positive effect of similarity on one factor neutralize the negative effect of difference on another? What if the two members differ in the salience they each attach to the same demographic factors? What are the effects of an assumed high level of consideration and support by one member and an assumed low level of loyalty and contribution by the other member? Interaction between the members may reveal assumptions that are not justified and, thus, may lead to changes in the categorization by either member. Whereas current evidence suggests that initial categorization is maintained over time, recategorization is possible with further exchange of information and behavior between the two members. Furthermore, given the awareness of the dysfunctional aspect of categorization, how do leaders and followers move beyond initial categorizations? What kind of environment is required to "discuss the undiscussable" and to avoid self-sealing ways of interacting with others (Argyris, 1990)? Are there other individual characteristics of both the leader and follower that may lead to revision of assumptions and beliefs formed in the initial stage of the relationship?

Another important issue relates to the context embedding the vertical dyad. We have used the work group's compositional demography as a context for examining contextual effects on any single dyad. What about the demographic composition of the entire organization? What role does this play in the supervisor–subordinate dyad? Some interesting ideas along this line are discussed in a recent paper by Tsui, Egan, and Xin (1994).

In addition, the VDL theory was developed within the American context. The social–psychological and sociological meanings and dynamics associated with the various demographic attributes presented in this chapter are also based primarily on the American culture. There may be cross-cultural differences in the role of relational demography in the leader–member relationship (Zalesny & Graen, 1993). For example, Graen and Wakabayashi (1994) have suggested that joint ventures or transplant organizations involving different cultures often result in a hybrid culture that may show some characteristics inherited from both cultures:

> Managers at a typical hybrid culture transplant have found that their associates see themselves neither as Japanese at the home plants nor as other Americans working in the same industry in the United States. Rather, they see themselves as part of a unique corporate culture that has developed. (p. 416)

Therefore, cross-cultural exchange relationships may take on a different meaning and dynamic if members of the dyad are of different national cultures. Each culture may have different norms and understandings of what constitutes a high-quality exchange relationship. The challenge for future leadership research is to understand how exchange processes operate in culturally heterogeneous teams.

In conclusion, we hope the ideas in this chapter have provided some basis for further conceptual and empirical work on the role of demographic factors in understanding the nature of exchange relationships between supervisors (or team leaders) and subordinates (or team members) in the demographically heterogeneous workforce worldwide.

REFERENCES

Argyris, C. (1990). *Overcoming organizational defenses: Facilitating organizational learning.* Boston: Allyn & Bacon.

Ashforth, B. E., & Mael, F. (1989). Social identity theory and the organization. *Academy of Management Review, 14,* 20–39.

Berscheid, E., & Walster, E. (1969). *Interpersonal attraction.* Reading, MA: Addison Wesley.

Blalock, H. M., Jr. (1957). Percent non-White and discrimination in the South. *American Sociological Review, 22,* 677–682.

Brewer, M. B. (1979). In-group bias in the minimal inter-group situation: A cognitive–motivational analysis. *Psychological Bulletin, 86,* 307–324.

Brockner, J. (1988). *Self-esteem at work: Research, theory, and practice.* Lexington, MA: Heath.

Byrne, D. (1971). *The attraction paradigm.* New York: Academic Press.

Byrne, D., Clore, G. L., Jr., & Worchel, P. (1966). The effect of economic similarity–dissimilarity as determinants of attraction. *Journal of Personality and Social Psychology, 4,* 220–224.

Dalton, G. W., Thompson, P. H., & Price, R. L. (1977, Summer). The four stages of professional careers: A new look at performance by professionals. *Organizational Dynamics,* pp. 19–42.

Dansereau, F., Jr., Cashman, J., & Graen, G. (1973). Instrumentality theory and equity theory as complementary approaches in predicting the relationship of leadership and turnover among managers. *Organizational Behavior and Human Performance, 10,* 184–200.

Day, D. V., & Crain, E. C. (1992). The role of affect and ability in initial exchange quality perceptions. *Group and Organization Management, 71,* 380–397.

Dienesch, R. M., & Liden, R. C. (1986). Leader–member exchange model of leadership: A critique and further development. *Academy of Management Review, 11,* 618–634.

Dockery, T. M., & Steiner, D. D. (1990). The role of the initial interaction in leader–member exchange. *Group and Organizational Studies, 15,* 395–413.

Duarte, N. T., Goodson, J. R., & Klich, N. R. (1993). How do I like thee? Let me appraise the ways. *Journal of Organizational Behavior, 14,* 239–249.

Duchon, D., Green, S. G., & Taber, T. D. (1986). Vertical dyad linkage: A longitudinal assessment of antecedents, measures, and consequences. *Journal of Applied Psychology, 71,* 56–60.

Fahr, J.-L., Podsakoff, P. M., & Organ, D. W. (1990). Accounting for organizational citizenship behavior: Leader fairness and task scope versus satisfaction. *Journal of Management, 16,* 705–721.

Fairhurst, G. T. (1993). The leader–member exchange patterns of women leaders in industry: A discourse analysis. *Communication Monographs, 60,* 321–351.

Graen, G., & Cashman, J. (1975). A role-making model of leadership in formal organizations: A development approach. In J. G. Hunt & L. L. Larson (Eds.), *Leadership frontiers* (pp. 143–165). Kent, OH: Kent State University Press.

Graen, G., Novak, M. A., & Sommerkamp, P. (1982). The effects of leader–member exchange and job design on productivity and satisfaction: Testing a dual attachment model. *Organizational Behavior and Human Performance, 30,* 109–131.

Graen, G. B., Orris, J. B., & Johnson, T. W. (1973). Role assimilation in a complex organization. *Journal of Vocational Behavior, 3,* 395–420.

Graen, G. B., & Scandura, T. A. (1987). Toward a psychology of dyadic organizing. *Research in Organizational Behavior, 9,* 175–208.

Graen, G. B., & Wakabayashi, M. (1994). Cross-cultural leadership-making: Bridging American and Japanese diversity for team advantage. In H. C. Triandis, M. D. Dunnette, & L. Hough (Eds.), *Handbook of industrial and organizational psychology* (Vol. 4, pp. 415–446). Palo Alto, CA: Consulting Psychologists Press.

Harrison, A. A. (1976). *Individual and groups: Understanding social behavior.* Belmont, CA: Wadsworth.

Hogan, E. A. (1987). Effects of prior expectations on performance ratings: A longitudinal study. *Academy of Management Journal, 30,* 354–368.

Ibarra, H. (1992). Homophily and differential returns: Sex differences in network structure and access in an advertising firm. *Administrative Science Quarterly, 37*, 422–447.

Kotter, J. (1973). The psychological contract: Managing the joining-up process. *California Management Review, 15*, 91–99.

Larwood, L., & Blackmore, J. (1978). Sex discrimination in managerial selection: Testing predictions of the vertical dyad linkage model. *Sex Roles, 4*, 359–367.

Lawrence, B. S. (1988). New wrinkles in the theory of age: Demography, norms, and performance ratings. *Academy of Management Journal, 31*, 309–337.

Lazarus, R. S. (1984). On the primacy of cognition. *American Psychologist, 39*, 124–129.

Liden, R. C. (1985). Female perceptions of female and male managerial behavior. *Sex Roles, 12*, 421–432.

Liden, R. C., & Graen, G. (1980). Generalizability of the vertical dyad linkage model of leadership. *Academy of Management Journal, 23*, 451–465.

Liden, R. C., Wayne, S. J., & Stilwell, D. (1993). A longitudinal study on the early development of leader–member exchanges. *Journal of Applied Psychology, 78*, 662–674.

Linton, R. (1940). A neglected aspect of social organization. *American Journal of Sociology, 45*, 870–886.

Linton, R. (1942). Age and sex categories. *American Sociological Review, 7*, 589–603.

Manogran, P., & Conlon, E. G. (1993, August). *A leader–member exchange approach to explaining organizational citizenship behavior.* Paper presented at the annual meeting of the National Academy of Management, Atlanta, Georgia.

McClane, W. E. (1991). The interaction of leader and member characteristics in the leader–member exchange (LMX) model of leadership. *Small Group Research, 22*, 283–300.

Merton, R. K. (1948). The self-fulfilling prophecy. *Antioch Review, 8*, 193–210.

Murray, M. (1982). *The middle years of life of middle class Black men.* Unpublished manuscript, Psychology Department, University of Cincinnati.

Parsons, T. (1942). Age and sex in the social structure of the United States. *American Sociological Review, 7*, 604–616.

Pettigrew, T. F. (Ed.). (1980). *The sociology of race relations: Reflection and reform.* New York: Free Press.

Pittman, T. S., & Heller, J. F. (1987). Social motivation. *Annual Review of Psychology, 38*, 461–489.

Scandura, T. A., & Graen, G. (1984). Moderating effects of initial leader–member exchange status on the effects of a leadership intervention. *Journal of Applied Psychology, 69*, 428–436.

Schreiber, C. T. (1979). *Changing places: Men and women in transitional occupations.* Cambridge, MA: MIT Press.

Sutton, C. D., & Woodman, R. W. (1989). Pygmalion goes to work: The effects of supervisor expectations in a retail setting. *Journal of Applied Psychology, 74*, 943–950.

Tajfel, H. (1982). *Social identity and intergroup relations.* Cambridge, England: Cambridge University Press.

Tajfel, H., & Turner, J. C. (1986). The social identity theory of intergroup behavior. In S. Worchel & W. G. Austin (Eds.), *Psychology of intergroup relations* (pp. 7–24). Chicago: Nelson-Hall.

Thomas, D. (1990). The impact of race on managers' experiences of developmental relationships. *Journal of Organizational Behavior, 11*, 479–492.

Tomkins, S. S. (1981). The quest for primary motives: Biography and autobiography of an idea. *Journal of Personality and Social Psychology, 41*, 306–329.

Tsui, A. S., & Egan, T. D. (1994, August). *Performance implications of relational demography in vertical dyads.* Paper presented at the annual meeting of the National Academy of Management, Dallas, Texas.

Tsui, A. S., Egan, T. D., & O'Reilly, C. A., III. (1992). Being different: Relational demography and organizational attachment. *Administrative Science Quarterly, 37*, 549–579.

Tsui, A. S., Egan, T. D., & Xin, K. R. (1994, February). *Diversity in organizations: Lessons from demography research.* Paper presented at the Claremont Graduate School Conference on Diversity in Organizations, Claremont, California.

Tsui, A. S., & O'Reilly, C. A., III. (1989). Beyond simple demographic effects: The importance of relational demography in superior–subordinate dyads. *Academy of Management Journal, 32*, 402–423.

Turner, J. C. (1985). Social categorization and the self-concept: A self-cognitive theory of group behavior. In E. J. Lawler (Ed.), *Advances in group processes: Theory and research* (Vol. 2, pp. 77–121). Greenwich, CT: JAI Press.

Turner, J. C. (1987). *Rediscovering the social group: A self-categorization theory.* Oxford, England: Basil Blackwell.

Vasudevan, D., & Graen, G. B. (1994). Team readiness: An antecedent to leader–

member exchange, job performance, and career progress. Unpublished manuscript, Department of Management, University of Cincinnati.

Vecchio, R. P., & Gobdel, B. C. (1984). The vertical dyad linkage model of leadership: Problems and prospects. *Organizational Behavior and Human Performance,* *34,* 5–20.

Vecchio, R. P., Griffeth, R. W., & Hom, P. W. (1986). The predictive utility of the vertical dyad linkage approach. *Journal of Social Psychology, 126,* 617–625.

Wakabayashi, M., Graen, G., & Uhl-Bien, M. (1990). The generalizability of the hidden investment hypothesis in leading Japanese corporations. *Human Relations,* *43,* 1099–1116.

Wayne, S. J., & Green, S. A. (1993). The effects of leader–member exchange on employee citizenship and impression management behavior. *Human Relations, 46,* 1431–1440.

Werner, C., & Parmelee, P. (1979). Similarity of activity preferences among friends: Those who play together stay together. *Social Psychology Quarterly, 42,* 62–66.

Zajonc, R. B. (1980). Feeling and thinking: Preferences need no inferences. *American Psychologist, 35,* 151–175.

Zalesny, M. D., & Graen, G. B. (1993). Exchange theory in leadership revisited: Same actors, different plot and location. In A. Kieser, G. Reber, & R. Wunderer (Eds.), *Handbook of leadership* (2nd ed., pp. 862–877). Stuttgart, Germany: Schaffer-Poeschel Verlag.

6

The Effects of Group Proportions on Group Dynamics

Pamela S. Tolbert, Alice O. Andrews, and Tal Simons

Two broad trends are reshaping contemporary organizations in the United States: increasing diversity in the workforce and widespread restructuring of work organizations into less hierarchical, more collaborative forms. The first trend is a consequence of large scale patterns of immigration and fertility that have affected the overall representation of racial and ethnic groups in the population, and of long-term shifts in women's patterns of labor force participation. As a result of these changes, by the end of the century White males will no longer be the majority group in the labor force (Johnston & Packer, 1987). As the absolute number of women and minorities in the workforce has increased, so has the dispersion of these groups into jobs and occupations in which they have been historically underrepresented. The second trend, toward more collaborative work structures, reflects efforts by many organizations to enhance economic competitiveness through the flattening of traditional management structures. Influenced by the employment arrangements of foreign competitors, U.S. firms have eliminated many middle management positions and created self-managing work teams charged with collective responsibility for managing and executing sets of interrelated production tasks (Applebaum & Batt, 1994).

Much attention has been given to the potential organizational benefits accruing from each of these trends. Increasing workforce diversity has often been extolled as offering renewal to stagnant firms through the provision of new perspectives and innovative approaches to problem solving (Jackson 1992). Similarly, autonomous work teams are viewed as stimulating creative problem solving and enhancing employees' sense of ownership in their work (Kochan, Katz, & McKersie, 1986). In tandem, however, these trends are also likely to result in common problems for the management of modern organizations. If teams become the loci of productivity and rewards, the ability of individuals to effectively communicate and cooperate with one another becomes even more critical for organizational success; high levels of active collaboration and support, not just passive tolerance, are required. In this context, social barriers associated with racial, ethnic, and gender differences in work groups can have a particularly deleterious effect on organizational performance.

We investigate some of the consequences of diversity for work teams in this chapter by examining the effects of the proportion of women faculty in academic departments on changes in the number of women at later points in time, using data from 50 departments over a 12-year span. Although the application of the label *work team* to academic departments may seem a bit odd, in fact, academic departments have many of the characteristics that are normally associated with self-managing teams. For example, Goodman, Devadas, and Hughson (1978, p. 296) characterize self-managing teams by a number of key elements: *groups* (versus dyads or whole organizations) that engage in *face-to-face interaction* around a set of *interdependent tasks* for which the group has *control* over the management and execution. They note that self-managing teams may be self-designing as well (i.e., responsible for defining appropriate technologies and group membership criteria).

Using these criteria, many academic departments easily fit the definition of self-designing, self-managing teams. Department faculty normally have collective responsibility for scheduling and providing classes, setting performance criteria for graduate and undergraduate degree recipients, evaluating student performance, and carrying out other activities that require collaboration and cooperation. Analogies to manufacturing teams' responsibilities for scheduling production, setting quality standards, and assessing the quality of output are not hard to draw. Departmental members also often have extensive decision-making power over faculty hiring, performance evaluation, and the termination of nontenured members. Because of these self-designing aspects, analysis of changes in the demographic composition of academic departments over time offers a unique opportunity to gain useful insights into processes associated with diversity in work teams.

DIVERSITY AND DEMOGRAPHY

Researchers' recognition of the effects of increasing diversity in contemporary organizations is reflected in the rapid growth of literature on organizational demography over the last decade. Studies of organizational demography focus on organizational groups that are defined by common status characteristics (e.g., race, sex, education levels) and examine both the causes and consequences of variations in the relative (or proportionate) size of such groups. Although demographic variation is only one aspect of diversity in organizations (see McGrath, Berdahl, & Arrow, chapter 2, this volume), given recent shifts in the racial, ethnic, and gender composition of the labor force, it is a key one for many contemporary organizations.

Proactive efforts by organizations to recruit women through affirmative action programs, as well as general changes in the representation of women in the labor force, have resulted in the entry of women into many jobs and occupations once held exclusively by men (Jacobs, 1989). Thus, it is not surprising that many of the recent demographic studies of organizations have been concerned specifically with the gender composition of organizations, investigating an array of outcomes ranging from individuals' work attitudes to compensation and staffing patterns (e.g., Davis-

Blake, 1992; Izraeli, 1983; Talbert & Bose, 1977; Tolbert & Oberfield, 1991; Tsui, Egan, & O'Reilly, 1992; Tsui, Xin, & Egan, chapter 5, this volume; Wharton & Baron, 1987).

Demographic analyses are based on the assumption that the distributions of status characteristics among the members of an organization affect social relationships above and beyond the aggregation of individual responses (see Pfeffer, 1983, for a review). The basic arguments can be summarized as follows. Individuals with similar status characteristics are more likely to interact frequently and to identify with each other than are dissimilar individuals (Blau, 1965, 1977; Kanter, 1977); thus, demographic characteristics affect the formation of informal coalitions among organizational members. The distribution of such characteristics among members fundamentally determines the size of coalitions, and the relative size of coalitions, in turn, strongly affects the nature of members' relationships. Therefore, all things being equal, an organization that is staffed almost entirely by members of one social group and an organization whose members are drawn in equal numbers from two different groups are likely to exhibit quite dissimilar patterns of interaction, information exchange, and conflict.

However, different theoretic perspectives posit very different group dynamics set in motion by shifts in group proportions and, hence, suggest different outcomes. One perspective, derived from social–psychological theories of intergroup contact, suggests that members of a majority group are more likely to engage in discriminatory behavior if a minority group is relatively small. An alternative perspective, focusing on competition between groups for control of material resources, suggests precisely the opposite hypothesis: Discrimination is more likely to occur as a minority group becomes proportionately larger.

The reasoning behind these hypotheses is developed in the following section, and empirical evidence for each is considered. The fourth section of this chapter describes sampling, measurement, and statistical techniques used to test these hypotheses. The fifth section presents the results of the analyses. Some of the general theoretic implications of the results and suggestions for further research are discussed in the conclusion.

SOCIAL CONTACT VERSUS COMPETITION: ARGUMENTS AND EVIDENCE

Early interest in the effect of changes in the relative size of minority groups on intergroup relations can be traced to post-World War II concerns with the social consequences of the large-scale migration of Blacks to previously segregated Northern urban areas (e.g., Allport, 1954; Myrdal, 1944; Williams, 1947). It was in this context that researchers first began systematic study of the relationships among social differentiation, discrimination, and minority group size. The recent revival of interest in the effects of minority group size accompanies another major social change: the influx of women into the labor force and, particularly, into traditionally male-dominated occupations (Jacobs, 1989). Out of the older and more recent literature on this topic, two opposing hypotheses have emerged, representing different theories of intergroup relations.

Social Contact Theories

One hypothesis is derived from social–psychological analyses of the effect of social contact on individuals' attitudes. Such analyses are predicated on the central assumption that greater contact and familiarity with members of a given social group reduces individuals' propensity to hold negative stereotypes and prejudices against the group (Allport, 1954; see Pettigrew, 1986, for a general discussion of this theoretic approach). Research in this tradition has identified a number of boundary conditions affecting the validity of this assumption, such as the existence of common goals (see Amir, 1969). But, if these conditions are met, increases in the size of a minority group should be accompanied by a declining level of discrimination by the majority, because the probability that majority members will have social contact with minority members is higher if the minority group is relatively large.

In line with this logic, Blau's (1977) analysis of the effect of group proportions on patterns of social interaction implies that, as a consequence of limited opportunities for cross-group interactions when a minority group is relatively small, majority members are more likely to hold negative attitudes toward minorities. Although Blau does not explicitly discuss discrimination as a consequence of minority group size, his assertion that "macrosocial integration . . . rests on the face-to-face associations between individuals from different groups and strata" (p. 11) is quite consistent with a social contact perspective, insofar as macrosocial integration refers to nonconflictual patterns of interaction across social groups.

Kanter (1977) elaborated the logic of this basic argument using an ethnographic study of a number of groups, varying in gender composition, in a large manufacturing organization. She posited a number of social–psychological processes as driving forces behind discriminatory behavior among majority members in "skewed" groups (i.e., groups in which minorities represent 15% or less of the total membership). Among these are a heightened consciousness of minority group members by the majority and consequent scrutiny of minorities' actions, a tendency to exaggerate the degree of differences between minority and majority group members and to experience strengthened identification with other majority members, and a propensity to rely on stereotypes when interacting with minorities. These processes, according to Kanter's arguments, should be alleviated by majority members' increased contact with minorities, leading to greater individuation among both minority and majority group members. Increased contact, in turn, is postulated to be linked primarily to increases in the size of the minority group.

In sum, the logic of both Blau's and Kanter's analyses suggests that increases in the proportionate size of a minority group should lead to less discrimination by the majority. Several empirical studies focused on group gender composition provide evidence consonant with this argument. For example, Spangler, Gordon, and Pipkin (1978), comparing data on students in two law schools, showed that women law students in a school with a small ratio of women to men scored significantly higher on measures of performance pressure and social isolation than their counterparts at the second school with a more balanced sex ratio. Similarly, research on labor union committees by Izraeli (1983) indicated that women on committees with a relatively small proportion of women were significantly more likely to feel constrained by the stereotype of being a "women's representative" and to feel less personally influential than women on demo-graphically balanced committees. Research by Segal (1962) on male nurses and by Wolman and Frank (1975) on small work groups of professionals also found a negative relationship between minority group size and the level of social isolation experienced by members of the minority group.

Competition Theories

At the same time, empirical evidence also exists for an opposing theoretic perspective, prominent in work on racial and ethnic conflict, that links the expansion of a minority group to increasing social differentiation and dis-crimination through a process of competition between groups for social and material resources. As summarized by Blalock (1957, 1967), the basic arguments underlying this approach are premised on the existence of a fi-nite set of desired resources that are competitively distributed. Given this condition, increases in the proportionate size of a minority group are likely to be perceived as a threat to the power of a majority group and, conse-quently, to the group's share of scarce resources. Perceptions of competi-tion and power threats lead to increasing hostility toward minorities by the majority and to widespread discrimination designed to prevent the erosion of the majority group's dominant position. However, once the size of a minority group reaches a threshold point, allowing them to counter discriminatory actions effectively, the impact of such actions is expected to decline.

Using similar reasoning, Bonacich (1972) posited economic competi-tion between social groups as a primary cause of social discrimination. Al-though the issue of relative group size is not addressed directly in this analysis, the logic of her argument suggests that competition and dis-criminatory behavior are intensified by the expansion of a minority group in a labor market, particularly a group with relatively few resources and, hence, limited power to determine conditions of work. Such groups are likely to become lower priced competitors to the established majority group; and the greater the number of minority members, the greater the threat of economic displacement to the majority. Thus, both of the forms of discrimination she discusses (exclusory and caste movements) involve efforts by a majority group to restrict the numbers of minorities in a given labor market. Although the analyses by Blalock and Bonacich differ in degree of emphasis on pure economic competition, both suggest that discrimination by a majority is more likely to occur as a minority group becomes proportionately larger. This postulated relationship has received support in a wide range of work on racial and ethnic conflict (Beck & Tolnay, 1990; Brown & Fuguitt, 1972; Frisbie & Neidert, 1977; Reed, 1972; Tienda & Lii, 1987).

The competition perspective has also received support in a number of studies focusing on gender relations. Using data from a survey of women employed by a government agency, South, Bonjean, Markham, and Corder (1982, 1987) found that as the proportion of women in a department increased, the amount of perceived support from male coworkers decreased significantly. This finding is consistent with the results from a survey of work groups in three large corporations by Tsui, Egan, and O'Reilly (1992) that indicated that men in work groups with a proportionately large representation of women exhibited lower levels of psychological attachment to the organization and were more likely to express intentions to leave. A study of orchestras by Allmendinger and Hackman (1993) produced similar findings.

More behavioral evidence supporting a competition perspective on gender discrimination was provided by a panel analysis conducted by Pfeffer and Davis-Blake (1987) of college administrators' salaries, showing that the presence of a relatively large proportion of women in administration was associated with a significant decline in salary levels for positions filled by women. Similarly, studies by Reskin and Roos (1990) of occupations undergoing demographic change documented a decline in wages paid to job holders in occupations that had an increase in the number of women in them. And in the same vein, a study of faculty in the humanities and in the natural sciences in three Israeli universities by Toren and Kraus (1987) documented a positive relationship between the proportion of women and the degree of gender disparity in rank.

It is possible that members of higher status groups do not experience the same consequences of being part of a numerically small minority. A number of studies of men in work groups with a high proportion of women have suggested that men are often not subject to the same negative pressures as female tokens (Fairhurst & Snavely, 1983; Gutek, 1985; Wharton & Baron, 1987). Although it is likely that general social status mediates the effects of proportionate representation in a group, the issue is not addressed here because there is a considerable body of research to support the contention that women hold lower status than men (e.g., Pugh & Wahrman, 1983).

We used data from academic departments over an extended time span to test competing hypotheses derived from the theoretic perspectives outlined earlier in this chapter. Specifically, we examined the effect of the proportion of full-time women faculty in departments at one point in time on subsequent changes in the number of women faculty.

Following the logic of social contact theories, an increase in the proportion of women faculty members should lead to increasing levels of social interaction among male and female department members. This increased interaction is expected to reduce resistance to the hiring of female faculty among male faculty and to create a more favorable social environment for women faculty in the department. Hence, we propose Hypothesis 1: The larger the proportion of women faculty in a department at a given point in time, the more likely are subsequent increases in the number of women faculty members to occur.

In contrast, a competition perspective suggests that increases in the proportion of women are likely to be perceived as a threat by male faculty and to lead to increasing opposition to further increases in the number of women in the department. This implies Hypothesis 2: The larger the proportion of women faculty in a department at a given point in time, the less likely are subsequent increases in the number of women faculty members to occur.

To effectively test this prediction with our data, it is necessary to distinguish the effects of competition from the effects of affirmative action policies on universities. During the 12-year period of this study, general pressure on organizations to demonstrate their commitment to principles of equality through affirmative action was relatively high (Edelman, 1992).

In this context, a plausible argument can be made that departments in which women were noticeably underrepresented should be more likely than other departments to increase the number of women faculty members. This argument leads to a predicted negative relation between the proportion of women faculty at one point and changes in the number of women at later time points—just as competition theories predict, although for very different reasons.

One way to explore the distinction between the effects of affirmative action pressure and competition is to examine the behavior of departments having a very low representation of women among their faculty and that of departments having a very high representation of women. If affirmative action pressures were the motor behind demographic change, departments in which women were substantially underrepresented should have felt such pressures most strongly, thus motivating greater efforts to attract and to retain women faculty. Theories of competition, on the other hand, do not imply that when the numbers of minorities are low, the majority will be particularly likely to support the addition of minority members to the group. Instead, they suggest that group proportions will be a determinant of behavior only when a minority group becomes comparatively large; under this condition, members of the dominant group are expected to perceive the minority as a threat and, hence, to mobilize to protect their interests. This logic implies that the likelihood of increasing the number of women faculty should have been lower in departments in which women were relatively *over*represented compared with departments with proportionately fewer women. It is unlikely that affirmative action pressure would produce this result; rather, such pressure should simply not be operative in departments with relatively large numbers of women.

Thus, assuming responsiveness to affirmative action pressure, Hypothesis 2a can be predicted: When the proportion of women in a department is much lower than average, the number of women faculty will increase at subsequent time points.

A competition perspective, on the other hand, leads to a different prediction, Hypothesis 2b: When the proportion of women on the faculty is much higher than average, the number of women in a department will decrease at subsequent time points.

It should be noted that these are not competitive hypotheses; it is possible that both of the processes suggested, produced through competition and affirmative action pressure, operate simultaneously. Thus, whereas competition or affirmative action pressure alone may be expected to produce a curvilinear relationship between group proportions and demographic change, the action of both forces may produce a linear pattern. This possibility is considered further below.

Blalock's formulation also suggests that discrimination arising from competition is likely to be checked if a minority group has countervailing power. Sheer size can be a source of power for a minority group, although size alone does not necessarily guarantee a group access to the resources necessary for the exercise of power, particularly in formal organizations. For example, assistant professors in a department with a large proportion of faculty at the assistant level do not necessarily have greater power than assistant professors in a department in which they are relatively few in number. In this particular context, a better indicator of the power of a minority group is the extent to which the minority is represented among the ranks of tenured faculty. Thus, a final hypothesis derived from competition theory is Hypothesis 3: The larger the proportion of women among tenured faculty at a given point in time, the more likely are subsequent increases in the number of women faculty to occur.

AN EMPIRICAL INVESTIGATION OF DEMOGRAPHY IN ACADEMIC DEPARTMENTS

Sample

To test these hypotheses, we collected data from 50 sociology departments offering graduate programs between 1976 and 1988. The sampling frame consisted of all departments in the United States that were listed during this period in the *Guide to Graduate Departments*, published annually by the American Sociological Association. Departments that were missing for

2 or more years from the *Guide* were eliminated from the frame, and a random sample of departments was then drawn.

A major advantage of this data source is that it provides detailed information on the demographic composition of similar types of organizational subunits (by providing lists of current faculty members and their rank) across a large number of organizations and over an extended period of time. Comparative data of this sort, which are necessary for the estimation of dynamic models of demographic change, are relatively rare.

Measures

For each department, we used the lists of faculty shown in the *Guide* to count the number of male and female faculty members in the ranks of assistant, associate, and full professors. In cases where the individual's sex was not known to us and could not easily be determined by the name listed, we took a number of steps. The first was to survey a set of other sociologists to see if they were familiar with the individual. Because sociology is a relatively small discipline and the graduate departments listed in the *Guide* consist of a visible subset of all sociology departments, this procedure allowed us to classify many of the ambiguous names. For the remaining 22 names, we used individuals' listed areas of specialization to make informed guesses about appropriate classification. We were able to check on a dozen of these names and found that we were wrong on four, for whom we corrected our classification. For the others—most of whom had left the department in the early to mid-1980s—we were not able to find a contact person within the department who could identify the person as male or female. Because the total number of faculty in the departments used in this study ranged from 790 to 877, errors created by misclassification of this remaining set are unlikely to substantially affect the analyses.

Key predictor variables in our analyses included lagged measures of both the proportion of women full-time faculty and the proportion of women among full and associate professors. A number of methodological analyses have questioned the use of proportional measures (ratios) as central predictor variables. However, recent work on this topic (Firebaugh

& Gibbs, 1985) indicated that the use of ratio variables is generally not problematic if specified conditions are met (e.g., regression rather than correlational analyses are used, the measures exhibit a high level of reliability). Because these conditions do hold for this analysis, our use of ratio variables is justified methodologically as well as theoretically, in that the theories that we are interested in testing focus specifically on group proportions.

Also included were two dummy variables indicating, respectively, whether a department was at least one standard deviation below the sample mean of the proportion of women faculty, or a standard deviation or more above the mean. In addition, a number of control variables were included in the analyses: measures of departmental prestige, the nature of institutional control (public or private), the total number of new hires in a department, and in the analyses of the ranks of full and associate professors, lagged measures of the number of women at the next lower rank.

More prestigious departments can be expected to have more resources with which to resist affirmative action pressure than do other departments and, thus, be less likely to have their hiring and promotion practices affected by such pressure. Two measures of departmental prestige were examined. The first was based on a survey by the National Research Council (NRC) of academic departments in 1981 in which selected faculty members were asked to rate different departments on the "scholarly quality" of the faculty. However, data from this source were available for only about half of the departments in our sample. Hence, a second measure, the number of PhD degrees annually awarded by a department, was considered. The correlation between the NRC's prestige ratings and the number of PhDs was .59. Because the latter measure had few missing values, we used it as our indicator of prestige.

Public institutions, heavily dependent on state and federal funding, can be expected to be more vulnerable to affirmative action pressures than are private institutions (Pfeffer & Ross, 1990; Tolbert, 1986). Institutional control was indicated by a dummy variable, coded 1 for public.

From 1970 onward, the number of women granted PhDs in sociology crept steadily upward; hence, departments that hired new faculty should have been likely to increase the number of women faculty simply as a consequence of their greater representation in the academic labor market. The number of new hires was measured by comparing the list of faculty names in a department in a given year with the names in the preceding year, and counting the total number of new names shown. As with virtually all archival data, there are some inaccuracies in these data. The most obvious problems stemmed from departments' failure to delete the names of faculty members who had left the department. Thus, we occasionally came across an individual listed at two institutions, one in which he or she had been listed previously and one that represented a move. Our coding in such cases was based on examination of department listings in later years; if the individual continued to be listed as a member of the new department (as was usually the case), he or she was coded as a member of the new department in the year of the double-listing. Such double-listings were relatively rare, and we did not observe any double-listings that spanned more than a single year. Hence, we do not believe this problem represented a serious threat to the reliability of the data.

Finally, assuming that changes at the ranks of full and associate professor were likely to reflect promotions from within a department, lagged measures of the number of women at the next lower rank within the department were included in the analyses of full and associate professors in order to control for the size of the internal labor pool of women faculty.

Analysis

The majority of research conducted thus far on group proportions and intergroup relations has been based on cross-sectional comparisons of groups that vary in their demographic composition. Dynamic models permit examination of rising or falling levels of discrimination against a minority group over time and, thus, provide more appropriate tests of social contact and competition theories.

Our analyses are based on autoregressive moving average models developed for pooled time series data. Examination of the autocovariances indicated that a two-period lag model provided the best fit to the data (see

Dielman, 1989; Kmenta, 1971; Sayrs, 1989). We also conducted analyses using an error components model (sometimes referred to as a variance components model) and an ordinary least squares regression model. Although the latter is technically inappropriate because of autocorrelation in errors and a key assumption of the former—that of constant correlation in error terms across time periods—seemed overly restrictive, it is worth noting that analyses from these models yielded the same substantive results in terms of key predictor variables as those reported here.

Results

Table 1 presents statistics illustrating the changes that occurred in the representation of women in sociology departments between 1977 and 1988. The overall percentage of women faculty increased fairly steadily over this period, rising from 14% in the mid-1970s to about 20% by the late 1980s. Although women remained concentrated in the ranks of assistant professors, the proportion of women among full and associate professors doubled during this period.

Table 2 shows the results of analyses predicting changes in the total number of women in a department. The first model includes only the lagged measure of percent women faculty, along with the control variables; the second model introduces the measure of minority group power, percent of women in tenured ranks; and the third model substitutes dummy variables for the lagged variable, percent of women faculty, allowing comparison of departments in which women were underrepresented with those in which women were overrepresented, relative to the mean. An additional model that included the square of the percent female variable was also examined. However, the quadratic term failed to reach significance, indicating that the linear model provided a more accurate fit to the data.

In both the first and second models, percent female faculty had a significant negative effect on changes in the overall number of women in the department, net of all other variables. This result is contrary to the prediction from social contact theories (Hypothesis 1) and is consistent with competition theories (Hypothesis 2). However, as noted, responses to affirmative action pressure may also produce these results. The third model

Table 1

Mean Percent Women Faculty, Total and by Rank, 1977–1988

Year	Total	Full	Associate	Assistant
1977	14.27	5.34	10.06	27.02
SD	9.07	12.24	15.17	19.55
1978	14.38	5.92	9.01	31.33
SD	8.49	13.08	13.74	21.03
1979	15.80	5.67	14.19	34.23
SD	9.71	12.60	19.79	23.41
1980	16.59	5.24	15.58	36.05
SD	8.59	11.83	19.83	26.37
1981	17.08	5.58	15.76	36.92
SD	9.74	11.65	20.67	25.92
1982	17.02	6.35	15.88	35.03
SD	8.68	12.46	18.15	23.12
1983	17.33	6.09	15.19	36.22
SD	8.33	11.95	16.37	25.84
1984	17.29	6.74	17.60	35.97
SD	7.98	12.37	18.35	25.36
1985	18.95	7.18	19.10	43.40
SD	8.12	12.67	18.45	31.90
1986	19.35	8.21	22.30	44.18
SD	8.63	11.85	21.50	30.47
1987	20.46	9.67	20.23	45.04
SD	8.26	12.11	17.42	29.74
1988	20.04	9.77	23.87	38.11
SD	10.23	12.98	21.27	33.03

Table 2

Autoregressive Moving Average Models of Change in the Total Number of Women Faculty

Variable	Model #1	Model #2	Model #3
Intercept	.242*	.388*	−.411***
SE	.128	.128	.094
LAGPCTF	−.019***	−.051***	—
(% women[a])			
SE	.003	.005	
LAGLOWF	—	—	.493***
(Below avg. % women = 1[a])			
SE			.099
LAGHIF	—	—	−.280**
(Above avg. % women = 1[a])			
SE			.099
LAGTENF	—	.037***	.017***
(% tenured women[a,b])			
SE		.004	.004
NPHD	−.021[ʜ]	−.025[ʜ][ʜ]	−.017
(No. of PhDs awarded)			
SE	.010	.010	.009
NEWHIRE	.346***	.341***	.354***
(No. new faculty)			
SE	.033	.031	.032
CONTROL	−.099	−.110	.021
(Public = 1)			
SE	.238	.084	.073
R^2	.24	.33	.26

[a]One-year lagged measure.   [b]Based on number of faculty at full and associate ranks.
*$p < .05$.   **$p < .01$.   ***$p < .001$.

Table 3

Autoregressive Moving Average Models of Change in the Number of Women Full Professors

Variable	Model #1	Model #2	Model #3
Intercept	.011	.066	.013
SE	.063	.065	.051
LAGPCTF	−.001	.002	—
(% women[a])			
SE	.002	.020	
LAGLOWF	—	—	−.023
(Below avg. % women = 1[a])			
SE			.051
LAGHIF	—	—	−.004
(Above avg. % women = 1[a])			
SE			.050
LAGTENF	—	−.002	.002
(% tenured women[a,b])			
SE		.002	.002
NPHD	.005	.005	.005
(No. of PhDs awarded)			
SE	.005	.005	.005
NEWHIRE	.014	.013	.012
(No. new faculty)			
SE	.016	.016	.016
CONTROL	−.035	−.040	−.039
(Public = 1)			
SE	.042	.044	.043
LAGFASSC	.060***	.058***	.058***
(No. women associates[a])			
SE	.017	.017	.017
R^2	.03	.04	.04

[a]One-year lagged measure.   [b]Based on number of faculty at full rank only.
*$p < .05$.   **$p < .01$.   ***$p < .001$.

Table 4

Autoregressive Moving Average Models of Change in the Number of Women Associate Professors

Variable	Model #1	Model #2	Model #3
Intercept	.038	.156	−.473***
SE	.099	.097	.094
LAGPCTF	−.007*	−.057***	—
(% women[a])			
SE	.003	.005	
LAGLOWF	—	—	.354***
(Below avg. % women = 1[a])			
SE			.089
LAGHIF	—	—	−.307***
(Above avg. % women = 1[a])			
SE			.085
LAGTENF	—	−.048***	.021***
(% tenured women[a,b])			
SE		.004	.003
NPHD	−.006	−.017*	−.005
(No. of PhDs awarded)			
SE	.008	.007	.008
NEWHIRE	.041	.023	.042
(No. new faculty)			
SE	.025	.022	.024
CONTROL	−.001	−.118	.063
(Public = 1)			
SE	.066	.067	.063
LAGFASST	.100***	.329***	.169***
(No. women assistants[a])			
SE	.024	.029	.027
R^2	.05	.23	.12

[a]One-year lagged measure.　[b]Based on number of faculty at full and associate ranks.
*$p < .05$.　**$p < .01$.　***$p < .001$.

Table 5

Autoregressive Moving Average Models of Change in the Number of Women Assistant Professors

Variable	Model #1	Model #2	Model #3
Intercept	.120	.234	−.211*
SE	.127	.130	.106
LAGPCTF	−.018***	−.025***	—
(% women[a])			
SE	.004	.005	
LAGLOWF	—	—	.443***
(Below avg. % women = 1[a])			
SE			.108
LAGHIF	—	—	−.075
(Above avg. % women = 1[a])			
SE			.108
LAGTENF	—	.009	.008*
(% tenured women[a,b])			
SE		.004	.004
NPHD	−.023*	−.024*	−.018
(No. of PhDs awarded)			
SE	.010	.010	.010
NEWHIRE	.268***	.267***	.277***
(No. new faculty)			
SE	.033	.033	.034
CONTROL	−.134	−.137	−.076
(Public = 1)			
SE	.083	.084	.083
R^2	.17	.18	.17

[a]One-year lagged measure.　[b]Based on number of faculty at full and associate ranks.
*$p < .05$.　**$p < .01$.　***$p < .001$.

permits examination of the potential effects of affirmative action policies. The significant positive coefficient for the first dummy variable (LAGLOWF), which delineates departments with a very low proportion of women, indicates that departments with a substantially lower proportion of women on their faculty than others were more likely to increase the number of women. This is consistent with Hypothesis 2a, predicated on the notion that affirmative action pressure would affect departments' staffing. At the same time, the significant negative coefficient for the other dummy (LAGHIF), which delineates departments with a very high proportion of women, provides support for a competition perspective (Hypothesis 2b) as well: Having a much higher than average proportion of women on the faculty at one point in time has a negative subsequent effect on the number of women in the department. The linear relation between proportion of women faculty and demographic change appears to be a product of the combination of these forces.

The strong positive coefficient for the variable percent of women at higher ranks is also consistent with predictions from competition theories. Taking this measure as an index of the relative power of women faculty, this result suggests that departments in which women have more power are likely to increase the number of women on the faculty.

Table 3 presents analyses of changes in the number of women at the rank of full professor. At this level, the only significant predictor of changes in the number of women is their representation in the internal pool of candidates for promotion, indicated by the number of women at the associate level. The lack of predictive power among the other variables may at least partly reflect the fact that changes in both the numbers and the proportion of women at the highest professorial rank were relatively small and slow over the period examined here (see Table 1).

As in the analysis of changes in the number of women overall, the analyses shown in Table 4 indicate that departments with a large proportion of women faculty were significantly less likely to increase the number of women associates. This is indicated both by the significant negative coefficients for LAGPCTF, the lagged measure of percent female faculty, in the first and second models, and by the coefficient for LAGHIF in the third model.

At the same time, changes in the number of women at the associate level were affected by affirmative action pressure, an interpretation supported by the significant positive coefficient for LAGLOWF in model 3 (indicating that departments with a relatively small proportion of women were more likely to increase the number of women associate professors). Increases in the number of women at this rank were also associated with the presence of a relatively large proportion of women faculty at the full and associate levels in the previous period. The effect of having a large proportion of tenured women faculty is particularly striking: The total amount of explained variance quadruples if this variable is added to the model. Thus, again, these results strongly support the arguments of competition theories and contradict those based on social contact theories.

Table 5 presents models of changes in the number of women assistant-professors. Once more, the coefficient for the lagged measure of percent women faculty is significant and negative. However, looking at the third model, this relationship appears to be driven largely by affirmative action: The coefficient for the dummy variable indicating below-average representation of women faculty is highly significant and positive, whereas the coefficient for the dummy indexing above-average representation of women is nonsignificant, albeit negative. As in the preceding analyses, the percent of tenured women faculty has a positive effect on changes in the number of women at the assistant level, although the impact of this variable is not as strong as at the associate level.

Summary

The bulk of the evidence presented here strongly supports predictions derived from competition theories. These predictions are based on the general argument that increases in the relative size of a minority group generate competition among groups for access to scarce resources and, thus, fuel intergroup conflict and discrimination. Our results indicate that departments with a high proportion of women faculty overall were significantly less likely to increase the number of women on their faculty. At the same time, this relationship was moderated by the degree to which women held power in a department, indexed by the percent with tenure. Departments with a higher proportion of tenured women faculty were more likely to increase the number of women faculty than others. The results directly contradict the prediction derived from social contact theories, which are based on the assumption that increases in the size of a minority group enhance opportunities for intergroup interaction and thereby enhance intergroup relations.

Interestingly, our findings also suggest that affirmative action policies may have some real effect on organizations' behavior beyond ceremonial activities (see Edelman, 1992). Departments in which the representation of women was clearly below average were much more likely to be characterized by increases in the number of women faculty, especially at the assistant level. In addition, the results of the analyses provide some tentative evidence that more prestigious departments have a greater propensity to exclude women from the faculty. Although the effects of our measure of departmental prestige are not consistently significant, they are negative in all analyses except for those focusing on changes at the rank of full professors. The negative coefficient for the prestige measure is consistent with the notion that there are differences across organizations in members' ability to indulge in "discriminatory tastes" (Becker, 1965; Tolbert & Oberfield, 1991).

CONCLUSIONS AND DIRECTIONS FOR FUTURE RESEARCH

This research extends previous studies of the gender composition of organizations in several ways. We derived our hypotheses from two central and competing theoretic paradigms of group proportions. Whereas the majority of work on this problem has focused on the effects of composition on individual attitudinal outcomes (e.g., Tsui, Egan, & O'Reilly, 1992; Wharton & Baron, 1987), our hypotheses addressed the question of the effect of changing proportions on organizational outcomes. In addition, by using data from a relatively large number of organizations over an extended period of time, we were able to investigate the relationship between group proportions and outcomes using dynamic models. Most previous studies have relied on cross-sectional data, often from a single organization. Our results, which suggest that women's growing representation in a group leads to an increasingly negative environment for them, are generally consistent with other studies that have also focused on structural consequences of variations in gender composition (Bach & Perrucci, 1984; Pfeffer & Davis-Blake, 1987; Toren & Kraus, 1987).

Differences in the findings of studies on the effects of gender composition may reflect the fact that changes in group proportions affect two separate dynamics: the attitudes and actions of minority members, and the attitudes and actions of majority members. Most work on individual-level outcomes of variations in minority group size has focused on the attitudes and actions of minority members. A few studies have examined the attitudes and actions of majority members, but studies focusing on both groups simultaneously are rare. However, variations in relative group size may produce strikingly different, even opposing, perceptions of and approaches to intergroup relations among minority and majority members. Thus, research that has documented a positive relationship between minority group size and perceptions by minorities of more favorable intergroup relationships may reflect only part of the dynamics involved in changing group proportions.

In other words, to fully understand the social–psychological processes that lie behind observed relationships between group proportions and behavioral outcomes in groups and organizations, careful examination of the impact of changing proportions on the attitudes and behavior of both minority and majority members at the same time is needed. And particularly in an organizational setting, this issue needs to be explored in the context of understanding how the hierarchical distribution of members of a minority group affects such attitudes and behaviors (e.g., Tsui, Xin, & Egan, chapter 5, this volume).

In addition, more research is needed to identify the general conditions under which group competition processes are most likely to be set in motion in organizations. Our research has focused on a single dimension of demographic diversity: gender. Whereas other research on race and ethnic relations provides evidence of the generality of competition theory, most of this research has focused on community, not organizational conflict. It is possible that somewhat different social dynamics will play out for other demographic groupings in organizations, such as race. This issue expands in complexity as the number of potentially salient demographic characteristics increases (e.g., White women compared with women of color).

A related problem that also needs to be addressed by future research is whether competition processes differ in nature and intensity among groups defined by ascribed characteristics (such as sex, race, and age) and those defined by achieved characteristics (such as professional affiliation and education). Much of the research derived from social identity theory relies on experimental designs, in which group membership is an achieved (temporarily assigned) characteristic (see the overview of this theoretic tradition provided by Brewer, chapter 3, this volume). The long-term salience of achieved identities and their power in affecting competitive behavior, compared with that of identities based on ascribed characteristics, merits exploration, particularly in the context of formulating strategies for managing conflicts associated with diversity within work groups. It may be that different strategies will be necessary for managing conflicts involving different forms of diversity (see both McGrath, Berdahl, & Arrow, chapter 2, this volume, and Northcraft, Polzer, Neale, & Kramer, chapter 4, this volume, for relevant discussions).

Likewise, the nature of the group—the length of its duration and the degree to which organizational rewards and security are directly controlled by its members—may affect the nature and level of intergroup competition. Academic departments are enduring work groups that normally have a high degree of control over the resources received by members from the larger organization (e.g., salaries, research support). Although some individual members may have relatively strong options for exit through mobility across universities, the relative permanence of social relationships in such units may exacerbate intergroup conflict over control of resources. Some corporate work teams are characterized by a similar degree of permanence, whereas others consist of individuals who are placed together only for a specified period of time and who all have equal tenure in the group. Under these circumstances, the majority group may have less reason to worry about losing resources to the minority group.

Although much remains to be learned about the effects of diversity on work teams, the results of this study suggest some immediate and important implications for organizations that are interested in creating self-managed work teams and are striving to increase the diversity of their workforce. In particular, they suggest that simultaneous pursuit of these objectives must be undertaken with some caution and a close awareness of the problems, as well as the advantages, offered by demographically diverse groups. Our analysis implies that programs designed to enhance workplace diversity, such as affirmative action, are by themselves insufficient for establishing conditions that will maximize the creativity and productivity of work groups and may actually run counter to these ends unless careful attention is given to the management of group relations. Fostering the sort of multiperspective, creative problem solving that is desired by contemporary organizations in the context of diversity requires that managers be attuned to group dynamics set in motion by demographic diversity and be prepared to provide training to make team members conscious of such dynamics (see Ely, chapter 7, this volume) along with other interventions, if necessary.

Given the changing nature of the workforce in the United States, learning to deal effectively with work teams characterized by racial, ethnic, and gender diversity is critical to the successful management of organizations in our society. Much research remains to be done, including research that furthers our understanding of the way in which different aspects of diversity affect different types of work groups and research that specifies and tests the practical implications of such understanding. The development of effective social policies and organizational arrangements must rest on a much fuller understanding of the impact of group proportions on intergroup relations than currently exists.

REFERENCES

Allmendinger, J., & Hackman, R. (1993). *The more, the better? On the inclusion of women in professional organizations* (Working Paper No. 94-005). Boston: Harvard University Business School, Division of Research.

Allport, G. (1954). *The nature of prejudice.* Reading, MA: Addison-Wesley.

Amir, Y. (1969). Contact hypothesis in ethnic relations. *Psychological Bulletin, 71,* 319–342.

Applebaum, E., & Batt, R. (1994). *The new American workplace.* Ithaca, NY: ILR Press.

Bach, R., & Perrucci, C. (1984). Organizational influences on the sex composition of college and university faculty: A research note. *Sociology of Education, 57,* 193–198.

Beck, E. M., & Tolnay, S. (1990). The killing fields of the Deep South: The market for cotton and the lynching of Blacks, 1882–1930. *American Sociological Review, 55,* 526–539.

Becker, G. (1965). Human capital. New York: National Bureau of Economic Research.

Blalock, H. M., Jr. (1957). Percent non-White and discrimination in the South. *American Sociological Review, 22,* 677–682.

Blalock, H. M. (1967). *Toward a theory of minority group relations.* New York: Wiley.

Blau, P. (1965). The comparative study of organizations. *Industrial and Labor Relations Review, 18,* 323–338.

Blau, P. (1977). *Inequality and heterogeneity.* New York: Free Press.

Bonacich, E. (1972). A theory of ethnic antagonism: The split labor market. *American Sociological Review, 38,* 547–559.

Brown, D., & Fuguitt, G. (1972). Percent nonwhite and racial disparity in nonmetropolitan cities in the South. *Social Science Quarterly, 53,* 573 582.

Davis-Blake, A. (1992). The consequences of organizational demography: Beyond social integration effects. In P. Tolbert & S. Bacharach (Eds.), *Research in the sociology of organizations* (Vol. 10, pp. 175–198). Greenwich, CT: JAI.

Dielman, T. (1989). *Pooled cross-sectional and time series analyses.* New York: Marcel Dekker.

Edelman, L. (1992). Legal ambiguity and symbolic structures: Organizational mediation of civil rights law. *American Journal of Sociology, 97,* 117–140.

Fairhurst, G., & Snavely, B. K. (1983). A test of the social isolation of male tokens. *Academy of Management Journal, 26,* 353–361.

Firebaugh, G., & Gibbs, J. (1985). User's guide to ratio variables. *American Sociological Review, 50,* 713–722.

Frisbie, W. P., & Neidert, L. (1977). Inequality and the relative size of minority populations: A comparative analysis. *American Journal of Sociology, 82,* 1007–1030.

Goodman, P. S., Devadas, R., & Hughson, T. L. (1978). Groups and productivity:

Analyzing the effectiveness of self-managing teams. In J. P. Campbell (Ed.), *Productivity in organizations* (pp. 295–327). San Francisco: Jossey-Bass.

Gutek, B. (1985). *Sex in the workplace*. San Francisco: Jossey-Bass.

Izraeli, D. (1983). Sex effects of structural effects? An empirical test of Kanter's theory of proportions. *Social Forces, 62*, 153–165.

Jackson, S. E. (Ed.). (1992). *Diversity in the workplace*. New York: Guilford Press.

Jacobs, J. (1989). Long-term trends in occupational segregation by sex. *American Journal of Sociology, 95*, 160–173.

Johnston, W. B., & Packer, A. E. (1987). *Workforce 2000: Work and workers for the 21st century*. Indianapolis, IN: Hudson Institute.

Kanter, R. M. (1977). *Men and women of the corporation*. New York: Basic Books.

Kmenta, J. (1971). *Elements of econometrics*. New York: Macmillan.

Kochan, T., Katz, H., & McKersie, R. (1986). *The transformation of American industrial relations*. New York: Basic Books.

Myrdal, G. (1944). *An American dilemma: The Negro problem and modern democracy*. New York: Basic Books.

Pettigrew, T. (1986). The intergroup contact hypothesis reconsidered. In M. Hewstone & R. Brown (Eds.), *Contact and conflict in intergroup encounters* (pp. 353–390). London: Basil Blackwell.

Pfeffer, J. (1983). Organizational demography. In L. L. Cummings & B. M. Staw (Eds.), *Research in organizational behavior* (Vol. 5, pp. 299–357). Greenwich, CT: JAI Press.

Pfeffer, J., & Davis-Blake, A. (1987). The effect of the proportion of women on salaries: The case of college administrators. *Administrative Science Quarterly, 33*, 588–606.

Pfeffer, J., & Ross, J. (1990). Gender-based wage differences: The effects of organizational context. *Work and Occupations, 17*, 55–78.

Pugh, M. D., & Wahrman, R. (1983). Neutralizing sexism in mixed groups: Do women have to be better than men? *American Journal of Sociology, 88*, 746–762.

Reed, J. S. (1972). Percent Black and lynching: A test of Blalock's theory. *Social Forces, 50*, 356–360.

Reskin, B., & Roos, P. (1990). *Job queues, gender queues*. Philadelphia: Temple University.

Sayrs, L. (1989). *Pooled time series analysis*. Newbury Park, CA: Sage.

Segal, B. E. (1962). Male nurses: A case study in status contradiction and prestige loss. *Social Forces, 41*, 31–38.

South, S. J., Bonjean, C. M., Markham, W. T., & Corder, J. (1982). Social structure and intergroup interaction: Men and women of the federal bureaucracy. *American Sociological Review, 47*, 587–599.

South, S. J., Bonjean, C. M., Markham, W. T., & Corder, J. (1987). Sex differences in support for organizational advancement. *Work and Occupations, 14*, 261–285.

Spangler, E., Gordon, M., & Pipkin, R. (1978). Token women: An empirical test of Kanter's hypothesis. *American Journal of Sociology, 84*, 160–170.

Talbert, J., & Bose, C. (1977). Wage-attainment processes: The retail clerk case. *American Journal of Sociology, 83*, 403–424.

Tienda, M., & Lii, D-T. (1987). Minority concentration and earnings inequality: Blacks, Hispanics and Asians compared. *American Journal of Sociology, 93*, 141–165.

Tolbert, P. S. (1986). Organizations and inequality: Differences in the earnings of male and female faculty. *Sociology of Education, 59*, 216–226.

Tolbert, P. S., & Oberfield, A. (1991). Sources of organizational demography: Faculty sex ratios in colleges and universities. *Sociology of Education, 64*, 305–315.

Toren, N., & Kraus, V. (1987). The effects of minority size on women's position in academia. *Social Forces, 65*, 1090–1100.

Tsui, A. S., Egan, T. D., & O'Reilly, C. A., III. (1992). Being different: Relational demography and organizational attachment. *Administrative Science Quarterly, 37*, 549–579.

Wharton, A., & Baron, J. (1987). So happy together? The impact of gender segregation on men at work. *American Sociological Review, 52*, 574–587.

Williams, R. (1947). *The reduction of intergroup tensions.* New York: Social Science Research Council.

Wolman, C., & Frank, H. (1975). The solo woman in a professional peer group. *American Journal of Orthopsychiatry, 45*, 164–171.

7

The Role of Dominant Identity and Experience in Organizational Work on Diversity

Robin J. Ely

The management literature is rife with advice that organizations should value diversity in order to enhance organizational effectiveness. Management experts have variously urged managers to learn about and be sensitive to cultural differences rather than succumb to ethnocentric bias (Cox, 1993); to respect differences, rather than seek to smooth them out (Thomas, 1990); and to use, rather than merely acknowledge, the ideas and skills of people from diverse backgrounds (Morrison, 1992). This approach represents a major shift in thinking from the management strategies of an earlier era, which called for color blindness and urged indifference to "irrelevant" cultural and physical characteristics such as race, sex, religion, and national origin. Clearly, if now managers are to value differences, they can no longer be blind to them.

However, because of this commitment to the spirit of color-blind strategies, which attempt to ensure that people have equal access to jobs and opportunities, the value-in-diversity message can be confusing. How should one think about people's identity group memberships at work? On the one hand, there is a tendency to ignore such memberships for fear of discriminating on the basis of them; on the other hand, one wants to value them for what they may contribute to the human resource pool.

In this chapter, I argue that this dilemma stems from the implicit assumption that it is only those in the oppressed position—women; people of color; gay, lesbian, and bisexual people—who constitute diversity. Phrases such as *the diverse group* or *the diverse person* used to refer to such people imply that the condition of diversity inheres solely in members of oppressed groups (Flax, 1990; Nkomo, 1992): Only people of color have a race; only women have a gender; only gay, lesbian, and bisexual people have a sexual identity. Hence, the assumption is that questions about the proper role of identity group memberships at work are questions about how to think or not think about those in the oppressed position.

It follows that changes required of those in the dominant position—men, Whites, heterosexual people—center on changes in their perceptions of and behavior toward these "others." Sensitivity training, an increasingly popular organizational intervention aimed at producing such changes, makes visible the experience of oppressed groups; it may or may not expose the existence of oppressive mechanisms within the organization. In any case, these interventions do not address the inner workings or logic of such mechanisms. As such, their prescriptions for change require little of dominant groups in the way of self-reflection. Diversity as a condition of relationship is lost to a notion of diversity as a set of attributes that reside in some people and not others. This leaves dominant groups fundamentally unchanged and relations of domination intact.

Therefore, I argue that psychologists must investigate the experience of privilege that accrues to those in the dominant position: how dominance "is established, how it operates, how and in what ways it constitutes subjects who see and act in the world" (Scott, 1992, p. 25). Here, I am borrowing from Scott's prescriptions for how to think more generally about difference. I do not mean to dismiss as in any way less important work that documents the experience of oppressed groups. This work, written primarily but not exclusively by members of these groups, has contributed to raising public consciousness of the myriad ways in which these groups have been excluded, denied, silenced, and otherwise devalued, often in the normal course of everyday organizational life; the act of producing and identifying with this work is also undoubtedly an important source of empowerment for those who locate their own experiences of oppression within it. (For examples of this work, see Abelove, Barale, & Halperin, 1993; Aguilar-San Juan, 1994; Anzaldua, 1990; Asian Women United of California, 1989; Brant, 1988; Gwaltney, 1981; Hull, Scott, & Smith, 1982; Moraga & Anzaldua, 1983; Weise, 1992; Woods, 1993.) Rather, I mean to suggest that by carving experiences along lines of dominance and oppression—experiences that reside simultaneously in everyone—and explicitly examining both, I may develop a more coherent and useful approach to workplace diversity. This approach appropriately places power at the center of my work on diversity; it recognizes previously unacknowledged aspects of dominant identity as potentially important sources of insight that organization members can use to enhance both their relationships and their work. By engaging multiple axes of identity—both dominant and oppressed—within each person, this approach creates the conditions for empathy among people who may otherwise feel frustrated with, guilty about, or angry toward one another.

The ideas I develop in this chapter are based on observations from my teaching and research. For the past 6 years, I have taught a course titled "Group Behavior and the Politics of Diversity" in a professional school of public policy and management. This course has afforded me the opportunity to observe the interactions and development of some 30 small (four- to seven-member) work groups engaged over the course of a semester in a range of tasks and experiential exercises. These groups have included men and women from over 20 countries, representing a wide range of races and ethnicities, ages, social class backgrounds, and sexual identities. On the basis of what I have learned from teaching this course, I will discuss here how to explore the experience of dominance and what to expect in the course of this exploration.

I will also use my research to demonstrate how observations from my course on diversity apply to organizations. The research is a case study of an organization that a colleague and I conducted as part of a larger investigation into the role of racial, ethnic, and gender diversity in organizations. The case involves a small, nonprofit, feminist organization. This organization espouses explicitly, as part of its governing ideology, a belief that engaging a multicultural workforce is essential to its ability to achieve its mission. They have worked hard to acknowledge, respect, and use explicitly the ideas and skills of the women of color on staff. Hence, this organization offered an ideal opportunity to explore the benefits and limitations of our current value-in-diversity approach, as well as ways that the approach I propose here may augment it.

EXPLORING DOMINANCE IN TEACHING ABOUT DIVERSITY

One goal I am striving toward in both my teaching and my research is to learn how to create organizations in which every member is able to bring all relevant parts of himself or herself to the work at hand. Thomas (1990) described this goal as one of "tapping fully the human resource potential of every member of the workforce" (p. 114). In my view, this is an emancipatory goal: emancipatory both in the traditional sense of freeing people from oppression and in the sense of freeing people to explore themselves and their relationships in ways that may release new energies and insights to be then harnessed productively. It seems to me that to pursue this goal, it is essential that people learn to acknowledge, embrace, and think critically about their various identity group memberships and that such learning can occur most meaningfully in the context of real, ongoing relationships. The course I teach is predicated on these ideas. In addition to lectures, readings, and cases, I use a series of experiential exercises in which students engage directly in the phenomena under study. The experiential component of the course is especially important because it acknowledges the affective as well as cognitive nature of learning about diversity-related issues and provides students with an opportunity to engage in the work both emotionally and intellectually.

Course Development

It first occurred to me that to achieve the goals of my course may require attention to dominant as well as oppressed group memberships when I confronted repeated subtle and not-so-subtle challenges from students about what I as a White person could teach them about race relations. These challenges came primarily, though not only, from students of color, who also sometimes took the view that, as people of color, they already knew all they needed to know about race relations. These students' challenges prompted me to consider whether there were aspects of my and others' experiences as White people that I could use to help educate people of color; in the same way, I was sure there were aspects of their experience that would help to educate White people. I knew from both theory (Alderfer, 1987) and experience that the powerless, of necessity, know more about the psychology of the powerful than the other way around. But I also knew that, as a woman, the less powerful sex, I did not fully understand men, the more powerful sex. It seemed that there were things I could learn about men both as a group and as individuals that might make my relationships with them more productive and that I suspected were related to who they were as variously male beings. Similarly, it seemed that there might be things about my experience as a White person that would be helpful for people of color who were trying to work with me and other Whites. It would only later occur to me that what I could learn about my own experience as a White person would help me to understand more about the experiences of men. Initially, however, I had only an inkling of this idea that dominance was an experience worth exploring in its own right.

There were other issues I encountered in teaching the course that reinforced this idea. One was the mutual irritation and frustration that arose between me and the men of color (African Americans, Latinos, and Asian Americans) in the class during my second year teaching the course. It seemed that any time I or another woman raised the issue of gender in class, one or several of the men of color would actively resist the issue, often wishing to recast it as a race issue. Similarly, I started feeling compelled to raise the problem of sexism when men of color raised the problem of racism, even though intellectually I knew that pitting these two forms of oppression against one another was counterproductive. I needed a way to break this pattern, and it occurred to me that one way to do this might be to acknowledge explicitly the identity group memberships people apparently wished to deny, at least in our dealings with each other. These were our respective dominant group memberships, White racial identity in my case and male gender identity in theirs.

Finally, I had not to my satisfaction decided on the best order in which to present material on race, gender, and social class, the three identity categories that had been the focus of the intergroup relations segment of the course. In particular, I struggled with whether to present race before gender or gender before race, anticipating that the order I chose would implicitly privilege one over the other.

When I first taught the course, I presented gender first, no doubt because that was for me—a straight, fast-becoming-upper-middle-class, White female—my most salient group membership, the one I knew the most about and the one it was, therefore, easiest and safest for me to explore with the class. This was not a particularly satisfying solution, however. I came to discover what White American middle-class feminists were also discovering, or as Donna Haraway described it, what they "were forced kicking and screaming to notice" (cited in Crosby, 1992, p. 131): Gender is not a unitary construct, but rather a complexly constructed social relation shaped by interaction with other social relations such as race, ethnicity, sexuality, nationality, and class (Flax, 1990; Fraser & Nicholson, 1990). I needed a meaningful and systematic way to address this in the course.

Each of these issues—the challenges I received as a White professor teaching about race relations, the tension in my relationship with the men of color in the class over racism versus sexism, and the order in which to present material on different intergroup relationships—eventually coalesced around a single solution. Rather than focus sequentially on particular kinds of intergroup relations, such as those based on race, sex, or class, I decided to highlight the feature that makes each of these identities worth examining in the first place: power. Each set of relationships has relatively easily specifiable dominant and oppressed group counterparts. Therefore, going against the *standpoint* theories of the radical feminists who argue that the subjugated social location of the oppressed is an epistemologically privileged position (e.g., Hartsock, 1985)—a view I had always found rather attractive—I decided to deprivilege the experience of oppression as the ground for knowledge and give equal status, for learning purposes, to the experience of dominance.

Course Design

I redesigned the intergroup relations segment of the course to include, first, an exercise on the experience of dominance and, then, one on the experience of oppression. These exercises are premised on the notion that everyone can identify some aspect of him- or herself that is both privileged—and therefore, at least potentially, an agent of oppression—and nonprivileged or disadvantaged—and therefore, at least potentially, a target of oppression.

To explore the experience of dominance, students form groups on the basis of some shared dominant group identity. They typically choose to work in a group of Whites, men, heterosexuals, middle- or upper-middle class people, native English speakers, U.S. nationals, Christians, or people who share some combination of these group identities. Occasionally, I have had students who are, for example, lesbians of color from poor family backgrounds in Third World, nonnative English-speaking countries and who, therefore, have difficulty finding a meaningful dominant identity group for this exercise. Some nonobvious dominant groups that have worked well for such people include able-bodied, physically attractive, or thin people.

For this exercise, people may also form their groups on the basis of additional shared group memberships that are not characterized by dominance. For example, gay men may choose to form a group for the exercise, but they must stay focused on their dominant status as men. By allowing for various subgroupings within a particular dominant group, the exercise reveals the similarities and differences in how that group's dominance operates, depending on other aspects of identity.

Once the groups have formed, they spend about an hour discussing questions such as the following:

1. What do you like about being a member of this group? What privileges have accrued to you as a member of this group? How do you

feel about these aspects of your experience?

2. Have you ever consciously taken advantage of your membership in this group?

3. When did you become cognizant of being a member of this group? What information did you get about how to behave, or how not to behave, as a member of this group?

4. Despite, or even because of, the privilege that accrues to your group, are there ways in which you feel you are systematically hurt by the "ism" that reflects that privilege?

After each group reports on its discussion of dominance to the class, we do a similar exercise to explore the experience of oppression. For this exercise, students form groups on the basis of some shared oppressed group identity. I find it important to define this group experience as *oppressed*, rather than *subordinate* or *subdominant*, for several reasons. First, that term more readily evokes group memberships based on identity rather than it does those based on organizational hierarchies; second, it emphasizes the historical relationships of power in which such groups are embedded; and finally, it acknowledges the emotional charge such relationships often evoke. For this exercise, students typically choose to work in a group of women, African Americans, Asian Americans, American Indians, Latinos, Latinas, nonnative English speakers, foreign nationals, Jews or other non-Christians, gays, lesbians, bisexuals, people from a working-class or poor background, or people who share some combination of these group identities. On occasion there have been straight, White, middle- or upper-middle-class, native English-speaking, American men who have difficulty imagining an identity group from which to work on their experience of oppression. As Miller's (1981) work on childhood suggests, one's experience as a child has proved for these people to be a productive group membership on which to focus for this exercise.

Again, people may also form their groups on the basis of additional shared group memberships that are not characterized by oppression. For example, gay men may choose to reconvene for this exercise, but this time stay focused on their oppressed status as gay.

Once the groups have formed, each group spends about an hour discussing questions such as the following:

1. What is it like to be a member of this group? What do you like and dislike about being a member of this group?
2. What are the advantages and disadvantages of being a member of this group?
3. In what ways do you think you perpetuate, reinforce, or collude in the oppression of your group?
4. In what ways do you resist colluding with the oppression of your group (that is, what strategies do you engage in to empower yourself as a member of this group)?

Again, we debrief after this exercise by having each group report on its discussion to the class.

Fear and Resistance

Students are uncomfortable when I ask them to identify and explore their experiences as members of a group that reaps the benefits and privileges of dominant status in our culture. They resist even naming the dominant groups to which they belong, and when we begin the exercise, there is much confusion about what is and what is not a dominant identity group.

I believe there are several reasons for people's resistance to acknowledging the ways in which certain of our group memberships bring us status and privilege. First, dominance is not salient when people are experiencing it. People take their dominant group memberships for granted, like the air. One does not have to think about them because the culture was organized with them in mind. This is consistent with social identity theory, which posits that those in the dominant group "do not think of themselves as being determined by their group membership or their social affiliation. They see themselves above all as individuals and human beings who are singular, 'subjects,' voluntary actors, free and autonomous" (Tajfel, 1982, p. 90). Similarly, Cox (1993) observed in his work on diversity in organizations that majority members are less likely to be aware of group membership than nonmajority members. Therefore, it is hard to get in touch with what dominant group memberships mean and how they shape members' experience. This may explain why there are relatively few writings on the experience of dominance. (The few examples that exist include Alderfer, 1982; Astrachan, 1988; Frankenberg, 1993; Kennedy, 1993; McIntosh, 1990; Pratt, 1988; Steele, 1990.)

Second, to explore the ways in which people are dominant makes them feel guilty—it suggests that perhaps they bear some responsibility for the consequences of racism, sexism, classism, and other systems of oppression. Moreover, it forces people to the difficult realization that if things are ever to change, they are going to have to exercise their power more responsibly and perhaps, under conditions where resources are fixed and scarce, relinquish some of that power.

Third, to recognize one's dominance seems somehow to delegitimize one's claims and concerns as a member of oppressed groups. It feels as though it may dampen or undermine any commitment to opposing the forces of oppression.

By contrast, when we turn to the exercise on oppression there is typically no resistance to naming oppressed groups, nor is there any confusion about what constitutes an oppressed identity group. Most students who elect to take this course understand perfectly well the importance of identifying, exploring, and discussing the ways in which members of oppressed groups (especially their own) are systematically denied opportunity and access to power.

This exercise can, however, fuel a competitive dynamic whereby oppressed groups vie for most oppressed status. Several years ago, a student in the class aptly named this dynamic "the Oppression Olympics." Latinos argue that they are more oppressed than Blacks—that in the fight over the crumbs left by Whites, it is the African Americans who win. Black men argue for the primacy of race over gender; White women fight to keep sexism on the agenda, often wishing to forget their role as agents of racism. Some women of color identify with men of color, casting their vote for race and cutting their connections to White women; other women of color emphasize sexism in their communities and risk alienation from their racial and ethnic groups. Yet if they join the White women, they know they may be the targets of racism from their White sisters. The White men are pleased, for once, not to be the direct targets of hostility. This scrambling for sovereignty in the territory of oppressions reflects the powerful need members of some groups have for recognition of their pain and suffering and their fear that to recognize others' pain will somehow weaken their group's demands for justice.

Lessons

My observations suggest that, both despite and because of these fears and resistances, these exercises can be transforming. They bring to light previously unacknowledged aspects of experience that can then serve as important sources of insight into people's work relationships. The more typical, non–self-reflective stance that people take in relation to their dominant group memberships, for example, limits the kind of responses available to dominant groups when confronted with charges of discrimination. The immediate responses available to the non–self-reflective dominant are guilt or defensiveness. Neither is productive; neither positions one to learn; and each limits one's capacity for engaging fully in relationships with others. Without self-reflection, one squanders the opportunities diversity offers for promoting more satisfying and productive human connections.

Exploring one's own experience as a member of a dominant group offers such opportunities in several ways. First, one can begin to understand and more easily recognize what the internal psychological and emotional processes are that attend privilege and, more importantly, that attend any attempts—not necessarily conscious, although sometimes so—to perpetuate and maintain that privilege. If the privileged are perpetuating racism and sexism in ways they fail to understand or have difficulty recognizing, it is doubtful they will ever rid themselves, let alone society, of them. This exercise makes students more attentive to their behavior, to the point where they have become able to identify, for example, how their stereotypes of other groups may be negatively influencing their interactions with members of those groups.

Second, attempting to understand the experience of dominance helps to take some of the responsibility off the oppressed for educating their dominant counterparts about racism, sexism, classism, heterosexism, and so forth. Members of dominant groups have information about these dynamics; they just have trouble accessing it. This knowledge can help to relieve the often burdensome expectation that women and people of color, for example, are the only parties capable of identifying behaviors, attitudes, or policies that may be sexist or racist, respectively.

Third, doing this work helps individuals who generally focus only or primarily on their less privileged group status(es) to empathize with those whom they experience as their oppressors. Such empathy, although difficult to achieve, can provide an incentive for those in oppressed groups to form crucial alliances for change with their more privileged counterparts. For example, a straight African American man who was quite sophisticated in his understanding of Black–White relations was in conflict for a good portion of the semester with a gay African American man in his group. The gay man consistently pointed to ways in which he felt the straight man was homophobic. It was only when the straight man was able to hear his responses to the gay man's accusations (e.g., "Some of my best friends are lesbians and gay men," or "OK, so I'm guilty; tell me how you want me to act") as classic dominant group responses similar to those he had often heard from Whites that he could engage more productively in a dialogue with the gay man about the problems they were having working together. His recognition about his own defensive reaction to his dominance, however, also gave him insight through empathy into his relationships with the White people in his group.

Finally, it is important to explore the ways in which being members of these privileged groups is not always a positive experience—these memberships also hurt members in systematic ways. Whites have described, for example, the pain and frustration of stressed race relations that limit their ability to engage in potentially satisfying, productive relationships with people of color. Men have described the burden they feel of others' expectations that they be strong, in control, and responsible, especially in their relationships with women. Understanding that interactions with members of certain groups may evoke such feelings and resentments can often help to explain tensions that have characterized such interactions.

The exercise on oppression, especially by following the exercise on dominance, also opens new opportunities for learning. First, it can instill in people who have led relatively privileged lives empathy for their less privileged counterparts as they find aspects of their own experience that provide new insight into the experiences of others.

Second, the competition for most oppressed status provides an immediate experience of the emotional dynamics that underlie many oppressed groups' inability to form constructive alliances with each other. The exercise gives people the opportunity to recognize aspects of their groups' rhetoric that engages this competition, makes visible the destructive nature of the competition, and consequently reveals whose interests it ultimately serves. To examine this dynamic at the intergroup level also helps to expose how it often manifests at the interpersonal level as one person's need for the other to recognize the injustices he or she has suffered as a member of an oppressed group. When the two people can recognize the competitive aspect of their respective needs for recognition, as well as the fact that intergroup comparisons only partially reflect each person's experience, the relationship often becomes a more constructive one.

Finally, the exercise on oppression can expose the ambivalent feelings members of oppressed groups often have about these aspects of their identity, aspects that can bring both pride and shame: pride for all the things they value in themselves that they associate with their group memberships, but shame for the negative stereotypes that they also sometimes associate with these same group memberships. Internalized oppression is that process whereby "a set of beliefs, attitudes, and misinformation about members of a target or oppressed group are put out by the dominant group to justify their subordination. That misinformation becomes embedded in the psyche—the emotional domain of that target group" (Love, cited in Njeri, 1994, p. 355). Uncovering the myriad forms of internalized oppression—all the ways one colludes in the oppression one experiences as a member of these groups—and resisting the collusion is perhaps the most important psychological and emotional work people can do from

173

their oppressed group positions. Once dominant groups have acknowledged their complicity in oppression, it is easier for oppressed groups to explore their own complicity.

This design for the intergroup relations segment of my course successfully addresses each of the issues that prompted it. It provides a coherent framework for exploring how White racial identity, as well as other dominant identities, can be used constructively to learn about race relations and other relations of domination. It also provides a basis for identification and differentiation among people in conflict over their different crosscutting dominant and oppressed group memberships. Finally, by encouraging multiple levels of subgroup categorization, this design motivates a more appropriately complex way of analyzing intergroup relations.

EXPLORING DOMINANCE IN ORGANIZATIONS

In this section, I use what I have learned from teaching about diversity, in particular what I have learned about dominance, to analyze the role of diversity in one organization, which I will call LHS. This case study demonstrates the benefits and limitations of a successfully implemented value-in-diversity approach that privileged the experience of those whose views traditionally have been ignored or distorted.

The Organization

LHS is a high-performing, nonprofit, feminist organization. The program at the core of the organization's work involves professional services in the area of advocacy and public policy to protect and advance the rights of women. Over a period of 10 years, LHS underwent a transition from a professional staff composed entirely of White women to one that included a program staff that was three-quarters women of color.

At the time of this case study, there were 12 members of the organization; 6 were White women and 6 were women of color, all of whom participated in this research. The organization's management staff was composed of four White women: an executive director who was a founder of the organization; an associate director who was responsible for development, media, and communications; a director of finance; and a manager of program staff. Each of these women had been with the organization for at least 10 years. Reporting to the manager of program staff were three additional program staff members: one Asian American who had joined the organization about a year earlier and two Latinas, one who had been with the organization 8 years and one who was an intern for the year. Another professional staff member worked in development, was White, and had joined the staff about 6 months earlier. There were four women in support staff positions: one African Caribbean who had been with the organization for 8 years, and two Latinas and one White woman, all of whom had joined the staff within the past year. Recently hired staff reflected growth of the organization, rather than staff turnover.

Three former members of the program staff also participated in the study. One, an Asian American, had been the first woman of color to join the professional staff. She remained on the staff for 1 year. Another, a White woman, had been with the organization for about 7 years and had witnessed the demographic change from an all-White professional staff to a multicultural one. The third was an African American woman who had recently left the staff after 6 years.

Data Collection

The data collection team consisted of an African American woman and me. With only a few exceptions, the African American woman interviewed the women of color in the study, and I interviewed the White women. The data I will discuss in this chapter are responses to a standard set of interview questions that focused on three areas: (a) the salience of the participant's race or ethnicity and other identity characteristics at work, (b) the impact of the participant's race or ethnicity and other identity characteristics on her work (processes or outcomes, including accomplishments, successes, difficulties, and failures), and (c) the impact of the organization's demographic composition on the way work was defined, organized, delegated, evaluated, and managed. (For a more complete analysis of this organization, see Ely, 1994.)

Results and Discussion

The results that I present here show how the particular perspective this organization developed on its racial and ethnic diversity had both positive and negative consequences. I will attempt to show that although the women of color were highly valued for certain kinds of contributions they could make to the organization, organization members' lack of insight into the role of dominant identity and experience, together with their resistance to acquiring such insight, created a kind of racial segregation that potentially limited all members' contributions in various ways. There were costs to both the organization and its members as a result.

The original motivation for diversifying LHS's program staff was to give the organization greater credibility with and access to the groups of women of color it hoped to serve better. By virtually all accounts, however, the change in staff composition moved far beyond this original goal: The change entirely reshaped the character and priorities of the firm's work in unanticipated ways in order to respond to the needs of low-income Black, Latina, and Asian women. As the executive director explained, "We were always interested in low-income women and women of color, but [as we became more diverse] we became more deliberate and strategic in our emphasis." The firm now works in coalition with a number of public interest, civil rights, and other "people-of-color" groups and, by all accounts, defines as relevant to its mission work that its former all-White program staff would have neither recognized nor undertaken.

All of the participants described LHS as successful, and virtually all attributed at least part of its success to its ability and willingness to bring the interests and perspectives of women of color "into the centerpiece of the organization." One woman summarized this as follows:

> [The demographic composition of LHS] has affected the work in terms of expanding notions of what are women's issues and taking on issues and framing them as women's issues in creative ways that would have never been done [with an all-White staff] and doesn't get done by other women's organizations. It's really changed the substance and in that sense enhanced the quality of our work.

White staff and staff of color, both support and professional, past and present, corroborated this view. In addition, current and past professional staff of color reported uniformly a feeling of being respected and "not simply brought along as window-dressing." As one woman of color put it, "The assumption about you is that you are competent."

Thus, LHS had achieved the value-in-diversity vision of not only hiring and retaining people from traditionally underrepresented groups, but also using their ideas and skills to enhance the quality of the organization's work. We speculated that their ability to do this may be attributable to organization members' commitment to feminist principles. This commitment provided them with an explicit and shared understanding of the nature and dynamics of oppression. This may have legitimized their use of oppressed racial and ethnic identity as a source of insight to be added to the organization's human resource pool while at the same time assuring that such use would not be—and would not appear to be—racist.

Clearly, this organization's ability to recognize and incorporate the views of women of color was a critically important step toward reaching the goal of a fully engaged and productive diverse workforce. A closer examination of work roles at LHS revealed, however, that by privileging the experience of oppression, this approach stopped short of fully realizing this goal.

A recurrent theme across virtually all of the interviews was the conviction that White women do not have direct access to the dynamics of racism through their own experience, are less capable of comprehending and analyzing racial dynamics, and, thus, are less competent than women of color to perform the central work of the organization (i.e., to advocate on behalf of low-income women, a disproportionate number of whom are women of color). No one entertained the possibility that White women may have relevant knowledge about racism on the basis of their direct experiences of privilege as members of the dominant racial group. The following excerpts are from White women's interviews:

> Clearly, in my experience, I have not experienced race discrimination myself. So it's not something that I kind of have an understanding of from the inside out.

I'm trying to think of a situation where I particularly made a decision that was affected by my being White. Huh. It's hard to say. I
think that what really happens in a situation where I perceive there
to be some question in any way about *who I am*, that I tend to go
in to talk to the women of color on staff and figure it out. [empha-
sis added]

My background doesn't always say to me, "You've got to think
about these [race] issues," because that wasn't part of my history. I
think that the women of color understand. It's just part of how they
think.

Women of color tended to corroborate this view. One woman, for example, felt that being able to understand the concerns of women of color
is "not natural to White women. Maybe my bias is that it can't be natural
to them unless they were women of color." Similarly, in the course of explaining why some White women in the organization responded to a particular event in a certain way, another woman commented, ". . . because
that group was all White, and they didn't know what the hell was going
on." Still another commented that "women of color have an added burden of monitoring [White women's activities] when you have White
women in your community."

Thus, White women came to depend on women of color to identify
issues and to provide the relevant race-related insights as if they had no
experiential basis themselves for sharing in this work. By this analysis, I
do not mean to suggest that White women and women of color were
somehow fungible resources to the organization. It is important to note
that there were some very real ways in which White women did need to
rely on women of color for the insights that accrued to them as a result
of their experience in their racial groups. My point is rather that White
women also had unique, race-based contributions to make that both
groups failed to recognize.

Although this role gave women of color opportunities to contribute
and excel in ways that are traditionally unavailable to them, there was a
price to pay as well. First, the women of color routinely reported feeling
burnt out from the weight of the responsibility they felt for needing al-

ways to monitor White women's work. In addition, by locating racial competence in the women of color, the organization had difficulty institutionalizing the work these women brought into the organization. For example, several people expressed the fear that the immigrant work of one of the Latinas would disappear if she were to leave the firm, just as the issues of greatest concern to African American women were less salient in the firm since the African American on staff left. Despite the fact that an African American had been on the program staff for 6 years, it was still the case that

> there are certain things we're not involved with because we don't have any Black professional women on the staff. So we worry about there being an entire community that we kind of can't really service, because [a representative of the African American community] doesn't exist here.

Finally, White women felt marginalized from the central work of the organization. As one woman said,

> Sometimes there's been a feeling here, that I have had at least, of being somewhat marginalized, because being a woman of color is more important than being a White woman.

When we presented these observations during our feedback session to the entire organization, one woman of color advanced the analysis further, suggesting that there was a flip side to this dynamic whereby women of color were de-skilled in management and finances:

> I think that the program is the most important part of LHS, but that there are things in society that are viewed as more important or difficult. Like management or finances. Somehow, program comes from your gut, from your experiential background, but the other stuff is more difficult. It takes more education. And I think that's part of what happens. It sounds weird to say "relegating" program to people of color, but [I use this word] just to highlight what I'm trying to say, which is that to some extent, it's leaving that part of what happens in an organization to the people who can do it just

out of instinct or something. Whereas the other stuff, the management stuff, is the property of the White people in the organization. And I think this dependency also works both ways. I think there's a fear on the part of people of color to take on management, economics, all that kind of work. The other stuff I do out of my [gut]. . . . Giving this one defined area to people of color in a sense seems like placing them in a place of importance. But it also keeps them out of other areas. And I mean everybody collaborates in that. . . . Both sides are participating in that.

This observation was consistent with the view a number of people expressed in their interviews, that management and finance were more "neutral" activities than the program work in the firm. In terms of decision making, they were "not sure how much it matters that administrative work is all White." That people in the organization held this view had been one of the themes we included in our feedback to them. We speculated that this view helped to justify the fact that management was all White and reflected their more general incognizance of Whiteness as a source of subjectivity. What this woman's comments suggested, moreover, was that this asymmetry between management and program work regarding the significance of race and ethnicity paralleled an asymmetry between opportunities for advancement available to White women and women of color. And although it was in the program that diversity mattered most, the sense that the value the women of color added there came somehow naturally to them suggested that other sources of competence and areas of expertise among the women of color may have been minimized or overlooked. By subtly undervaluing some of their qualifications relative to others, this shared belief may have blocked women of color from developing to their fullest potential.

This notion generated some discussion among the staff at our feedback meeting, and although they reached no consensus or conclusions, it raised an important hypothesis: Women of color, as well as White women, were being de-skilled. By relegating women of color to program activities and reserving management positions for White women, this organization invented a kind of racial segregation in its internal labor market in which both White women and women of color colluded.

We suspected, however, that the two groups' reasons for colluding were different. We surmised that White women were invested in believing they had no direct experiential access to the dynamics of racism. One reason for this investment may be that it protected them from having to acknowledge what they do know from their experience, not as victims to the oppressive dynamic, but rather as its agents. Thus, it was not surprising to hear from most White women that their racial identity was "not especially" salient to them at work. One typical response by White women to our question about the salience of their racial identity was to focus on the gaps in knowledge and awareness that their White racial identity represented to them. As one White woman put it, "[It is salient] only in the context of what I hope is my awareness of what I'm not aware of." Similarly, when asked whether she thought she had anything to teach women of color, another said, "We can teach them that we have more in common than we think we do and that the world around us has just exacerbated the differences." Her part in the learning process was

> being educated [by women of color] and at times breaking down the defenses and letting them know we can talk about this. It doesn't have to be an us-versus-them competition. And the other thing that draws us together here is the issue of gender. That commonality. There's that sameness that cuts through all the differences.

A second possible reason for White women's investment in maintaining their stance of ignorance was that it kept at bay a potential competitive dynamic that could erupt among them. If they were to acknowledge that White women are capable in their own right of doing some (even if not all) of the important work with communities of color, they would also have to acknowledge the fact that some of the White women have the skills and experience to do it better than others. As it was, the White women tended not to differentiate along these lines, noting, for example, that "everybody screws up, and one White woman is just as likely to screw up as another White woman."

Women of color, it seemed, were also invested in maintaining these beliefs about who has relevant racial knowledge. Their investment centered, however, on the fact that, without representation in the management ranks of the organization, their only real access to power and decision-making authority was in the program-related work. The de-skilling of White women was, thus, a source of power for the women of color. Several of the women of color acknowledged this dynamic:

> I think that I have been part of a process that has led to the marginalization [of White women]. . . . I think it is the role of women of color to make sure that their work stays at the center of the organization and that their communities' interests stay at the center of the work, but you have to do that while you balance and recognize the importance of the [White women's] work.
>
> I think that we as women of color have been a bit possessive about our cases here. Although I don't think other women of color would admit that. And part of the possessiveness is also the worry that we're not quite where we . . . could just turn it over to the White women. Now, I think that part of the possessiveness may be well-founded, but it's less a problem with some of the White women than with others.

Finally, both groups' explicit belief in the asymmetry of knowledge about racial dynamics may have helped to obfuscate their implicit belief in the asymmetry of knowledge about management and finances. This made the fact that the management staff was entirely White, a source of "embarrassment" among the White management staff, easier for everyone to overlook.

SUMMARY AND CONCLUSIONS

In this chapter, I have forwarded the notion that our current approach to diversity in organizations, which treats diversity as a condition that resides solely within oppressed groups, can be liberating in some ways, but limiting in others. I argue that one must acknowledge the role of dominant identity and experience as well in order to reach the goal of a fully engaged and productive diverse workforce. My observations from teaching about dominant as well as oppressed group experiences suggest that people resist examining their own experiences as members of dominant groups, but that this resistance is well worth overcoming. In addition to the insights it affords about the ways dominance operates in ourselves and others, this self-examination also creates conditions that make it easier to reflect on important, but often unacknowledged, ways in which people sometimes collude in their own oppression. As a result, people engage more fully, more consciously, and more productively in their relationships and their work.

The case study of LHS illustrated both the potential value of drawing on people's experiences of dominance in a multicultural work setting and the limitations of failing to do so. The results I presented here suggest that failing to acknowledge the role of dominant identity and experience can marginalize some groups while ghettoizing others in ways that may ultimately compromise any goals for a diverse workforce. This finding is especially relevant to organizations, such as LHS, whose missions serve directly the needs and interests of those in oppressed groups. But it is important for other organizations, too. Exposing the subjectivity of dominant groups reveals at once the dominant group position as both less and more authoritative than is typically acknowledged: It deauthorizes it as a source of neutrality and reauthorizes it as a subjective source of insight into relations of domination. Any organization that takes up the challenge of examining dominance in this way, regardless of its mission, will be radically transformed.

To take up this challenge is not, however, a panacea. Its logical extension ultimately discredits all claims to neutrality within the organization. All policies and procedures then become questionable. In addition, de-privileging any one group's experience as the ground for knowledge inevitably raises the difficult question of whether and how to reconcile competing claims to authoritative interpretation. If the evidence of experience conflicts, as it inevitably will, this approach nevertheless affords conflicting parties an unprecedented opportunity to generate rules for mediation on equal footing. It also encourages these parties to generate such rules with a conscious and shared commitment to exposing the ways in which previously unacknowledged dominant group interests may be at stake. In addition, mutual risk taking, preferably initiated from the dominant group position, can provide important bases for building trust.

The research implications of the approach I introduced here are many. Most obviously, the ideas I have outlined call for more systematic investigation into the ways in which the dominant group position shapes dominants' experience. By forcing us to recognize the subjectivity of dominant groups—to understand their perspectives as located, bounded, and interested—this lens can bring new insights to a range of organizational phenomena. A self-consciously developed perspective on dominance may dramatically alter both how and what psychologists know about, for example, leadership, group dynamics, team effectiveness, and a whole host of human resource concerns. Its implications for research on diversity in organizations abound. This perspective on dominance will help, for example, to resituate work on identity group differences, which has traditionally relied on the essentializing paradigms of socialization and assimilation (Nkomo, 1992), more squarely within the paradigms of social constructionism. These new paradigms move us away from the concept of identity as unitary, fixed, and internally consistent toward one in which identity is best seen as a set of contradictory, fluid, contextually constrained positions within which people are capable of exercising choice. It then makes sense to examine the impact of organizations as historically situated contextual constraints that can shape and reshape, create and re-create identity in potentially infinite ways. This represents a radical reframing of the role of identity in organizations.

The kind of inquiry into dominance I propose is risky. No doubt, this chapter itself will raise a suspicious eyebrow or two: To suggest a legitimate role for members of dominant groups in understanding oppression may read to some as merely the defense of a straight White woman wishing to appropriate some sovereign locus of truth for herself and her dominant groups. Yet I believe those of us doing this work must risk such readings, "engage in the dangerous practice of having public conversations with each other" (Jones, 1993, p. 193), for it can only be by engaging ourselves and each other, calling upon our full human capacities, including empathy, affinity, anger, rage, and disgust, that we can hope to advance any measure of meaningful change.

REFERENCES

Abelove, H., Barale, M. A., & Halperin, D. M. (Eds.). (1993). *The lesbian and gay studies reader.* New York: Routledge.

Aguilar-San Juan, K. (Ed.). (1994). *The state of Asian American activism and resistance in the 1990s.* Boston: South End Press.

Alderfer, C. P. (1982). Problems of changing White males' behavior and beliefs concerning race relations. In P. Goodman (Ed.), *Change in organizations* (pp. 122–165). San Francisco: Jossey-Bass.

Alderfer, C. P. (1987). An intergroup perspective on group dynamics. In J. Lorsch (Ed.), *Handbook of organizational behavior* (pp. 190–222). Englewood Cliffs, NJ: Prentice Hall.

Anzaldua, G. (Ed.). (1990). *Making face, making soul: Haciendo caras.* San Francisco: Aunt Lute Foundation Books.

Asian Women United of California (Ed.). (1989). *Making waves: An anthology of writings by and about Asian women.* Boston, MA: Beacon Press.

Astrachan, A. (1988). *How men feel.* New York: Anchor Press/Doubleday.

Brant, B. (Ed.). (1988). *A gathering of spirit: A collection by North American Indian women.* Ithaca, NY: Firebrand Books.

Cox, T. (1993). *Cultural diversity in organizations.* San Francisco: Berett-Koehler.

Crosby, C. (1992). Dealing with differences. In J. Butler & J. W. Scott (Eds.), *Feminists theorize the political* (pp. 130–143). New York: Routledge.

Ely, R. J. (1994). *Multiculturalism at work: The role of racial and ethnic diversity in a feminist organization* (Working Paper No. RAS-2). Cambridge, MA: John F. Kennedy School of Government, Harvard University.

Flax, J. (1990). Postmodernism and gender relations in feminist theory. In L. J. Nicholson (Ed.), *Feminism/postmodernism* (pp. 39–62). New York: Routledge.

Frankenberg, R. (1993). *White women, race matters: The social construction of whiteness.* Minneapolis: University of Minnesota Press.

Fraser, N., & Nicholson, L. J. (1990). Social criticism without philosophy: An encounter between feminism and postmodernism. In L. J. Nicholson (Ed.), *Feminism/postmodernism* (pp. 19–38). New York: Routledge.

Gwaltney, J. L. (Ed.). (1981). *Drylongso: A self-portrait of Black America.* New York: Vintage Books.

Hartsock, N. C. M. (1985). *Money, sex, and power.* Boston: Northeastern University Press.

Hull, G. T., Scott, P. B., & Smith, B. (Eds.). (1982). *All the women are White, all the Blacks are men, but some of us are brave.* New York: The Feminist Press.

Jones, K. B. (1993). *Compassionate authority.* New York: Routledge.

Kennedy, D. (1993). *Sexy dressing etc.* Cambridge, MA: Harvard University Press.

McIntosh, P. (1990). White privilege: Unpacking the invisible knapsack. *Independent School,* pp. 31–34.

Miller, A. (1981). *The drama of the gifted child: The search for the true self.* New York: Basic Books.

Moraga, C., & Anzaldua, G. (Eds.). (1983). *This bridge called my back: Writings by radical women of color.* New York: Kitchen Table: Women of Color Press.

Morrison, A. M. (1992). *The new leaders.* San Francisco: Jossey-Bass.

Njeri, I. (1994). Who is black? In D. McQuade & R. Atwan (Eds.), *The writer's presence* (pp. 351–357). Boston: Bedford Books of St. Martin's Press.

Nkomo, S. M. (1992). The emperor has no clothes: Rewriting "race in organizations." *Academy of Management Review, 17,* 487–513.

Pratt, M. B. (1988). Identity: Skin, blood, heart. In E. Bulkin, M. B. Pratt, & B. Smith (Eds.), *Yours in struggle* (pp. 11–57). Ithaca, NY: Firebrand Books.

Scott, J. W. (1992). Experience. In J. Butler & J. W. Scott (Eds.). *Feminists theorize the political* (pp. 22–40). New York: Routledge.

Steele, S. (1990). *The content of our character.* New York: St. Martin's Press.

Tajfel, H. (Ed.). (1982). *Social identity and intergroup relations.* Cambridge, England: Cambridge University Press.

Thomas, R. R. (1990, March–April). From affirmative action to affirming diversity. *Harvard Business Review, 68,* 107–117.

Weise, E. R. (Ed.). (1992). *Closer to home: Bisexuality and feminism.* Seattle, WA: The Seal Press.

Woods, J. D. (1993). *The corporate closet: The professional lives of gay men in America.* New York: Free Press.

8

Managing Distances and Differences in Geographically Distributed Work Groups

David J. Armstrong and Paul Cole

I n the rush to go global, corporations are asking their employees to be effective across distances never before mastered, depending on new innovations in communication technology to tie everyone together. These leaner companies are simultaneously emphasizing flexible team structures as the organizational molecule most responsive to rapid developments in products and markets. Teams of professionals, armed with laptop computers, fax-modems, E-mail, voice mail, videoconferencing, interactive databases, and frequent-flyer memberships, are being sent out to conduct business in this global arena.

However, managers responsible for leading such teams have found that distance remains a very real dimension in human relations, despite electronic media and jet travel. A decision made in one country elicits an unexpected reaction from team members in another country. Remote offices fight for influence with the head office. Telephone conferences find

This chapter is based on an earlier version, "Managing Geographic, Temporal and Cultural Distances in Distributed Work Groups," presented at the 102nd Annual Convention of the American Psychological Association in Los Angeles, California, August, 1994.

distant members struggling to get onto the same page, literally and figuratively, in terms of a shared viewpoint or strategy. Conflicts escalate strangely between distributed groups, resisting reason. Group members at sites separated by even a few kilometers begin to talk in the language of "us and them."

Working with a *Fortune* 100, United States–based computer company, which we refer to by the pseudonym *Compute Company*, we served as consultants to product development teams with members located in separate offices, sometimes on different continents. This chapter summarizes the lessons we learned from consulting with two such *distributed groups* and from interviewing managers and staff consultants involved in seven other distributed groups. All of these groups were part of the software engineering organization, involved with product development, and consisted of software engineers, marketing specialists, and technical writers.

FACTORS AFFECTING DISTRIBUTED WORK GROUPS

The dynamics of distributed work groups may be usefully considered from several different perspectives. Findings in communications research indicate that the degree of physical proximity among members and their use of different electronic media affect their work relationships. Similarly, stages of group development and other key parameters of group process are affected differently by distances and media. Differences among the national and organizational cultures of group members also add new dimensions of distance between them.

Face-to-Face Versus Electronic Communication in Groups

Relevant research scattered across separate fields of inquiry generally suggests that communication and relationships unfold differently face-to-face than they do across electronic media. Research on the effects of physical proximity on collaborative working relationships indicates that technology fails to provide some important qualities of face-to-face contact. For example, Allen (1977) showed that communication frequency between research-and-development (R & D) researchers dropped off logarithmically after only 5 to 10 m of distance between offices. Kraut, Egido, and Galegher (1990) found that people in adjacent offices communicated twice as often as those in offices merely on the same floor, including via E-mail and telephone transmissions.

It appears that electronic links do not substitute for face-to-face communication, particularly if there are higher levels of complexity and ambiguity in the messages (Nohria & Eccles, 1992). People prefer face-to-face contact for subtle and complex exchanges (Allen & Hauptman, 1990; Davenport, 1994; Trevino, Lengel, & Daft, 1987). Face-to-face contact is particularly crucial to the initiation of relationships and collaborations.

Studying distributed R&D sites, De Meyer (1991, 1993) found that researchers needed regular face-to-face contact to be confident that they accurately understood each others' work, particularly if it involved innovative ideas. He found that the *half-life* of confidence decayed over time as researchers communicated through telephones and computer conferences. Sooner or later, they needed to meet face-to-face again to renew their trust in their mutual comprehension.

Computer-mediated communication (CMC) appears to produce different kinds of exchanges and relations among people compared with face-to-face contact (Hiltz & Turoff, 1993), perhaps because people react to each other with less politeness, empathy, or inhibition if they cannot sense the other's social presence (Short, Williams, & Christie, 1976). Sproull and Kiesler (1991) found more diversity of input and debate in CMC because of the fewer signs of status, prestige, or visible differences transmitted in the medium. People tended to focus more on the content of the task and less on the direction of high-status opinion leaders. CMC was more democratic and less hierarchical in this way, with bad news being conveyed upward to superiors with less delay. At the same time, they found there was less awareness of the needs of other group members or the group's needs (see also McGrath, 1990). With more rudeness and less inhibition, conflicts in CMC were sharper and escalated more quickly. Consensus was more difficult to reach in complex, nontechnical issues (Hiltz, Johnson, & Turoff, 1986).

Research specifically on work groups suggests that they form more slowly, and perhaps never fully, if face-to-face contact is lacking (De Meyer, 1991; Kraut et al., 1990). McGrath (1990), studying groups working through computer conferences, described chaotic consequences of relying exclusively on CMC, especially during early phases of group formation and problem definition. CMC worked best for routine tasks done by a defined group with established roles and motives (McGrath & Hollingshead, 1994). Creative, collaborative work required group members to resolve tough conflicts over who does what and who gets what out of the effort, conflicts best resolved face-to-face.

Perhaps most important, some findings suggest that the effects of electronic media arise not so much from the properties of the media themselves, but from the way the group evolved its style of use over time (Cole & Johnson, in press; Cole & Nast-Cole, 1992; Orlikowski, 1992). Studying the adoption and use of computer conferences in different work groups, Cole (1995) described how a group's leadership, learning, culture, and work task all interacted over time to guide whether and how work groups used technology. The group process of evolving norms defined the technology's use.

The Role of Communication in Work Group Dynamics

A work group is a collection of interdependent workers who share responsibility for an outcome (Sundstrom, De Meuse, & Futrell, 1990). The members share a general understanding of who is and who is not a member of the group, called the identity boundary (Hirschhorn & Gilmore, 1992). Work groups demonstrate internal integration through the development of a group culture consisting of shared assumptions and mutual expectations about how members work together, including roles, procedures, standards, and norms (Schein, 1985). This integrated culture produces the subtle understanding among members about the group's accepted and proper way of working and enacting roles.

Over time, a work group develops a culture, which evolves through stages where members negotiate and define the group's core work and how it should be done. Groups are unified in general, especially across distances, through a shared understanding of the group's purpose or goal (Bartlett & Ghoshal, 1991; Lipnack & Stamps, 1993). The group leader has great influence in this process (Schein, 1985), which often involves conflict between members facing tough questions (McGrath, 1990; see also Tuckman, 1965; Tuckman & Jensen, 1977).

Face-to-face group meetings appear to be particularly important to forming a group, cementing shared commitments to key decisions, and resolving major conflicts among members (De Meyer, 1991; Kraut et al., 1990; Sproull & Kiesler, 1991). In distributed groups, technology seems to close only partially the physical gap. For example, Abel (1990) described an engineering work group, located in two offices 1,000 km apart, that experimented with an omnipresent video wall and cameras in all offices to link the sites together. Generally, the engineers interacted across the distance as one cohesive group. But there were some key exceptions. Video links were not so effective in generating new relationships or in resolving divisive differences, and miscommunication was experienced as rudeness. Members of an arguing design team were unable to listen to each other's ideas until they met face to face for 3 days, where they reached effective consensus.

The Role of Cultural Norms in Shaping Communications in Groups

Corporate Culture

Experts in corporate strategy have noted that some organizational structures and cultures permit great local autonomy, whereas others exert more uniform global control (Bartlett & Ghoshal, 1991; Ghoshal & Nohria, 1993). Galbraith (1994) described two types of corporate structures that support competition across distance. In the *parent–child* relationship, headquarters deals separately with each subsidiary. In the *peer-to-peer* model, responsibilities are shared equally across sites. The peer-to-peer model requires more intensive communication across sites and depends on reciprocal, mutual dependency among sites to achieve the cooperation needed. Corporate cultures support or limit the success of distributed work groups through their norms toward distance (Bartlett & Ghoshal, 1991; Galbraith, 1994). A culture of teamwork is needed to work effectively in a peer-to-peer model.

The policies of some corporate cultures promote better relations with remote offices. According to one study, multinationals that exercise fairness and procedural justice in their decision making with subsidiaries enjoy a higher level of compliance with those decisions; remote offices are more willing to implement the full spirit of decisions if there is two-way communication and the remote site believes that the head office is familiar with the local context (Kim & Mauborgne, 1993). The flow of information in a company across sites depends on informal networks of personal connections for full understanding (Bartlett & Ghoshal, 1991; Davenport, 1994; Galbraith, 1994).

National Culture

Driven by the challenges faced by companies expanding into international markets, studies of multicultural differences and their impacts on work relations have proliferated in recent years. Hofstede's description of *Culture's Consequences* (1984) was followed by Adler's (1991) analysis of multicultural differences in organizational behavior.

Many writers have emphasized the subtlety and pervasion of multicultural differences in values, norms, assumptions, and expectations (Schwartz, 1994; Triandis, 1994). These differences are particularly important in the complex negotiations that collaborative work projects require, where misunderstandings can easily produce offense. Multicultural confusions seem to be most insidious in the routine organizational exchanges Gudykunst (1991) called *scripts*, including exchanges such as giving instructions to subordinates or participating in meetings. Often, these unexamined behaviors express unspoken expectations and assumptions about work roles.

On the basis of a review of a large body of literature in psychology and sociology, Triandis (1994) concluded that different cultural groups are more likely to get along when they (a) share superordinate goals and equal status, (b) have frequent contact and a shared network of acquaintances, (c) have knowledge and accurate understanding of each other, and (d) are encouraged by their peers and supervisors to view each other positively. Under these conditions, group members are likely to experience each other as more similar, more understandable, and, therefore, more predictable. On the other hand, a history of prior conflict, competing goals, and power differences between groups combines to focus members on the details of their differences, leading to an exaggeration of perceived differences, increased conflict, negative stereotypes, and dislike. Ingroup–outgroup dynamics such as these are very relevant to groups working across distances and differences, as our case study of Compute Company illustrates.

A CASE STUDY OF DISTRIBUTED WORK GROUPS

We used interviews and document reviews to study nine distributed work groups in Compute Company's software engineering organization. The groups included software product development groups, a product management group, and a group responsible for producing software manuals. We interviewed 38 managers, individual contributors, and staff consultants associated with these groups. In addition, we conducted extensive organizational consultations with two of the groups and visited their work sites.

These distributed work groups ranged in size from 25 employees to 450 (in this largest group, we studied the management team). The groups ranged in dispersion from 2 to 9 sites, located from 15 km apart to worldwide distribution. All groups had offices in or near the software engineering head office (HO) on the United States' east coast. Other group sites in the United States were located in the states of Massachusetts, New Hampshire, New Jersey, California, and Washington. Groups had international offices in the United Kingdom, France, Germany, Italy, Israel, Hong Kong, Taiwan, and Japan.

Members of these distributed groups were linked by E-mail, voice mail, fax, telephone conferences, and computer conferences that allowed sites to work in shared text files. Some sites had videoconference links with their HO counterparts. Computer networks allowed the engineers to ship their software products to other sites for testing, trial assembly, or joint inspections.

Problems Across Distances and Differences

The members of these distributed work groups experienced two problem areas that they considered uniquely difficult when working across distance and differences: (a) misunderstandings in communications and (b) strangely escalating conflicts.

Communications were often fragmented, with gaps and misunderstandings among distant group members. There was confusion in telephone conferences, with people on different pages of documents. Group members failed to return telephone calls or respond to inquiries from distant members. Key group members at remote sites were left off E-mail distribution lists. Distant members were not informed of key decisions or information. Misunderstandings developed on the basis of different assumptions about the tasks and assignments. Messages were interpreted differently in different places, sometimes fueling ongoing conflicts among office sites.

Conflicts among sites went unidentified and unaddressed longer than conflicts among members of colocated groups and flared up more suddenly, surprising distant managers. Leaders were surprised by unexpected reactions to their decisions from distant sites. Some of these conflicts seemed to resist reason and play a role in self-perpetuating feuds among different sites. Members of the same group treated each other as if they were members of different groups, with colleagues at one office site described as *us* and group members at distant sites labeled *them*. As a consequence of the conflicts and communication problems, projects often took longer than planned to start up, with frequent delays in work progress.

In addition, managers reported difficulty analyzing performance problems and coaching from a distance. Distances interfered with communications that depended on subtle, often nonverbal behaviors, which were needed to be effective in group work roles such as project leader. In particular, managers had difficulty transferring group culture subtleties (e.g., "how we do things around here") across distance.

Proximity Effects on Work Relations

Chatting in the Hall

Communication with colleagues who worked nearby, on the same floor of the same building, was more frequent and occurred in more situations, in both scheduled and coincidental encounters, than with distant colleagues. Communication with people at the same site occurred through many media, permitting a broader range of messages and immediate responses. One informal study by an engineer revealed, in fact, that more E-mail messages were sent to colocated group members than to group members on another continent, despite the fact that nearby members were easily accessible face-to-face.

Beyond a very short distance, people began to miss out on spontaneous exchanges and decision making that occurred outside of formal meetings. Many people commented on how often key exchanges occurred after meetings and in chance encounters in the hallway, over work-cube walls, and in the cafeteria. The "postmortem" analysis of one canceled international project zeroed in on the lack of casual connections: "There was no day-to-day coffee machine conversation, which was needed to make it succeed." Remote group members felt cut off from the key conversations, over lunch or in the hall, that often followed videoconferences.

Feedback

Distance blocked the corrective feedback loops provided by chance encounters. Misunderstandings built up between sites that lacked the casual opportunities that close proximity offered to identify and discuss disagreements. One manager contrasted how employees who worked in his home office related to his decisions, compared with employees 15 km away. Engineers would drop by his office, or catch him in the hall or at lunch. "I heard you were planning to change Project X," they would say. "Let me tell you why that would be stupid." The manager would listen to their points, clarify some details they were lacking, and all would part better informed.

In contrast, employees at the remote site would greet his weekly visits with formally prepared group objections, which took much longer to discuss and were rarely resolved as completely as the more informal hall-way encounters. He concluded that "you don't get coincidental chances to detect and correct perceptions at a distance. Informal channels of face-to-face encounters allow things to be corrected more easily."

Learning by Watching

Distance blocked casual visual observation, which was invaluable to mon-itoring and mentoring performance. In colocated groups, managers found it useful to simply watch the person work or eavesdrop on casual conver-sations. Likewise, some of the more subtle work roles, such as project leader, were best learned through direct observation and modeling. These roles tended to be unique to particular organizational cultures. The in-ability of remote employees to watch successful project managers enact their roles, along with the inability to observe the learning employee in action, served as a barrier to effective coaching of such subtle interper-sonal skills across distance.

Out-of-Sight, Out-of-Mind

Distant employees tended to be left out of discussions and forgotten—"out-of-sight, out-of-mind." Remote sites "fell off people's radar screens" and were ignored even during telephone and videoconferences. "The de-fault behavior is to ignore the speaker phone. This is magnified if the smaller group is on the phone [distant]." In a case where the larger part of a group was in the home office, while the smaller part was in Europe (and also not native English speakers), the larger face-to-face subgroup would start talking and "just roll over" the silently listening Europeans. The manager of this group explained that it took discipline and coaching to adequately integrate the smaller, distant group of employees into the meetings, but that it was "less of an exercise" in video conferences than in telephone conferences.

Short Is Long

People described how the effects of close proximity died off quickly, with relatively little distance, making short distances equal to long ones in their effects on group interaction. Managers felt there was as much conflict be-tween sites 15 km apart as between sites 800 km apart. One manager, referring to the HO buildings that were joined by a common cafeteria, explained, "Even if you are on the other side of the cafeteria, you are in another sphere of influence. Outside of that range, the next major jump is across a different time zone." Echoed another manager, "You make the same mistakes if the distance is 4,000 miles or 10. You still tend to turn to the person in front of you for the answer. I respond more to people I see more often."

Time Is Distance

Time differences amplified the effects of physical distance. Distributed group members faced the challenge of "finding each other at the same time, in different times." Global conference calls caught people at different times of day. One consultant made conference calls only late at night or early in the morning (her time) because the group members (in Japan, the United States, and Europe) literally spanned all hours of the day(s). A global group leader listed endurance as one trait necessary in his role, both for the jet lag and the conference calls.

Time differences sometimes highlighted cultural differences. One group, based in the United States and Italy, celebrated a project milestone in their weekly videoconference by sharing foods on the video screen and fax. The east coast U.S. team, at 9 A.M., sent images of bagels and coffee. The Italian team, it being 15:00 in their time zone, sent images of champagne and cookies—different times, different tastes.

Several managers felt that time was more of a barrier than physical distance alone for engineers who were used to solving technical problems in spontaneous meetings. They called distant peers into spontaneous video- or telephone conferences when they could, but often global time differences meant their counterparts were not available.

The Home Group

People tended to think of their home group as the people they sat beside at work. Geographic sites promoted an informal, spontaneous group identity. This first group identity was reinforced by close physical proximity and the dense communication it promoted. Office site colleagues shared the metacontext of the locale, including similar occupational beliefs and concerns, cultural perspectives, and political viewpoints. People working in an office tended to have friends at the same nearby competitors, hear the same industry rumors, and share similar beliefs about technological trends.

People working at the same geographic site also tended to feel that they shared related organizational fates. In sites that included people from several groups and departments, layoffs in one group would threaten all site members. In other sites, all members relied on the same project in one way or another for their livelihood. As a result, sometimes distant group members did not feel like members of the home-site group and were treated accordingly (e.g., left out of decision making).

Site Cultures With Site Attitudes

Site cultures developed shared viewpoints and beliefs about the site in relation to the rest of the company. A site's perspective gave unique meaning to messages sent from other sites or the HO. These shared filters tended to perpetuate the expectations that they were based on, acting as self-fulfilling prophecies. Site cultures seemed comparable to national cultures as sources of misunderstandings and conflicts.

One site, founded by a "rogue pirate" engineer who was too brilliant for the company to lose, developed the belief that the HO always stole the site's best project ideas by reassigning the products to HO teams. Various groups at this site shared similar beliefs and acted accordingly, sometimes actually hiding promising new ideas. Visitors from the HO complained that site members had a "chip on their shoulder," holding a resentment that resisted solutions.

Recognizing Conflicts

Conflicts were expressed, recognized, and addressed more quickly if group members worked in close proximity. A manager could walk across the hall, "nip it in the bud," and solve the problem quickly. Over distance, the issues were more likely to just get dropped and go unresolved, contributing to a slow buildup in aggravation.

Conflicts among sites were often nurtured within sites by shared at-

titudes, beliefs, and values. People complained to their neighbors, rein-
forcing local perceptions of events, but did not complain to distant leaders until feelings reached high levels. One experienced manager of distributed groups stated, "With conflicts at a distance, thresholds for
expressing the conflicts are higher the greater the geographic and cultural
distance. Charges build up to higher levels in remote players before being
discharged to the central manager."

Group Dynamics and Distances: Groups Are Formed, Not Assigned

Distributed work groups could be described by the degree of psychological closeness among members. This psychological closeness (or experienced proximity) consisted of many interrelated variables, including
(a) the degree of identification with group membership; (b) the similarity of work goals, norms, role, and procedure expectations (task cohesion);
(c) the accuracy of mutual comprehension; (d) the degree of motivation
toward shared goals; (e) the amount of interdependency and mutual trust;
and (f) the frequency of communication among members.

Lines of Conflict Reveal Group Boundaries

Assigning people from distant sites or different departments to one group
did not necessarily form a group. A voluntary group identity had to be
forged and integrated across distance. Some formally assigned groups were
not experienced by the designated members as being groups. They had
not coalesced around a genuine, shared commitment to the group and its
goals.

Fragmented communications or patterns of conflicts between members sometimes revealed the true functional boundaries of working groups
(as opposed to assigned boundaries to which few members felt loyalty).
In one case, the members of an international group with four sites fought
among themselves as if they were enemies. Interviews revealed that the
group was not a single group, but rather four groups under one manager.
Employees indicated that their alliances were stronger to other employees

located in different departments at their sites than to their functional colleagues across the continent. Their use of *we* most often referred to people at their site, regardless of work group assignment.

Distributed Groups Coalesce Slowly

The formation of a distributed group had to overcome the lack of physical proximity in order to coalesce across distance. Similarities of shared goals, norms, and expectations were built over time among group members, evidenced by a more frequent spontaneous use of *we, us,* and *our way.* Accurately shared expectations and understandings between members were experienced as a growing group closeness, described by some as a group identity or culture. This group culture integrated members from different office sites and national cultures, spanning distances between members.

The group culture that seemed to matter most to work groups entailed accurate understandings about how to work together. It was easy to assume that distant members understood each other's expectations and meant the same thing with words such as *project review, phase completion,* and *test procedure.* Experience usually called such assumptions into question, as subtle yet profound differences generated strong feelings of resentment toward the "other" site.

In the case of one failed engineering project, a postmortem analysis revealed significant differences in expectations between the U.S. and European subgroups. Even careful planning did not prevent misunderstandings about specific processes vital to the project's success. The two sites had different definitions of completed product quality and tested their work with different procedures. These differences caused unexpected conflicts and delays and were taken by either side as signs of bad faith and political maneuvering by the other. These two sites were unable to overcome the mistrust that existed between them and never developed a unified group identity.

Distributed groups that reached an invisible line of formation across distances tended to show developmental changes over time. The leader of one global organization described how the management group of 12 site managers and staff developed over time from two separate organizations into one organization with a formal hierarchy and, finally, into a collaboration of team peers.

Multicultural Differences Observed Within Groups

Differences in national and office site cultures could be observed even within integrated groups. Several U.S. managers characterized European engineers' relations with management as more formal and hierarchical than they were used to with U.S. engineers, who were more verbally confrontational with objections and questions.

Compute's recognition and reward programs, designed for U.S. engineers, did not always fit the cultures of subgroups in other countries. The leader of a global group met with his Japanese manager to revise the corporate excellence awards. "We agreed that they were not correct for a team culture, not appropriate for some of our Asian sites. They reflected more of the individual hero ethos of our Western sites."

This manager also delegated tasks differently during group meetings, depending on the site manager's nationality. He adjusted his style in telephone conferences, depending on what he felt was most culturally appropriate. In delegating to the manager from the United Kingdom, he would ask the manager's opinion and then try to sell him on the merits of a particular approach, whereas he might later turn to the Japanese manager and tell him precisely what to do, with very specific instructions. He then followed up often with the U.K. manager, while leaving the Japanese manager alone.

Managers were particularly surprised when they encountered differences in work cultures in engineering groups within the United States: "I underestimated and was surprised when I found just as strong differences in the U.S. groups, like the New Jersey group. They have a distinct culture, . . . they want to be left alone and autonomous and fear being gobbled up." Another manager experienced a similar surprise with a group located just 15 km from the HO when it delayed individual pay raises to save money for a team-building consultation: "They have a very different socialist culture compared to our hero, capitalist culture where some get more and others get less." He was describing two teams in the same U.S. state, but it sounded like he was describing groups from different continents.

Personal and Cultural Style Factors Were Easily Confused

It was difficult to distinguish the source of differences among members of a distributed group. The subtle interplay of personal style, national culture, and organizational and occupational cultures often made accurate attribution of style differences difficult for group members. Deciphering the precise cause of conflicts or performance problems at a distance was almost impossible.

National, Organizational, and Professional Cultural Factors

National cultural differences interacted not only with individual style differences, but also with differences in company and professional cultures. One U.S. manager described a problem that her U.S. group had with an Italian superior. Engineers in her group complained that the superior overdirected them and did not ask for or listen to their opinions enough. The U.S. manager was unsure how much of the superior's style was an expression of an Italian management style, his own personal style, or a reflection of the fact that he was new to Compute Company and came from a marketing instead of software engineering background. She wondered specifically whether her manager related differently to her than to male professionals. She spent a weekend with him and his family, and observed his enthusiastic encouragement of his daughter's professional development. She concluded that the issue was probably not a gender-based dynamic, but rather his history in a more hierarchical company and profession. Notice the complex levels of factors she analyzed (Italian male marketeer from a European company).

Effects of the Organizational Context

In many cases, the larger organizational context was a determining factor in the effectiveness of the distributed group.

Conflicts Detoured Into the Distributed Group

Often, there was a host organization that sponsored the distributed work group. Conflicts within the host organization were sometimes detoured into the distributed group and played out there. Because the cause of the fight did not originate among group members, resolution of the conflict within the distributed work group was impossible. In one such case, members of a distributed group responsible for product marketing fought among themselves. Interviews revealed that their conflicts paralleled the conflicts of the larger, more influential engineering sites they each served. The distributed product managers acted as proxies for the larger organization, carrying out its duels on the periphery.

Home Office and the Periphery

Most distributed groups included offices in or near the HO, plus one or more sites that were distant from the HO, located on the metaphorical (and often geographically literal) periphery of the organization. The structure of geographic distribution of people and resources was echoed in the language used by managers, who spoke of *remote* sites on the company's *periphery*, and the *core*, or home office region. This HO-centric language reflected the fact that many distributed groups had a greater mass of people and resources at or near the HO complex. This distribution of resources gave the HO-based people more connections and easier access to upper management in software engineering, as well as people in other departments of the company. Many of the issues within distributed groups reflected dynamic tensions between the HO and sites on the periphery.

Home Office Sponsorship and Assigned Group Mission

A critical factor in the life of a distributed group and its remote sites was the work assignment or mission given to each site. The mission was the site's central assignment, the reason for the site's existence, and the area of work owned and controlled by engineers at the site.

From the perspective of the larger company, remote software engineering sites were established for many overlapping reasons, such as to reassure local customers, meet import requirements, and even retain star engineers who insisted on moving to remote locations. From the site's perspective, however, the group wanted responsibility for challenging projects that would gratify their needs for achievement. In practice, the remote sites were often given responsibility for small tasks and treated as subcontractors rather than getting critical, strategic projects. In other cases, remote sites had multiple HO sponsors (such as sales and design engineering) with conflicting expectations of the remote site.

Influence of Changes Between the Home Office and Periphery

No matter how clearly the founding reason was specified, over the years, the reason for a site's existence drifted from the original one. Markets and technologies changed, projects were completed, and the site staff looked for new work. Sometimes, the site matured and began to lobby for more ownership of strategic, challenging assignments. In other cases, headquarters changed strategies, or reprioritized projects, rendering a remote site's mission extinct. The negotiation of changes in missions and associated changes in site resources, budget, and location involved some of the strongest feelings among group members: "Giving things up and getting new things [assigned] is where the pain and suffering is."

The consequences of strategic changes initiated by the HO were often far more dire for remote sites than for the HO. Smaller sites were more vulnerable in that their limited staffs had been hired for one technical purpose. Retraining this same staff in another technology took one site a year and a half. In other cases, it simply was not possible. By contrast, groups within the HO were more easily dissolved and reconfigured around new assignments because of the much larger mass of talent available to call on.

The forces of change, of course, worked both ways. The remote sites existed, in part, to bring awareness of new technology and market trends into the core, pushing the company to change. Just as the periphery could drag, so, too, did the HO resist needed changes. In one case, a remote site made a proposal that the company change its strategy in some key areas where new technology was developing quickly. The company ignored the suggestion for 2 years, while competitors developed advantages over them in this field.

Such mutual resistance was aggravated by the lack of shared context, making mutual understanding more difficult. The periphery existed partly because it offered insight into developments that were foreign to the core. The sites also often had different cultures of influence, informal rules guiding them in to successfully influencing others. Remote sites without a lot of contact with people in the HO often did not know how to influence the HO. "Out there is almost a naiveté, as with novices," explained one HO manager. The HO culture could be confusing and obscure, however, to remote managers used to different styles of conducting business. One remote manager thought he had succeeded when his contact in the HO agreed to support his proposed new project. But then, mysteriously, the contact told him he now had to go "work" the proposal with other colleagues in the HO, leaving the manager to wonder what that actually meant.

Acculturation to Home Office Work Culture

Newly established remote sites had to import and set up both the physical connections to Compute's core (i. e., broadband data networks, computer systems, and telephone links) and, just as critically, the human infrastructure of work roles and procedures. This more subtle infrastructure of shared expectations was often difficult to export to remote sites without at least some learning errors.

Different Meanings in Different Contexts

Remote sites, with unique site cultures and contexts, tended to interpret messages from within their own sets of assumptions and expectations. These filters were not always accurately accounted for in transmissions from the HO, especially in broadcasts from the HO to multiple remote sites. The remote sites often perceived messages that the HO did not intend to send, usually pertaining to power and control over projects and budgets.

Integrating Practices That Span Distances and Differences

Face-to-Face Contact

Group formation was difficult across distances using electronic media alone. The integrating degree of psychological closeness needed to form the group was aided strongly by face-to-face discussions and agreements on the group's purpose, norms, roles, and procedures for working together and communicating effectively across distances. Frequently distributed groups were formed when people from various sites were reassigned to a new project and placed in a newly designated group. Face-to-face contacts allowed group members to form initial relationships around a group identity, which could then be supported on the "reduced bandwidth" of E-mail, telephone, and videoconferences.

Face-to-face meetings first focused on gaining commitment to the group's purpose. Developing an accurately shared awareness of a group's mission and goals is a unifying exercise in any work group. Such shared understandings were even more vital when working across distances. The group as a whole, as well as each remote site, required a well-articulated mission and set of goals. Promoting a common vision of the group's mission and strategy was central to promoting a cohesive group culture across distance.

To promote strong group cohesion among site managers around the globe, the leader of a newly designated organization committed his management staff to meeting face-to-face every 6 to 8 weeks. They rotated the location of each meeting around the globe so that they visited each other's country and office several times. Telephone conferences were held every 3 weeks between the face-to-face meetings. During their first round of visits to each other's site, the assembled management team also met face-to-face with each site's staff in discussions facilitated by a consultant. The group even developed shared humor and jokes, such as requiring each site manager to sing a song in his or her native tongue to the assembled management team at his or her first meeting. This became an entry ritual for new managers as membership turned over.

Group Leadership

Group leadership was important in guiding group members to articulate and embody group norms, roles, and procedures in working together and communicating. An effective leader convened and facilitated repeated group discussions of these issues, captured and followed through reliably on agreements reached, modeled the norms, and coached group members to maintain norms. Sometimes, this leadership was distributed among several people and sites.

Leadership took the form of bringing up issues of distance and leading group discussions about the challenges of communicating across distance. Discussions had to reach into the details of procedures, roles, and expectations in order to avoid later confusions. Effective leaders organized discussions of how to use various technologies, such as computer conferences, to communicate across distance. They modeled the desired use of the technology, coached and directed others, and reviewed its use in later meetings.

Leadership was required in showing diligence in monitoring the group's communication practices to ensure that people were not left out. It was demonstrated in articulating norms for videoconferencing, including how to structure the meetings, where to point the cameras, who controlled them, and how to talk in conferences . The manager in one group helped the engineers learn how to ask each other for input; just saying "would you guys read my stuff" would produce no action. She coached them to make their requests very specific during conferences, such as "I need you two to review these lines of code for issue X, by next Monday if possible."

Group Learning

Some groups developed an escalating cycle of learning, where members experimented with and shared their developing insights on techniques for communicating, comprehending, and working together smoothly across distances. Such techniques included, for example, habits of updating or checking in with each other, use of computer conferences for information exchange, effective video and teleconferencing procedures, and operating procedures for working together.

Engineers located in the HO learned to bring up hallway discussions and check out decisions in weekly videoconferences with distant counterparts. Traveling to the other site of a conference was particularly enlightening. One manager of a remote site regularly invited staff from the HO out to his site on some pretext so that they would end up sitting in on his site's end of a videoconference. Similarly, HO staff were sensitized to their relation to remote sites when they observed their own HO colleagues turning up on the video screen. When traveling members returned home, they might be given feedback that they "talked too fast." In various ways, group members learned how to be effective with the technology and, more important, learned how to maintain awareness of the other sites rather than "rolling over" them during conferences or forgetting about them outside of conferences.

Developing Group Norms About Cultural Differences

Cultural differences were addressed by managers who discussed the topic directly with their distributed groups, providing leadership in modeling how cultural differences could be identified and discussed. With such leadership, over time the group developed its own knowledge about cultural differences and the best way for the group to handle them. This group knowledge became part of the culture of the group.

One of the clearest examples of such leadership was provided by the manager of a globally distributed group responsible for translating products into local languages and markets. His company badge listed his name in Latin, Cantonese, and Japanese characters. He coached his managers to watch for and address possible culturally based misunderstandings during their meetings. He would interrupt staff who were discussing an issue to check if one was not fully understanding the other. He encouraged his managers to do the same. He would also meet with his managers privately, like a diplomat, to bring up more sensitive issues, such as the possibility that one manager's style might be offensive to another.

Leadership and Management Practices

One experienced manager explained that leading a distributed group required "focus and discipline," meaning a highly structured, clear style with careful follow-up on action items (assigned tasks). In a distributed group, the great distances involved required that decisions be made clearly, not reversed often, and reliably followed-up over time to ensure implementation and necessary revisions. Examples of useful structure in leadership activities included (a) structured, frequent conference calls or video meetings; (b) agendas, slides, and written material distributed in advance, and meeting minutes with action items published quickly afterward; (c) customized, but structured formats, revised over time to fit the group's needs, including such practices as polling all silent members before making key decisions. Reliably updating distant colleagues on hallway conversations and even delaying key decisions until distant peers could comment on them were related aspects of "focus and discipline."

Personal Relations Bridge Distance

Frequent face-to-face contacts among members of a distributed group served to renew their trust in mutual comprehension. Visits to different sites, staff rotations, and large face-to-face meetings convened at junctures of key change in the group all helped to maintain a level of mutual comprehension and trust. This trust then acted as a buffer, keeping misunderstandings from escalating into conflicts. One manager had better relations with distant sites than with sites near his office. He attributed this to the fact that he tended to visit nearby sites with a very tight schedule of formal meetings, then rush back to his office that same day. With distant sites, he would go for 10 days and spend much time in unstructured conversations where he learned useful details about the site's work and concerns.

Layered Communication Technology With Norms for Use

Distributed groups were supported by having ready access to multiple, simultaneous channels of communication among members. Such a layered network ideally included voice mail and E-mail (both of which bridge time differences), fax, telephone conferencing, computer conferencing, and videoconferencing. Work group software support (groupware) that allowed group scheduling or the sharing of technical designs and convening of technical review meetings across distance were also very useful.

A shared agreement across distance concerning how to use the technology was just as important as the technology itself. Much of the critical group leadership and learning involved facilitating and teaching clear group norms and skills about how to use the communication technology effectively.

Integrated Leaders Sent Out to the Periphery

An old joke in the United States is that organizational failure leads to an assignment "to Alaska." Sending a manager to a distributed group's remote site as punishment would, in fact, be destructive to the site and to the organization as a whole. Remote sites of distributed groups prospered best when they had leaders or staff who were successful in the HO and who brought with them informal contacts, influence, and knowledge that greatly improved the remote site's connection to the HO. Sending out leaders who had already peripheralized themselves while at the HO (through clashes in style, fundamental disagreements, or rebellious relations) only made remote sites more remote.

CONCLUSIONS

Our findings lead us to three propositions, which may be used as testable hypotheses, but which can only be informally supported by the experiences described in our findings.

1. Distance among members of a distributed work group is multidimensional. Objective measures of distance include not just geographic distance (m/km), but also time difference (time zones), organizational distance (different departments, functions, and levels), and cultural difference (both national culture and organizational office site culture).

   Our findings suggest that national and organizational cultures are experienced as dimensions of distance in distributed work groups, along with kilometer and time zones. The culture that matters most to work groups is that concerning work roles, procedures, and methods. Surprisingly, members can have very different national cultures but establish closer work cultures, or be very close nationally and geographically but be very different in work cultures (as between an engineer and a marketing specialist).

2. The impact of such distances on the performance of a distributed work group is not directly proportional to objective measures of

distance. Some work groups are more effective than others, even if their memberships span a greater geographic distance and encompass more time zones and cultures than other, less effective groups. This proposition is supported by the experiences of managers who have worked in several distributed groups with varying degrees of success. It may be judged more accurately with controlled outcome measures.

3. The differences in the effects that distance seems to have on work groups is due at least partially to two sets of integrating practices: (a) practices that help members effectively span distances, and (b) an organizational context and structure that support the group as its members work across distance.

The integrating practices within distributed groups emphasize group and leadership *process* variables in work groups (Hackman, 1983). Personal contacts serve to refresh De Meyer's (1991) "half-life" of trust among members. In a manner akin to Bartlett and Ghoshal's flow of knowledge (1991), informal networks of relations transmit knowledge about subtle work processes, such as how to influence the HO, that are needed to span distances in multinational corporations. The larger organizational contexts that help distributed groups to span distances include *structure* and *design* variables such as stable, long-term sponsorship and a clear mission.

Geographically distributed work groups are inherently diverse, at least on some dimensions. Managing a distributed group requires addressing its diversity so that the group forms effectively across distances. McGrath, Berdahl, and Arrow (chapter 2, this volume) point to the importance of time as a process variable in groups. They observed that groups grow less diverse over time on some dimensions. This fits closely with our observation of how groups form across distances over time. To form successfully, group members become much less diverse in their definition of work culture, including goals, methods, roles, and procedures for collaborating across distance. This decreasing diversity is along the dimension of group *task* cohesion (Bernthal & Insko, 1993).

We do not consider distributed work groups to have qualitatively different dynamics than colocated groups. Many of the integrating practices are the same for both, such as gaining commitment to shared goals and articulating and monitoring norms. In distributed groups, these common factors were essential for even basic group formation. Other practices are more uniquely crucial to groups operating across distances, such as structured communication practices, informal networks of relations, face-to-face contacts, and a reliance on layered communication technology. Distributed work groups are very sensitive to the structural features of their host organization, but then, the ability of any work group to integrate differences is affected by the structure and values of the larger organization.

Many of the integrating practices that help form a work group across distances and differences are similar to the positive factors Triandis (1994) has described in multicultural research on ingroups–outgroups and social distance. The conditions that promote greater understanding and liking between cultural groups (such as equality, superordinate goals, frequent contact, and mutual knowledge) also promote cohesion in distributed work groups. We can even say that the leadership and group learning necessary to articulate detailed work norms and procedures contribute to *isomorphic attributions* (accurate understandings of each other). The networks of personal relationships provide a buffer of trust that slows down *nonisomorphic attributions* that can fuel ingroup–outgroup rivalries.

According to this same model, members of cultural groups that have a history of prior conflict, competing goals, and power differences tend to exaggerate the perceived differences, thereby increasing conflict and mutual dislike. This conclusion from Triandis (1994) reads like a case description of a distributed group gone bad. Several of the failed distributed work projects we studied met these criteria closely: a history of resentment and conflict with the home office or other sites, competition for limited resources, and lack of influence in the HO.

As with current group theory, based largely on face-to-face contact, the cultural models of ingroup–outgroup dynamics often assume that physical proximity is the source of cultural contact and networks of connecting acquaintances. It will be of interest to study cultural relations between physically distant groups linked by media and technology, such as sister cities in the United States and Russia.

Distributed work groups are created entities, formed over time for the accomplishment of defined goals and for the provision of work and income to its members. The groups that formed and performed most effectively competed with the local work scene to capture a degree of commitment to a common goal from its scattered members. Aided by leadership, group members developed a shared sense of group culture that clarified role and procedure expectations. They became less diverse and more of an ingroup. Clearly articulated norms on how to use technology to communicate across distance and on how to handle cultural differences were of key importance in this process, as were frequent face-to-face contacts.

Success served to solidify the group identity and ingroup culture, whereas serious setbacks taxed group identity. Distributed work groups that achieved major success in high visibility projects were remembered fondly by their former members years after the group was dissolved, much like a circle of friends or a winning sports team.

REFERENCES

Abel, M. (1990). Experiences in an exploratory distributed organization. In J. Galegher, R. E. Kraut, & C. Egido (Eds.), *Intellectual teamwork: Social and technological foundations of cooperative work* (pp. 489–510). Hillsdale, NJ: Erlbaum.

Adler, N. J. (1991). *International dimensions of organizational behavior* (2nd ed.). Belmont, CA: Wadsworth.

Allen, T. J. (1977). *Managing the flow of technology.* Cambridge, MA: MIT Press.

Allen, T. J., & Hauptman, O. (1990). The substitution of communication technologies for organizational structure in research and development. In J. Fulk & C. Steinfield (Eds.), *Organizations and communication technology* (pp. 275–294). Newbury Park, CA: Sage.

Bartlett, C., & Ghoshal, S. (1991). *Managing across borders.* Boston: Harvard Business School Press.

Bernthal, P., & Insko, C. (1993). Cohesiveness without groupthink: The interactive effects of social and task cohesion. *Group and Organization Management, 18,* 66–87.

Cole, P. (1995, January). *The impact of group context on patterns of groupware use: A study of computer conferencing as a medium of work group communication and coordination* (CCS Working Paper No. 182, Sloan School WP No. 3795-95). Cambridge, MA: Massachusetts Institute of Technology, Center for Coordination Science.

Cole, P., & Johnson, E. (in press). Lotus deploys team room: A collaborative application for work teams. In R. Whitehead & P. Lloyd (Eds.), *Transforming organizations through groupware: Lotus notes in action.* London: Springer-Verlag.

Cole, P., & Nast-Cole, J. (1992). A primer on group dynamics for groupware developers. In D. Marca & G. Bock (Eds.), *Groupware: Software for computer-supported cooperative work* (pp. 44–57). Los Alamitos, CA: IEEE Computer Society Press.

Davenport, T. (1994). Saving IT's soul: Human-centered information management. *Harvard Business Review, 72,* 119–131.

De Meyer, A. (1991). Tech talk: How managers are stimulating global R&D communication. *Sloan Management Review, 32,* 49–58.

De Meyer, A. (1993). Management of an international network of industrial R&D laboratories. *R&D Management, 23,* 109–120.

Galbraith, J. (1994). *Competing with flexible lateral organizations.* Reading, MA: Addison-Wesley.

Ghoshal, S., & Nohria, N. (1993). Horses for courses: Organizational forms for multinational corporations. *Sloan Management Review, 34,* 23–35.

Gudykunst, W. (1991). *Bridging differences: Effective intergroup communication.* Newbury Park, CA: Sage.

Hackman, J. (1983, November). *A normative model of work team effectiveness* (Tech. Rep. No. 2). New Haven, CT: Yale School of Organization and Management, Research Program on Group Effectiveness.

Hiltz, S. R., Johnson, K., & Turoff, M. (1986). Experiments in group decision making: Communication process and outcome in face-to-face versus computerized conferences. *Human Communication Research, 13,* 225–252.

Hiltz, S. R., & Turoff, M. (1993). *The network nation* (rev. ed.). Cambridge, MA: MIT Press.

Hirschhorn, L., & Gilmore, T. (1992). The new boundaries of the "boundaryless" company. *Harvard Business Review, 70,* 104–115.

Hofstede, G. (1984). *Culture's consequences.* Newbury Park, CA: Sage.

Kim, W. C., & Mauborgne, R. (1993). Making global strategies work. *Sloan Management Review, 34,* 11–27.

Kraut, R. E., Egido, C., & Galegher, J. (1990). Patterns of contact and communication in scientific research collaborations. In J. Galegher, R. E. Kraut, & C. Egido (Eds.), *Intellectual teamwork: Social and technological foundations of cooperative work* (pp. 149–171). Hillsdale, NJ: Erlbaum.

Lipnack, J., & Stamps, J. (1993). *The teamnet factor.* Essex Junction, VT: Wright.

McGrath, J. (1990). Time matters in groups. In J. Galegher, R. E. Kraut, & C. Egido (Eds.), *Intellectual teamwork: Social and technological foundations of cooperative work* (pp. 23–62). Hillsdale, NJ: Erlbaum.

McGrath, J., & Hollingshead, A. (1994). *Groups interacting with technology.* Newbury Park, CA: Sage.

Nohria, N., & Eccles, R. (1992). Face-to-face: Making network organizations work. In N. Nohria & R. Eccles (Eds.), *Networks and organizations: Structure, form and action* (pp. 288–307). Boston: Harvard Business School Press.

Orlikowski, W. (1992, August). *Learning from Notes: Organizational issues in groupware implementation* (rev. ed.; CCS TR No. 134, Sloan School WP No. 3428-92). Cambridge, MA: Massachusetts Institute of Technology, Center for Coordination Science.

Schein, E. (1985). *Organizational culture and leadership.* San Francisco: Jossey-Bass.

Schwartz, S. (1994, August). *Values, meanings and goals: Views of the world in different cultures.* Master Lecture presented at the 102nd Annual Convention of the American Psychological Association, Los Angeles.

Short, J., Williams, E., & Christie, B. (1976). *The social psychology of telecommunications.* London: Wiley.

Sproull, L., & Kiesler, S. (1991). *Connections: New ways of working in the networked organization.* Cambridge, MA: MIT Press.

Sundstrom, E., De Meuse, K., & Futrell, D. (1990). Work teams: Applications and effectiveness. *American Psychologist, 45,* 120–133.

Trevino, L. K., Lengel, R. H., & Daft, R. L. (1987). Media symbolism, media richness and media choice in organizations: A symbolic interactionist perspective. *Communication Research, 14,* 553–574.

Triandis, H. (1994). *Culture and social behavior.* New York: McGraw-Hill.

Tuckman, B. W. (1965). Developmental sequence in small groups. *Psychological Bulletin, 63,* 384–389.

Tuckman, B. W., & Jensen, M. (1977). Stages of small-group development revisited. *Group and Organization Studies, 2,* 419–427.

PART TWO

Future Directions

9

Closing the Gap Between Research and Practice

Ann M. Morrison

I n many organizations, managers are struggling with a number of goals: to improve the relationship between supervisors and their subordinates; to create a more effective partnership to better serve the organization's mission; and to remove the dysfunctional effects of prejudice with respect to race, sex, and other differences. One would hope that research on the topic of diversity within work teams would offer guidance to these struggling managers. For example, Tsui, Xin, and Egan (chapter 5, this volume) described how personal characteristics affect the supervisor–subordinate relationship. Such research sounds as if it may be useful, but can managers really use it? One implication of the research seems to be that teams can be recomposed to reduce the salience of characteristics such as race and sex. That may mean, however, that several team members must be reassigned at the same time. If openings occur one at a time, as they typically do in organizations, is this technique feasible? If not, what options exist?

There has been a long-standing gap between research and practice that makes questions such as these very difficult to answer. Increasingly, however, researchers are making an effort to put their work to use in businesses, agencies, and institutions throughout the world. For example, Ely (chapter 7, this volume) described her attempt to use her understanding of the dynamics of diversity to benefit the work of a not-for-profit organization. Her intervention, in turn, sheds new light on her conceptual approach to understanding diversity. Thus, she encourages discarding the concept of identity as "unitary, fixed, and internally consistent" and moving toward one in which "identity is best seen as a set of contradictory, fluid, contextually constrained positions within which people are capable of exercising choice" (p. 184). For Ely, research is clearly not divorced from the struggles of managers and their subordinates; applying knowledge seems to be at least as important as generating knowledge.

The unusual nature of Ely's chapter also reveals that a pioneering spirit is needed to bring research and practice together. Researchers in academic settings who embark on such adventures must be willing to take career risks, because they are forced to rely on their intuition rather than on precedent. Ultimately, these barriers to action-oriented research are detrimental to both the generation of new knowledge and the application of available knowledge.

BARRIERS TO THE APPLIED USE OF RESEARCH

Several interrelated problems continue to make it extremely difficult to move information from the research domain into practice. One problem is that research papers are typically written in a cumbersome style that keeps them from circulating beyond strictly academic circles. For example, Brewer's research (chapter 3, this volume) seems likely to appeal to a wide array of managers and professionals struggling to develop diversity within their companies, agencies, and institutions. The intriguing title is "Managing Diversity: The Role of Social Identities." Yet reading this chapter may be a daunting task for a chief executive officer or even a human resource director. In fairness to Professor Brewer and the other authors of chapters in this volume, I recognize that the intent here is not to communicate to a lay audience. As a practicing consultant, however, I believe it may be helpful if the ideas in a volume such as this can be made accessible to managers.

Unfortunately, however, there are two separate bodies of literature on the topic of diversity—one written and read by university faculty and students, and one written and used by practitioners (including many of the managers who earned an advanced degree in the social sciences). Although this division may serve some useful purposes, it does not encourage application of research findings. For the topic of diversity in particular, which is posing almost overwhelming challenges to most organizations today, the separation seems particularly dysfunctional.

Language is not the only barrier that prevents the application of research findings in organizations. Another problem, it seems, is that some researchers have little concern for the practical utility of their work. In some cases, researchers simply stop short of drawing implications for practice. A question put to several researchers at a recent conference was the following: On the basis of your research, what do you tell policymakers? One researcher contended that there are no simple answers regarding issues of diversity and so no simple recommendations can be made. When pressed to make recommendations appropriate to the complex situation, this researcher stated, "You can't make complex recommendations." With regard to applying research findings to help solve current problems, the most this researcher was willing to contribute was to advise practitioners to "read the literature and draw your own conclusions."

What seems to be a lack of interest on the part of some researchers for serving as an agent of change may be something else entirely. Perhaps researchers feel they are out of their element when it comes to creating research-based policies and tools for use in companies and other organizations. Some may even feel helpless to use their knowledge constructively because of the politics that they see operating. One researcher at a recent conference commented that "knowledge is socially constructed" and that any recommendation to practitioners "depends on their or my purposes." If researchers are not certain that their purposes and values are in line with those of the managers they may advise, some may prefer to make no recommendations at all rather than get involved in a political situation. As one researcher put it, "You have to understand the context to make a useful intervention."

Once the context is understood, the wisest thing to do may, in fact, be to walk away. In dealing with a controversial issue such as diversity, some researchers have come to understand that in many organizations, the foxes are left in charge of the henhouse and that little will be changed there, regardless of their recommendations. Perhaps these researchers generalize unfairly and withdraw from participating in any intervention because they refuse to be used as political pawns by those with decision-making power. Researchers who feel helpless to prevent such political manipulation may willingly retreat from taking an active role in applying their research findings.

For many researchers, retreating from organizational interventions is not a major career sacrifice. Career rewards are not generally contingent on the utility of their work, and this factor preserves the gap between research and practice. In the university community, teaching and publishing in traditional academic journals are generally given more weight in career decisions than consulting on interventions. In some cases, researchers may be viewed skeptically within the academic community if they spend more of their time with practitioners than in academic pursuits. Many researchers find little encouragement or incentive to apply their research and few negative consequences if they do not.

The lines have been drawn to keep research "pure," uncontaminated by its potential utility. In a recent article in *The Wall Street Journal*, Professor Marianne Jennings (1994) addresses this problem as "Business Schools' Formula for Irrelevance." She worries that the educational system ignores applied knowledge in favor of equations and models. She quoted a colleague as saying, "No one can get anything published in the top journals in finance if it has any business application." Her conclusion is, "What we research and teach in business schools is so far removed from what businesses do that even our MBA students sell back their textbooks." Many argue that the same conclusion can be drawn about educational programs in other disciplines as well.

The emphasis on purity means that researchers' credibility may be damaged if their research appears to be too application-oriented or even too "trendy." Researchers may give in to pressure to distance themselves from current problems for fear that they are seen as opportunists more concerned with practical outcomes than with adequate theory-building. With respect to research on the issue of diversity, the pressure may be especially powerful. Researchers who are people of color, women, people with disabilities, and others who are "different" sometimes find that they are suspected, even accused, of lacking adequate objectivity in pursuing research involving people like themselves. Diversity is still not seen as a legitimate area of scholarship in many institutions, particularly if demographic differences of race and sex are involved. A low profile may often be required to study these issues, prohibiting some researchers from participating in interventions.

CLOSING THE GAP

Both academics and practitioners need to help close the gap between research and applications concerning diversity. Individuals and organizations in both groups can be more proactive in forging partnerships that encourage field research and practical application of the findings. Many businesses and other organizations are willing to invest in on-site research that will help them to manage people more effectively. Academics who do some consulting are likely to be aware of current business needs and business contacts who could arrange a research partnership. In other cases, several departments of a university may cooperate to organize a mini-conference for the local business community to identify areas of mutual interest. Organizing a symposium for a national or regional professional conference that blends theory and practice in an area of interest can also be a first step in building a research partnership.

A partnership that involves on-site research can benefit both the participating businesses and the academic agenda of the researchers themselves along with their institutions of learning. For a large-scale project, a combined team of perhaps six or eight individuals may be willing to commit to working together for 2 years. This team defines the specifics of the research project, such as the sample, methods, use of data, anticipated publications, and so forth. Periodic team meetings help ensure that everyone has current information about the project and a say in resolving any problems that come up. The businesses, which may cover many of the research expenses, get considerable expertise and a tailored approach to solving key business problems that they perhaps cannot otherwise afford. The researchers get valuable experience in a "living laboratory," the opportunity to use their knowledge to solve real-world problems, and career-building publications. The learning institution, which may receive some funding, becomes better connected with neighbor organizations and better able to find additional projects and placements for faculty and students. A variety of collaborative arrangements are available for gaining these kinds of benefits and bridging the gap between research and its application.

Some professional organizations are also finding ways to close the gap. For example, the Academy of Management uses its practitioner-oriented journal, *The Executive*, to summarize research papers appearing in academic journals. These summaries are written crisply and with a general audience in mind. At the individual level, academics who advise students and who edit and review manuscripts for professional publications can encourage research with greater utility for a wider audience.

Professors and students, managers and professionals, must be proactive to remove the stigma associated with doing research on some diversity issues and the stigma associated with taking a practical approach to applying these research findings in organizations. Certainly, some research will continue to be foundation-building work that should not be prematurely applied, but there are plenty of opportunities to focus on the potential applications. Research is not only a worthwhile intellectual exercise. It is also a valuable tool that psychologists and laypeople alike can use to solve some burning problems and change the world for the better.

REFERENCE

Jennings, M. (1994, November 28). Business schools' formula for irrelevance. *The Wall Street Journal*, p. A18.

10

The Importance of Contexts in Studies of Diversity

Harry C. Triandis

T he main theme of this chapter is that diversity is a socially constructed issue that must be examined in a cultural–historical context. Acknowledgment of such context is missing from most of the chapters of this volume. These chapters also fail to recognize the importance of several variables that may usefully be included in future research on diversity, such as cultural distance, differences in the levels of adaptation on key perceptual variables in the two cultures, the emotional effects of the history of intergroup relations, the pattern of acculturation of the relevant cultures, and the tendency of members of each cultural group to make isomorphic attributions.

DIVERSITY IS SOCIALLY CONSTRUCTED

Diversity is a socially constructed phenomenon. Consequently, what appears as an issue in one culture may not appear as an issue in another culture. Specifically, diversity is more likely to be viewed as an important issue in settings where there is group heterogeneity and the power rela-

I thank D. Bhawuk and M. Gelfand for comments on an earlier draft of this chapter.

tionships among social categories are changing. For instance, in cultures where everyone is Black, the Black–White contrast is of little consequence; other contrasts are more important. In cultures where the power relationships of men and women are more or less frozen (e.g., the conservative parts of the Muslim world), there is little concern about gender diversity. Of course, oppression does exist, and the oppressed often protest, directly or indirectly, or become apathetic. Unfortunately, these societies lose half of the talent in their population.

The chapters in this volume are focused on diversity in the context of modern-day, U.S. culture. Thus, readers should be cautious about making generalizations from these chapters to related phenomena in other cultures or countries. For example, as Tsui, Xin, and Egan (chapter 5, this volume) acknowledged, age-based diversity effects found within the United States may bear little resemblance to effects found in some Asian cultures. Similarly, although the minimal categories paradigm Brewer (chapter 3, this volume) uses in her research shows that even trivial differences can cause people to favor their ingroup, it is nevertheless limited because in most cases intergroup conflict has a history. Because this is missing from the paradigm, the external validity of the findings is open to question.

Consider, for instance, the case of some African Americans and European Americans, where there is a long history of conflict. If we reflect on the nature of this history, we realize that we must pay attention to a differentiation, outlined by Ogbu (1994), between voluntary and involuntary minorities. Voluntary minorities (e.g., the recently arrived Vietnamese) came to this country voluntarily, expecting to have jobs at the bottom of the social structure until they learned enough about their new country to advance upward. Consequently, when they encounter discrimination, they can consider it the price for having a better standard of living than they had in the country from which they came. As a result, they may be able to more easily assimilate to the new culture.

Involuntary minorities include many African, some Hispanic, and most Native Americans, who were brought here involuntarily or were conquered by European Americans. Ogbu argues that such minorities often have an "oppositional framework" for reacting to actions of the majority.

That is, if the majority says that something is "good," they may say that it must be "bad." I argue, then, that Brewer's approach to managing inter-group relations through the use of crosscutting assignments may be helpful only in the case of voluntary minorities or other groups where historical factors play a relatively minor role.

CONTEXT HAS BOTH UNIVERSAL AND CULTURE-SPECIFIC ASPECTS

Cross-cultural psychologists call the universal *etic* and the culture-specific *emic*. For example, what is sexual harassment? Can a male understand what it means? The etic perspective argues that males can understand it; the emic argues that they cannot. The emic perspective is that if you are not a woman, you cannot understand the phenomenon.

Etics apply outside the system; emics apply within the system. Etics apply to more than one culture or point of view; emics apply to only one culture or point of view. The variables used by etic researchers are theoretic, assumed rather than extracted from data, and checked with constructs that are presumed to be appropriate in all cultures. They are "imposed" on the problem. McGrath, Berdahl, and Arrow (chapter 2, this volume) presumed this approach. McGrath et al. provided a valuable, but rather abstract, analysis of different kinds of diversity, as well as useful hypotheses of the way these types of diversity will affect various organizational outcomes. Although they adopted an etic approach, they nevertheless made the useful point that some kinds of diversity are likely to have positive consequences, whereas other aspects of diversity are likely to have negative consequences. This agrees with some of my own research (Triandis, Hall, & Ewen, 1965), which showed that for dyads, dissimilarity of attitudes resulted in higher creativity, but dissimilarity of abilities resulted in lower creativity.

The variables that are used by emic researchers are discovered from within, through "thick descriptions" (Geertz, 1973). The data are only descriptions of one culture. For example, Ely (chapter 7, this volume) provided a valuable "thick description" of the way dominant identity is negotiated in groups and a case study from an organization. However, this is an unusual organization that is providing a specific kind of service. A production organization would probably be very different.

The criteria for evaluating research used by etic researchers are universal (i.e., applicable to all cultures and social categories). The criteria for evaluating research used by emic researchers are internal to one culture. Comparing research that uses these differing approaches is like comparing apples with oranges (Triandis, 1994). Fruit have etic attributes: weight, size, price, and so forth. But the emic theorists may argue that if one provides information about the weight, size, and price of a fruit, one does not know if it is an apple or an orange. One needs the culture-specific attributes, such as orange flavor, to really "understand" it. My view (e.g., Triandis, 1992) is that it is possible to use both emic and etic perspectives, and that makes for good research.

For example, categorization and social identity processes are probably universal, but they may acquire different forms in different settings. It is important to examine phenomena from both the etics of social identity (e.g., how do individuals relate to their ingroups) and the emics of social identity (e.g., how does an African American, 30-year-old woman with an MBA define herself in an organization that consists predominantly of European American, 50-year-old males with high school educations).

A study that is done in a specific context will generalize to other contexts with some difficulty. As psychologists and researchers learn more about etic dimensions of context (e.g., individualism and collectivism), they can extrapolate theoretically from studies done in individualistic cultures to studies done in collectivist cultures. However, if the study reflects emic context, generalization outside that context is bound to be minimal. For example, the fixed pie bias mentioned by Northcraft, Polzer, Neale, and Kramer (chapter 4, this volume) may be especially important for some subgroups. There is literature in anthropology about the image of limited good (Foster, 1965) that suggests that peasant societies tend to see "the good" as limited. Thus, if their competitors get some "good" (e.g., high yielding seeds), they feel threatened. That is presumably a consequence of the good deriving from the land: Land conflicts are distributive, and rarely integrative. This way of thinking is then carried to other situations. Furthermore, those who are most ethnocentric are most likely to see issues in distributive rather than integrative ways. Some cultures (e.g., nationalistic, collectivist cultures) have especially strong propensities to view the ingroup–outgroup relationships as distributive (Triandis, 1995). Thus, in the case of Northcraft et al., cultural factors may augment or diminish the effects that are discussed. Having said this, I nevertheless think the Northcraft et al. chapter makes an important contribution. The authors point out that similarity within the organization can be dysfunctional because sometimes individuals actually want the same things, making distributive conflicts more likely. When individuals want different things, integrative solutions become more available. I think that is an important point, because theories of diversity, such as my own (Triandis, Kurowski, & Gelfand, 1994), have not considered it.

The chapter by Tolbert, Andrews, and Simons (chapter 6, this volume) also reminds me of the importance of attending to context. Their research results support the competition hypothesis on the effects of group proportions on group dynamics. I agree with the conclusions, which are consistent with Pettigrew and Cramer's (1959) findings. However, in this study, the contact hypothesis was unlikely to be supported because one of the bases of the hypothesis is that people are prejudiced because of ignorance of the other group and, when they come in contact with the other group, they discover similarities, which reduces their prejudice. But ignorance is unlikely to be an important factor in the relationships of men and women, especially among sociologists who must have seen many extremely competent women in graduate school. Such contact did not necessarily increase their knowledge of or change their attitudes toward women.

I also noted that Tolbert et al. assumed that there is a lot of contact among faculty members, another condition necessary for a meaningful test of the contact hypothesis. But in very large departments, most of the contact is likely to occur through electronic mail. As Armstrong and Cole (chapter 8, this volume) have shown, such contact may not be sufficient for fostering understandings among dissimilar people. Furthermore, professors often behave like prima donnas, doing their research with their students and contacting other professors only to solve departmental problems. Is that kind of contact meeting the assumptions of the contact hypothesis? Again, the specific context in which the data were collected makes generalization to other contexts unlikely. Similarly, although Armstrong and Cole provided fascinating real life quotes from the work of computer engineers scattered on different continents, the very fact that they are computer engineers engaged in what appear to be extremely interdependent tasks makes the generality of the findings minimal. In many international teams people have considerable autonomy and do not need to interact with each other with as much urgency as is described in that chapter.

MISSING VARIABLES AND FUTURE RESEARCH NEEDS

Future research on diversity must take the issue of context more seriously. Some contextual variables that I consider very important in the diversity debate, but that are missing from the chapters in this volume are *cultural distance, level of adaptation, history of intergroup relations, acculturation,* and *isomorphic attributions.* There is no space here to present the full argument concerning why these variables are important, but it is available elsewhere (Triandis et al., 1994).

Cultural Distance

Briefly, cultural distance refers to the dissimilarity in the language, social structure, religion, politics, aesthetic standards, economic conditions, and basic assumptions about the nature of reality between two cultural groups. People who cannot communicate, who come from cultures with different social structures, different assumptions, religions, economic conditions, and standards, will have a very hard time working together.

I note that in almost all of the chapters in this volume the cultural distance is very small. For example, Armstrong and Cole dealt with European and American computer engineers. The fact that they are computer engineers already reduces their cultural distance markedly. The demographic differences described by Tsui, Xin, and Egan or Ely do not necessarily involve large cultural distances. Even McGrath, Berdahl, and Arrow visualize relatively minor differences. Major differences involve people from different cultural regions (Burton, Moore, Whiting, & Romney, 1992), such as sub-Saharan Africa and North America. Brewer makes the important point that crosscutting group assignments can be helpful in reducing intergroup differentiation, but this can work only if the cultural distance among the individuals who are included is relatively small. If cultural distance is great, a simple crosscutting strategy does not address the sources of misunderstanding that are present.

Level of Adaptation

The way people make judgments on any continuum depends on the level of adaptation that they use (Helson, 1964). As you may recall, the level of adaptation is the neutral point of any judgmental continuum. Helson reviewed work in psychophysics showing that it is the geometric mean of the salient stimuli on any judgmental continuum, such as whether this person is acceptable or not acceptable for that job, or whether this job is "difficult" or "easy."

If one group has a lot of experience with heterogeneity, the level of adaptation will be on the heterogeneity side of the continuum, and other groups that are only slightly heterogeneous will be perceived as homogeneous. The very same groups, however, will be perceived as heterogeneous in settings with minimal heterogeneity. Whether group members see other group members as similar or different from themselves is a crucial factor in attraction, readiness to cooperate, and the like. The position of the level of adaptation determines expectations. An executive who has been exposed to many women chief executive officers (CEOs) will be less likely to oppose the promotion of a competent women to the CEO position than will an executive who has been exposed to no women CEOs. This phenomenon occurs in innumerable judgments in the area of diversity.

History of Intergroup Relations

History refers to the relationships of two groups such as the ones discussed by Ogbu (1994). For instance, relationships between men and women have distinct histories in the West and in Islam. Hispanic and Anglo peoples have a distinct history of relationships that must be taken into account.

Native Americans, Korean Americans, Japanese Americans, and each other variety of Americans also have specific histories of relationships. As Ely's chapter illustrated, these unique histories must be incorporated into an understanding of modern relationships.

Acculturation

Acculturation is important because cultural groups do change as they come in contact with one another. If cultural distance is very large, they are likely to seek separation; if it is minimal, they are likely to accommodate to each other. Mental health is optimal when they retain their culture and also learn the other culture (Berry, Kim, Minde, & Mok, 1987). If people interact with members of other cultures, they must develop skills, such as learning the language of the other group, in order to have good interpersonal relationships. Future research should take into account the degree of acculturation that is likely to have occurred among members of different subgroups. In addition, the process of acculturation itself, and the conditions that inhibit or facilitate it, require further study.

Isomorphic Attributions

One of the most important skills is learning to make isomorphic attributions: that is, learning to assign causes to the social behavior of members of the other group that are more or less like the causes that the members of that group assign to explain their own behavior. There is evidence that people who use isomorphic attributions experience less culture shock and have better interpersonal relationships with members of other cultures than do people who use very different attributions. Thus, future research that improves our understanding of the conditions that support the process of learning to make isomorphic attributions can greatly improve our understanding of how to manage diverse work groups more effectively.

In sum, future research should examine how context influences the findings reported in the chapters of this volume. For example, what is the effect of small versus large cultural distance between cultures on the findings of any one of the studies? How are differences in the level of adaptation found in the relevant cultures likely to affect the findings of each of the studies? Are the findings the same when the history of conflict between the relevant cultures is one of no conflict as when the history is one of major conflict? What happens to the findings of each of the studies in societies that have adopted a multicultural as opposed to a unicultural policy? How are the findings affected when people from one or both of the relevant cultures have been trained to make isomorphic attributions? These directions of future research will complete the picture so ably sketched out in the chapters of this volume.

REFERENCES

Berry, J. W., Kim, U., Minde, T., & Mok, D. (1987). Comparative studies of acculturative stress. *International Migration Review, 21*, 185–206.

Burton, M. L., Moore, C. C., Whiting, J. W., & Romney, A. K. (1992, February). *World cultural regions.* Paper presented at the meeting of the Society for Cross-Cultural Research, Santa Fe, NM.

Foster, G. (1965). Peasant society and the image of limited good. *American Anthropologist, 67*, 293–315.

Geertz, C. (1973). *The interpretation of cultures.* New York: Basic Books.

Helson, H. (1964). *Adaptation level theory.* New York: Harper & Row.

Ogbu, J. U. (1994). From cultural differences to differences in cultural frames of reference. In P. M. Greenfield & R. R. Cocking (Eds.), *Cross-cultural roots of minority child development* (pp. 365–392). Hillsdale, NJ: Erlbaum.

Pettigrew, T. F., & Cramer, M. R. (1959). The demography of desegregation. *Journal of Social Issues, 15*, 61–71.

Triandis, H. C. (1992). Cross-cultural research in social psychology. In D. Granberg & G. Sarup (Eds.), *Social judgment and intergroup relations: Essays in honor of Muzafer Sherif* (pp. 229–244). New York: Springer-Verlag.

Triandis, H. C. (1994). *Culture and social behavior.* New York: McGraw-Hill.

Triandis, H. C. (1995). *Individualism and collectivism.* Boulder, CO: Westview Press.

Triandis, H. C., Hall, E. R., & Ewen, R. B. (1965). Member heterogeneity and dyadic creativity. *Human Relations, 18*, 33–55.

Triandis, H. C., Kurowski, L., & Gelfand, M. (1994). Workplace diversity. In H. C. Triandis, M. Dunnette, & L. Hough (Eds.), *Handbook of industrial and organizational psychology* (Vol. 4, pp. 769–827). Palo Alto, CA: Consulting Psychologists Press.

11

The Complexity of Diversity: Challenges and Directions for Future Research

Taylor Cox, Jr.

I n this essay I identify and comment on several themes that reoccur throughout this volume. In doing so, my objectives are to illuminate linkages among the individual chapters and suggest promising directions for future research relating to the intersection of diversity and teamwork.

A recent discussion with a colleague has provided me with what I think may be a helpful unifying lens through which to view this volume. She asked me, "What is the core puzzle that psychologists are trying to solve in diversity research?" After some reflection, my answer was that psychologists are trying to understand the impact of diversity as a characteristic of social systems—whether they be single work teams or organizations—on work behavior and outcomes. I then pointed out that, because the existing research has shown that diversity can either enhance or hinder organizational performance, the core puzzle of diversity research is to discover under what conditions one may capitalize on the potential benefits of diversity while minimizing the potential for diversity-related phenomena to adversely affect performance. All the chapters in this volume touch on this basic puzzle.

With this unifying lens in mind, I want to address the following three themes, which I believe link the chapters and suggest areas of needed research: (a) Diversity is a broad concept with many overlapping yet distinct dimensions; (b) the effect of diversity on work teams is a complex function of the interaction of member identity structures and various contextual factors; and (c) the effect of diversity in work teams occurs within and is significantly influenced by a social–cultural landscape that extends, in time and space, beyond the boundaries of existing organizational relationships.

BREADTH AND MULTIDIMENSIONALITY OF DIVERSITY

Perhaps the most difficult challenge in diversity research is dealing effectively with the multidimensionality of the concept. This requires acknowledging the uniqueness of each dimension of diversity while also identifying effects and relationships that occur across many dimensions. The particulars of this challenge are especially prominent in the chapter by McGrath, Berdahl, and Arrow (chapter 2, this volume). Among other things, they point out that diversity is more than demographic differences and that not all effects of diversity are generic. They also offer a categorization scheme for types of diversity, producing a list of five diversity clusters. Their discussion of the distinctions among these clusters immediately leads us into the difficulty of dealing adequately with the overlap among the dimensions. For example, they treat organizational status, culture, and demography as separate dimensions of diversity, yet there is considerable evidence to suggest that demographic categories (such as gender and national origin) also differentiate people in terms of status and culture within specific social contexts (e.g., Belenky, Clinchy, Goldberger, & Tarule, 1986; Cox, 1993; Hall, 1976; Ridgeway, 1991).

The extent to which it is difficult to address the challenge of multiple identities in a given research project is vividly illustrated in the research of Tsui, Xin, and Egan (chapter 5, this volume) on leader–member dyads. In an acknowledgment of the problems posed by the multidimensionality of identity, the writers prefaced propositions 5 through 10 by stating,

"Given the potential interaction among different demographic variables, these propositions focus on the main effect of each relational demographic variable and assume constancy of all other demographic factors" (p. 114).

In theory development, and to a lesser extent in the conduct of laboratory research, the constancy assumption may be viable, but it will seldom apply in real organizational work teams. Instead, researchers are confronted with situations in which members are similar on some dimensions of diversity and different on other dimensions, and these complexities probably should not be ignored.

The importance of the interrelationships among diversity dimensions is also explicitly addressed by Northcraft, Polzer, Neale, and Kramer (chapter 4, this volume). These authors argue that the effect of cognitive diversity on the performance of work teams is more potent than the effect of demographic diversity, but at the same time they note that the latter often acts as a surrogate for the former. One way in which this surrogate effect occurs is that members assume or expect certain qualities to be present in others on the basis of these physical or other types of differences (e.g., female, Asian, an accountant). These expectations become determinants of the effects of diversity, regardless of the extent to which they are accurate. Northcraft et al. illustrated this point in their discussion of the potential effects of diversity on the process of negotiation. For example, they pointed out that the quality of negotiations is often impaired because stereotypic thinking leads each party to exaggerate the extent to which the other party's interests are in conflict with their own (i.e., there is a false presumption of distributiveness).

In terms of the basic puzzle that I have posed here, the fact that diversity has many overlapping dimensions raises the following question: Which types of diversity have effects on which organizational outcomes? There is some indication that many "diversity effects" have wide application. For example, McLeod, Lobel, and Cox (in press) found that ethnic diversity can enhance creative performance by teams, at least for identity-relevant tasks such as developing marketing strategies in a global context. Likewise, creativity and innovation have been shown to be positively related to diversity of cognition (Amabile, 1983), age, organizational tenure, functional area, and education (e.g., Bantel & Jackson, 1989; Murray, 1989). As a second example, for a variety of dimensions, increasing diversity in work teams has been shown to potentially lower outcomes on measures of group cohesiveness and organizational commitment (e.g., Ancona & Caldwell, 1992; Tsui, Egan, & O'Reilly, 1992). Thus, it appears that at least some effects of diversity may occur over a wide range of diversity dimensions. However, scholars and researchers need to establish these generic effects by systematic research, not assumption.

The multidimensionality of diversity and the interrelationships among diversity dimensions present some formidable challenges for the development of theory and methodologies for use in work on diversity. I believe that researchers may begin to tackle these challenges by following a few basic principles. Specifically, in designing future research scholars need to (a) be very explicit about the definition of diversity and the specific dimensions that their theory and empirical research are intended to address; (b) increase the use of field experiments in order to increase control over extraneous variables without limiting generalizability, which is often a problem for laboratory research; (c) replicate completed research using different dimensions of diversity as the point of focus (with the same work group or organizational outcomes) and, to the extent justified by the data, use combinations of studies to generate general principles about the interrelations of diversity and work outcomes; and (d) develop measures that attempt to track specific behavioral patterns associated with specific aspects of respondent identities.

In order for researchers to reach the deeper understanding of diversity suggested in item (d), they need more research designed to test alternative explanations of behavior. They also need to know more about such things as (a) the cultural identity structure of subjects (not just their demographic categories), (b) the identities that are salient at a particular point in time or for a particular task, and (c) the thought processes that occur as subjects make behavioral choices and interact in groups and organizations. This combination of needs is at least partially illustrated in the work of Ely (chapter 7, this volume). In her research, she explicitly asked subjects about identity salience and about the impact that a particular identity had on their behavior at work.

DIVERSITY EFFECTS AS THE INTERACTION OF IDENTITY AND ENVIRONMENT

A second dominant theme throughout this volume is that the specific effect of diversity on organizational behavior and performance is largely determined by contextual factors. In terms of the basic puzzle of diversity, this theme raises the following question: Under what environmental circumstances do links between specific types of diversity and specific work outcomes occur? In presenting the interactional model of cultural diversity, I have argued elsewhere (Cox, 1993) that various aspects of the "diversity climate" of organizations interact with the identity structures of individuals who work there to produce effects (both positive and negative) related to diversity at both the individual and organizational level. The chapters in this volume represent considerable theoretic and empirical advancement toward identifying the important contextual factors and their effects.

For example, McGrath, Berdahl, and Arrow (chapter 2, this volume) discussed task and technology as context factors that interact with characteristics of team members to produce what they call work team "fit." Presumably, work outcomes are better when the fit is good than when it is poor. The technology construct refers to all tools used to perform the work, including rules, procedures, and norms. McGrath et al. pointed out that neither members nor the contexts in which they work are static over time. When new members enter or old members mature in their relationships, the fit of task, technology, and members is altered. These ideas shed additional light on previous empirical findings indicating that the work outcomes of diverse teams relative to homogeneous teams are greatly affected by the length of time that members have worked together (e.g., Watson, Kumar, & Michaelsen, 1993).

A second contextual factor highlighted in this volume is that of group or organizational demographic composition. In her analysis of a social service organization, Ely (chapter 7, this volume) treated demographic composition not only as referring to the overall proportion of each identity category for the particular diversity dimension of focus in the study (i.e., racioethnic identity), but also as an analysis of power distribution (e.g., all managers were White). This treatment parallels what I have previously referred to as "structural integration" (Cox, 1993). Similarly, in propositions 11 and 12 of their chapter, Tsui et al. (chapter 5, this volume) included the level of demographic heterogeneity as a contextual factor that moderates the relationship between relational demographic similarity and the quality of the exchange relationship between the supervisors and their subordinates. Also, Tolbert, Andrews, and Simons (chapter 6, this volume) found that the likelihood of women being hired in university faculty jobs over time is inversely related to the proportion of women already on the payroll. Thus, the context factor of proportionate representation of women seems to be an important factor in determining the relationship between the gender identity of a prospective hire and the outcome of hiring or organizational entry.

Perhaps the most far-reaching determinant of how increasing diversity will affect work team and organizational performance is the extent to which the diversity is managed. By "managed," I mean taking proactive steps to create a climate in which cultural norms, values, work practices, and interpersonal relations reinforce rather than hinder the full participation of all organizational members. This point was cogently made by Adler (1986) in her description of the effect of cultural diversity on work team productivity:

> Highly productive and less productive teams differ in how they manage their diversity, not, as is commonly believed, in the presence or absence of diversity. When well managed, diversity becomes a productive resource to the team. When ignored, diversity causes process problems that diminish the team's productivity. (p. 111)

Most of the research that has been done on the relationship between diversity and organizational behavior has been done on "unmanaged" diversity. For example, one may ask whether the apparent lowering of support for the hiring of women by male-dominated faculties found by Tolbert et al. (chapter 6, this volume) is inevitable or just an example of what happens when demographic diversity is increased with no organizational intervention. Likewise, Tsui, Egan, and O'Reilly (1992) found that when gender and race diversity increased in work groups, the commitment and morale of White men declined. But is this result an unavoidable consequence of diversity or merely an indicator of the need to manage it?

This aspect of context was addressed explicitly in some of the chapters in this volume and indirectly in others. For example, several possible interventions for work teams containing physical and cultural distance were discussed by Armstrong and Cole (chapter 8, this volume). Brewer and Northcraft et al. (chapters 3 and 4, this volume) advocated enhancing the diversity–performance relationship by paying attention to the social architecture of groups. Specifically, Brewer suggested that many of the potential dysfunctions of diversity can be alleviated if managers systematically avoid the convergence of categorical identities and functional roles in teams (e.g., avoid the situation where all engineering representatives are male).

As already noted, McGrath et al. (chapter 2, this volume) suggested that diversity will enhance the performance of work groups only if there is a good fit between the specific type of diversity and the specific task at hand. One implication of their framework is that leaders of organizations can leverage diversity for positive effects if they alter the technology (which includes such things as work procedures and norms) to better reflect and respond to the diversity of team members. Finally, Ely (chapter 7, this volume), in her analysis of the effect of increasing racial–ethnic diversity on the organizational outcomes of a social service agency, stated that the firm "achieved the value-in-diversity vision" not only because it recruited non-White women, but also because the organization took steps to use "their ideas and skills to enhance the quality of the organization's work" (p. 177).

In summary, the relationship of diversity to work performance in teams and organizations will be greatly influenced by contextual factors such as the demographic profile of the group, the task to be done, the technology used to accomplish the task, and the extent to which the organizational climate is conducive to leveraging diversity. In general, the extent to which diversity's potential positive impact is maximized and its negative impact minimized will depend on the extent to which effective interventions are used to proactively address the dynamics of diversity. Future research on context should focus on (a) the development of theory that specifies which aspects of the work environment are relevant to the diversity–work-performance relationship, (b) empirical examination of the ideas about context advanced in this volume, and (c) the evaluation of interventions designed to effectively manage diversity (e.g., culture awareness training, modification of organizational reward structures) to determine which are most useful and how they should be implemented to achieve the best results.

HISTORY AS THE LANDSCAPE OF DIVERSITY

Triandis (chapter 10, this volume) has already noted the importance of history in understanding issues of diversity. His observation deserves elaboration.

The basic phenomena of diversity are intergroup dynamics. When people with different group identities interact in a social system, contemporary transactions are influenced by the legacy of prior interactions among members of those groups. Thus, the history of intergroup relations is the social–cultural background on which the effects of diversity in any particular work team are constructed (Alderfer & Smith, 1982). Often, this "landscape" for diversity includes both a societal component and an organizational component. An example of the former is the legacy of bitter conflict over land and sovereignty that characterizes the history of relations between European Americans and many Native American tribes. An example of the latter is the history of distrust and antagonism that marks prior transactions in the United States between management and organized labor in many companies. It is important to acknowledge in these instances that the character of prior relations is psychologically connected to the social group (i.e., Native Americans vs. European Americans, management vs. labor) more so than to individual members.

Although the vital role of history as social landscape is not addressed in all of the chapters presented here, it is an explicit theme in at least some and implied in others. For example, Northcraft et al. pointed out that the false assumption of distributive interests that often hinders negotiations and cooperation is due to such factors as mistrust, untested assumptions, and poor communications. To a large degree, what they are describing is the character of the history of intergroup relations between the parties. In terms of the basic puzzle of diversity, these authors wrote: "Simply put, if the benefits of diversity are inaccessible because of faulty perceptions, organizations must change those perceptions" (p. 84). Although supporting this statement as far as it goes, I think it is important to acknowledge the role of history as a potentially potent obstacle to changing intergroup perceptions and assumptions. A part of this acknowledgment is to make the explicit discussion of history a part of the process of promoting change.

A second example of the theme of history occurs in the chapter by Ely. She wrote: "It then makes sense to examine the impact of organizations as historically situated contextual constraints that can shape and re-shape, create and re-create identity in potentially infinite ways" (p. 184). Thus, the writer made explicit the role of history in shaping the impact of identity diversity on work groups. I believe we can deepen the insight given concerning the role of history in the context of the Ely research. Her findings that occupational roles tended to be segregated by race on the basis of assumptions about race-related competencies have roots in the history of the labor market and in race differences in educational opportunities. Competent mathematics and science teachers are particularly scarce in inner-city communities where most Blacks attend school in their formative years. Also, the labor market has historically been more open for Blacks in jobs dealing with the external community of firms such as public relations, community relations, and urban affairs, as compared with occupations such as finance and management of internal operations (Collins, 1989). Both of these historical circumstances not only translate into stereotypic views of what type of work is appropriate for Whites versus Blacks, but also may be responsible for real differences in vocational interests and skills. Thus, the fact that the Black women gravitated toward case work while the White women gravitated toward management and finance can be interpreted as a manifestation of historical effects of race on educational and occupational opportunities. The writer came close to making this point when she attributed the role of the Black women in maintaining the job segregation to a quest for a base of power in a system that denies them access to managerial jobs. However, the problem posed by this organizational history is greatly compounded by the legacy of the societal history. In this respect, I believe Ely's conclusion that the organization "invented a kind of racial segregation in its internal labor market in which both White women and women of color colluded" (p. 180) should be amended to acknowledge that women of both races are subject to a history that has created a certain distribution of job skills and career interests that are indeed influenced by race. In this case, more attention to the role of history suggests that the organization reinforced rather than invented the form of racial segregation observed there.

In the future, research on diversity should give more attention to these history effects. For example, in measuring organizational climate with regard to diversity, researchers may ask questions about the quality of past relations among members of focal groups (interfunction, interracial, etc.). As a second example, organizational scholars can develop theory about how differences in the historical legacies of intergroup relations lead to differences in the contemporary relationships between people of different groups. To illustrate, the fact that Native Americans are arguably the most difficult of any of the non-European racial–ethnic groups in the United States to successfully recruit on a large-scale basis to work in White-dominated firms is undoubtedly related to unique aspects of their history. This history includes such specifics as the forced assimilation of Native Americans in White schools during the late 19th century, the repeated breaches of treaties governing land possession, and the forced changes in lifestyle imposed on Native Americans by White government officials and military leaders (e.g., forcing a shift from hunting and gathering to farming and ranching).

In conclusion, the core puzzle of diversity with regard to work teams is to understand the conditions under which the potential performance benefits of diversity can be maximized while simultaneously minimizing the potential performance detriments. To solve the puzzle, we need to know more about the impact of diversity. The impact of diversity, in turn, will be better understood as researchers (a) develop theory and research methods that better accommodate the multiple dimensionality of group identity; (b) learn more about contextual factors that influence the link between diversity and work outcomes; and (c) approach diversity as a phenomenon that occurs within, and is significantly influenced by, a landscape of social and cultural history that extends beyond organizational boundaries in space and time.

REFERENCES

Adler, N. (1986) *International dimensions of organization behavior*. Boston: Kent.

Alderfer, C. P., & Smith, K. K. (1982). Studying intergroup relations embedded in organizations. *Administrative Science Quarterly, 27*, 5–65.

Amabile, T. M. (1983). The social psychology of creativity. *Journal of Personality and Social Psychology, 45*, 357–376.

Ancona, D. G., & Caldwell, D. F. (1992). Demography and design: Predictors of new product team performance. *Organizational Science, 3*, 321–331.

Bantel, K. A., & Jackson, S. E. (1989). Top management innovations in banking: Does the composition of the top team make a difference? *Strategic Management Journal, 10*, 107–124.

Belenky, M. F., Clinchy, B. M., Goldberger, N. R., & Tarule, J. M. (1986). *Women's ways of knowing*. New York: Basic Books.

Collins, S. M. (1989). The marginalization of Black executives. *Social Problems, 36*, 317–331.

Cox, T., Jr. (1993). *Cultural diversity in organizations: Theory, research and practice*. San Francisco: Berrett-Koehler.

Hall, E. T. (1976). *Beyond culture*. New York: Doubleday.

McLeod, P. L., Lobel, S. A., & Cox, T., Jr. (in press). Ethnic diversity and creativity in small groups. *Small Group Research*.

Murray, A. I. (1989). Top management group heterogeneity and firm performance. *Strategic Management Journal, 10*, 125–141.

Ridgeway, C. (1991). The social construction of status value: Gender and other nominal characteristics. *Social Forces, 70*, 367–386.

Tsui, A. S., Egan, T. D., & O'Reilly, C. A., III. (1992). Being different: Relational demography and organizational attachment. *Administrative Science Quarterly, 37,* 549–579.

Watson, W. E., Kumar, K., & Michaelsen, L. K. (1993). Cultural diversity's impact on interaction process and performance: Comparing homogenous and diverse task groups. *Academy of Management Journal, 36,* 590–602.

12

Identities and the Complexity of Diversity

Stella M. Nkomo

After reading these chapters and participating in the discussions and poster sessions at the conference on which this volume is based, I cannot help being struck by the complexity of the topic of diversity and work teams. The complexity of diversity is reflected in two core questions: What is diversity? And how can the barriers to work team performance created by diversity be removed without losing the very benefits expected from diversity? Each of these questions raises a host of additional issues. The very variety of the theoretic frames used by the authors of the chapters in this volume offer a glimmer of hope that psychologists may eventually find a way to understand the complexity of diversity. This understanding will eventually advance theory and practice. As McGrath, Berdahl, and Arrow (chapter 2, this volume) argue, one must first "unpack the complexities" of diversity.

THE CONCEPT OF DIVERSITY

The implied central construct underlying the meaning of diversity is *identity*. The essential debate is whether diversity should be broadly defined or narrowly defined. Those preferring the former approach argue that diversity encompasses all the possible ways work team members can differ in identity (Jackson, May, & Whitney, 1995; Thomas, 1991). Therefore, differences in individuals due to race, gender, age, and other demographic categories and differences due to values, abilities, organizational function, tenure, and personality can all be understood using a single, integrative theory. Those who favor more narrow definitions argue for restricting the domain of diversity research to focus attention on identity based on race, gender, and other cultural categories. The reason behind this approach is that the key issues are those that arise because of discrimination and exclusion of cultural subgroups from traditional organizations (Cross, Katz, Miller, & Seashore, 1994; Morrison, 1992). In my opinion, neither approach is entirely satisfactory for capturing the basic complexity of the concept of diversity.

The broad view is problematic because it implies that all differences among people are the same. That is, diversity due to, for example, organizational function (marketing vs. production) and diversity due to gender identity (male vs. female) are the same or will have the same effects in work teams. Another risk with this approach is that it leads to a reductionist conclusion that "everyone is different." If this conclusion is accepted, the risk is that the concept of diversity becomes nothing more than a benign, meaningless concept. Yet, diversity has its effects exactly because the distinctions made are not benign. It is important, as Tsui, Xin, and Egan's chapter on relational demographics (chapter 5, this volume) points out, to be aware of the "relational" dimension of diversity. Dichotomies are created (e.g., Black vs. White, male vs. female, ingroup vs. outgroup, sales vs. production). However, dichotomies are not symmetric. Someone or some group becomes the "other" (Ely, chapter 7, this volume), and otherness has a very unique meaning for the sociohistorically embedded categories of race, ethnicity, and gender (Triandis, Kurowski, & Gefland, 1994). Differences between people based on these categories are grounded within structures of power inequalities and unequal access to resources. Given this, can diversity based on race, ethnicity, and gender be understood in the same way as diversity based on organizational function, abilities, or cognitive orientation? Or, is the content of a particular identity important to understanding its effects in a work team?

On the other hand, narrow definitions that restrict discussions of diversity to race and gender are problematic for other reasons. First, the research on these identities usually focuses on one dimension at a time (e.g., race *or* gender). Such research fails to recognize the interactions among the categories. Second, too often race and gender are treated as if they were characteristics that have consequences only for minorities or women. For example, as Ely (chapter 7, this volume) notes, the tendency is to study experiences of oppression as if only Blacks have race and only women have gender. Her work reminds psychologists that everyone has a race and gender.

An individual has multiple identities, not a single identity (Hall, 1991), and the multidimensional nature of identity is particularly important in understanding work team dynamics. Race and gender can interact with each other as well as with other aspects of identity, including organizational function, personality, and cognitive style (McGrath et al., chapter 2, this volume). If individuals enter a work group or are assigned to a team because of particular knowledge, skills, abilities, or functional specialties, they also bring along identities grounded in their race and gender. Thus, a work team will rarely be diverse on a single dimension of identity. The challenge before psychologists and researchers is to understand the interactive effects of multidimensional diversity. This raises the thorny research problem of how to determine the relative salience of the different identities an individual brings to a work team.

As scientists, psychologists should try to develop an approach that specifies the different types of diversity and their effects. This means identifying and describing the particular content and nature of the different bases of identity. Researchers should be explicit in recognizing the multiple sources of identity—racial identity, gender identity, ethnic identity, and functional group identity, for example—and not assume that they all operate the same in a work team or that one can be a surrogate for another (Skevington & Baker, 1989; Tinsley, 1994).

Furthermore, in developing this more complex approach to understanding diversity, we must keep in mind that identity is neither stable, fixed, nor innate. Rather, it is socially constructed (Wharton, 1992). In other words, the meanings of identities can change across contexts and over time (Bhavnani & Phoenix, 1994). For example, Tsui and her colleagues (chapter 5, this volume) argue that being a male subordinate with a female manager takes on a different meaning in a work group that is female-dominated versus a work group that is male-dominated. Similarly, although race has been a salient issue in the United States, the meaning of race is neither stable nor obvious. Racial discourse, racial meanings, and racial categories have changed over time (Winant, 1994). Even among members who are in the same social category, the salience and meaning of their identity may not be the same. Merely being part of a social category does not mean one is psychologically attached to that category. Not all women share the same gender identity, and not all marketing specialists share the same occupational identity. To address such complexities, psychologists clearly need better theories and more sophisticated methods for measuring identity.

MINIMIZING THE NEGATIVE EFFECTS OF DIVERSITY

Social identity theory makes a major contribution to understanding one of the basic effects of diversity in identities: the creation of ingroups and outgroups. According to social identity theory, mere categorization (regardless of the basis of such categorization) into distinctive groups has detrimental effects on collective goals. Once ingroup and outgroup distinctions become salient, stereotyping, distrust, and competition occur and interfere with group functioning (Armstrong & Cole, chapter 8, this volume; Brewer, chapter 3, this volume). Or, as Northcraft, Polzer, Neal, and Kramer (chapter 4, this volume) may say, subgroup members come to believe that conflicts are distributive.

A common theme in prescriptions for overcoming the barriers to work team performance is breaking down group boundaries that result from categorization—for example, by increasing intergroup contact. It is ironic that the major prescription for reaping the benefits of diversity is to find ways of minimizing attention to subgroup differences. Furthermore, the research results presented by Tolbert, Andrews, and Simons (chapter 6, this volume) shed considerable doubt on the efficacy of the contact hypothesis. They found that increases in the proportionate size of a minority group did not decrease discrimination. From a practical point of view, this finding calls into question diversity management strategies that focus on awareness training or other efforts that imply the problem is essentially a lack of familiarity with those who are different. The problem is obviously much more complex. Specifically, as Tolbert et al. found, the power status of the minority group moderated the relationship between the proportionate size of the minority group and intergroup relations. These results suggest that change strategies must attend to the relative power of groups, not merely numbers.

The relative power of subgroups is one important aspect of the context that must be attended to as psychologists attempt to minimize the potential negative effects of diversity, but it is not the only important aspect of context. For example, Northcraft et al. (chapter 4, this volume) describe how orientations toward conflict shape the context in which interactions occur. They suggest several strategies for creating a productive context. For example, team education can be used to change members' perceptions so they appreciate the constructive nature of differences in beliefs rather than viewing differences as distributive conflicts. Team architecture can be used to create a climate for cross-disciplinary cooperation, including attention to physical proximity of team members. Close proximity of team members allows for more casual contact, which may ameliorate negative stereotyping. The case studies reported by Armstrong and Cole (chapter 8, this volume) also highlight the role of proximity in shaping work team interactions. Interestingly, they found that the effects of distance were equally dramatic in work sites that were a few kilometers apart and in those that were continents apart. Finally, Northcraft et al. remind us that team infrastructure, including performance appraisal and reward systems, can support cooperative efforts. Again, this is consistent with Armstrong and Cole's (chapter 8, this volume) observation that formal, explicit procedures for group communication and a clear charter from the larger host organization are key to the effective functioning of teams working across distances.

If psychologists accept the notion that context is so important to understanding the consequences of diversity, they must then consider this question: Can results from studies using artificially created work groups be applied to real situations, especially situations where distinctions are based on socially and historically marked categories like race and gender? Is it reasonable, as suggested by Brewer (chapter 3, this volume), to cross-cut roles with category membership in organizations, or would this require dismantling deeply rooted notions of race and gender differences held by individuals? To what extent can we "script" team behavior in real organizational settings?

Solutions rooted in social identity theory appear to assume that the basic problem lies in faulty cognition and perceptual error. For solutions to the problem, suggested strategies emphasize recategorizing group members, changing perceptions about group members, and imparting knowledge about the "other." Will these strategies work equally effectively in situations where work team diversity is based on cognitive variety and in situations where diversity is a function of race? Is it important to consider the specific form and content of the different bases of diversity? May not the type of task also determine the effectiveness of a particular intervention strategy, adding another level of complexity? Research in field settings is needed to test the generalizability of strategies developed in laboratory studies. A research approach that emphasizes experimental control and universal psychological processes may not be appropriate if the objective is to illuminate the more contextually structured and socially constructed aspects of diversity. Psychologists are more likely to advance theory and practice if they expand research methodologies to include field studies. In this volume, the chapters by Armstrong and Cole, and by Ely illustrate the rich understandings such methodologies can yield.

REFERENCES

Bhavnani, K. K., & Phoenix, A. (1994). *Shifting identities shifting racisms: A feminism and psychology reader*. Newbury Park, CA: Sage.

Cross, E., Katz, J. H., Miller, F. A., & Seashore, E. (1994). *The promise of diversity*. Burr Ridge, IL: Irwin Professional.

Hall, S. (1991). Ethnicity: Identity and difference. *Radical America, 23*, 9–20.

Jackson, S. E., May, K. E., & Whitney, K. (1995). Understanding the dynamics of diversity in decision-making teams. In R. A. Guzzo & E. Salas (Eds.), *Team decision-making effectiveness in organizations*. San Francisco: Jossey-Bass.

Morrison, A. (1992). *The new leaders: Guidelines on leadership diversity in America*. San Francisco: Jossey-Bass.

Skevington, S., & Baker, D. (Eds.). (1989). *The social identity of women*. Newbury Park, CA: Sage.

Thomas, R. R. (1991). *Beyond race and gender: Unleashing the power of your total workforce by managing diversity*. New York: AMACOM.

Tinsley, H. (Ed.). (1994). Special issue on racial identity and vocational behavior. *Journal of Vocational Behavior, 44*.

Triandis, H., Kurowski, L., & Gefland, M. J. (1994). Workplace diversity. In H. C. Triandis, M. Dunnette, & L. Hough (Eds.), *Handbook of industrial and organizational psychology* (Vol. 4, pp. 769–827). Palo Alto, CA: Consulting Psychologists Press.

Wharton, A. (1992). The social construction of gender and race in organizations: A social identity and group mobilization perspective. *Research in the Sociology of Organizations, 10*, 55–84

Winant, H. (1994). *Racial conditions: Politics, theory, comparisons*. Minneapolis: University of Minnesota Press.

Author Index

Subject Index

About the Editors

Susan E. Jackson is Professor of Management at New York University. She received her MA and PhD degrees from the University of California at Berkeley. Her work on the topic of workforce diversity emphasizes the consequences of diversity for teamwork in organizations and the importance of linking diversity issues to strategic business issues. This perspective is reflected in her book, *Diversity in the Workplace: Human Resources Initiatives*, (1993, Guilford Press) which describes how several major companies have been attempting to improve their ability to use effectively a workforce that is diverse along many dimensions.

Marian N. Ruderman is a research scientist at the Center for Creative Leadership in Greensboro, North Carolina. Her research interests are in how managers develop through job assignments and how gender and ethnicity affect management practice and development. She has published several articles and reports on these topics. She is a member of the American Psychological Association, the Society for Industrial and Organizational Psychology, and the Academy of Management. She received her BA in psychology from Cornell University and her PhD in organizational psychology from the University of Michigan.